The AiA Gluten and Dairy Free Cook Book

of related interest

Diet Intervention and Autism
Implementing the Gluten Free and Casein Free Diet
for Autistic Children and Adults – A Practical Guide for Parents
Marilyn Le Breton
Foreword by Rosemary Kessick, AiA
ISBN 1 85302 935 1

A User Guide to the GF/CF Diet for Autism,
Asperger Syndrome and AD/HD
Luke Jackson
Foreword by Marilyn Le Breton
ISBN 1 84310 055 X

Allergy Busters
A Story for Children with Autism or Related Spectrum
Disorders Struggling with Allergies
Kathleen A. Chara and Paul J. Chara with Karston J. Chara
Illustrated by J. M. Burns
ISBN 1 84310 782 1

The AiA Gluten and Dairy Free Cook Book

Compiled by Marilyn Le Breton

Foreword by Rosemary Kessick

Jessica Kingsley Publishers
London and Philadelphia

Every effort has been made to ensure that the information contained in this book is correct, but mistakes happen! Please ensure that you check through each recipe used carefully to make sure that is suitable for the individual it is intended for. The author does not take any responsibility for any decision taken as a result of the information contained in this book.

The author does not endorse, approve or assume responsibility for any recipe, product, brand or company. The presence (or absence) of a product does not constitute approval (or disapproval) by the author.

None of the information contained within this book is designed to be taken as medical advice. Always consult a qualified medical practitioner before implementing any dietary intervention.

First published in the United Kingdom in 2002
by Jessica Kingsley Publishers
116 Pentonville Road
London N1 9JB, UK
and
400 Market Street, Suite 400
Philadelphia, PA 19106, USA

www.jkp.com

Second impression 2005

Library of Congress Cataloging in Publication Data
A CIP catalog record for this book is available from the Library of Congress

British Library Cataloguing in Publication Data
A CIP catalogue record for this book is available from the British Library

ISBN-13: 978 1 84310 067 6
ISBN-10: 1 84310 067 3

Printed and Bound in Great Britain by
Athenaeum Press, Gateshead, Tyne and Wear

Contents

Please Read Before Starting to Cook

Recipes

Appendices

Index

Foreword

Up until now it seems that it hasn't been possible to pick up a single recipe book in the certain knowledge that it contains a comprehensive variety of meals and treats suitable for people with differing intolerances and allergies.

This recipe book is different! Marilyn Le Breton has done a fabulous job in compiling recipes and ideas from round the world. Many well-known names in the catering fraternity, touched by the plight of our AiA children, have been generous in time and spirit allowing AiA to use some of their most successful recipes.

Having bought this book, I'm confident that you will share my enthusiasm and gratitude to all the contributors, in particular the parents and their own little expert tasters who take no prisoners! When they approve a recipe - you know it's a success!

Many perennial questions are addressed here such as,

"What do I do for packed lunches?"

Well, you'll find plenty of ideas between these pages!

Although this book will become an invaluable resource for those catering for a variety of food intolerances, it has been compiled primarily to help children and adults on the autistic spectrum, that is, those who find themselves on any point from dyslexia through dyspraxia, ADHD, Asperger's and autism.

Many people on the autistic spectrum are unable to eat certain foods. In particular any animal milk based products or gluten, from oats, rye, wheat, barley and spelt. When they do, they can suffer from distressing reactions ranging from sleeplessness to hyperactivity and aggression.

Marilyn Le Breton's first book, 'Diet Intervention and Autism', was an overnight success, helping many hundreds of parents and professionals world-wide in their quest to implement the diet. The charity is indebted to Marilyn for her unstinting generosity in editing this book on behalf of AiA, which will be the sole beneficiary of any royalties.

Finally I should like to add my personal thanks to Marilyn for so many things, not least of which is her unfailing dedication and humour as she tackles the day to day difficulties of manning AiA's volunteer helpline.

I know that Marilyn, with her determination for detail, has personally experimented with most of the recipes in this book and I will happily bear witness to the fact that she is an excellent cook. If, however, any of you are feeling faint at the idea of donning your aprons, then take heart with me as I look back with a giggle, because this remarkable woman's first comment to me, many months ago, before she embarked on the diet for her own son was:

"I don't do cooking" !

Rosemary Kessick
CEO Allergy induced Autism
May 2002

AiA is a charity promoting research into the causes underlying ASD dietary and medical difficulties. For further details of our work see the AiA website at *www.AutismMedical.com.*

Preface

This recipe book's primary purpose is to help parents who are implementing a gluten, casein, DGa and artificial sugar free diet for their child who is on the autistic spectrum. But this book will also be of help to coeliacs following a gluten free diet, those who are lactose or dairy intolerant, those who are allergic or intolerant to wheat and, it is hoped, to many others who have food intolerances or allergies.

One of the first thoughts to fly through the mind of a parent who is about to embark on any diet with their child is, 'They will never eat normal food again', quickly followed by, 'Oh they love to eat… What on earth will they eat now?' If this book does nothing else, it will put paid to any ideas that the diet is a restrictive one.

Converting main meals into suitable replacements for a child poses few problems for parents. Finding suitable and tasty replacements for bread, biscuits and cakes can cause headaches. Shop-bought alternatives are expensive and the choice is limited. For those parents whose children have additional food intolerances, the only choice sometimes is to 'forget it'. A quick flick through the recipes in this book will illustrate the wealth of alternatives available. All the recipes in this book come either from parents with children on the diet or from those who have food allergies or intolerances themselves. So all the recipes have been tried and tested by the true experts, those implementing the diet and those on the diet.

I hope that you will be inspired to start baking and cooking by this book and that your efforts will dispel any fears that 'special' food cannot be tasty food. I've really enjoyed putting this book together, developing new recipes and trying some of the others that have been sent in. I hope that you and your family enjoy the book too.

Wishing you all happy, tasty and safe baking.

Marilyn Le Breton

Acknowledgements

I would like to give my heartfelt thanks all the people and companies who were kind enough to take the time to send in recipes for this book. Without these people this book could not have happened. In particular I would like to mark out for a 'special thank you' the following:

Barbara Powell of Barbara's Kitchen, who seems to be single-handedly teaching those in the UK with food allergies and intolerances, how to bake scrummy food. Thank you Barbara, for your friendship, help, humour, time and patience.

To my good friend Debby Anglesey, who has contributed far more than recipes to this book. Thank you for your tireless research and kindness.

To Diane Hartman, whose energy for converting practically every recipe in the world for those with food intolerances is awesome.

To Rosemary Kessick and all at Allergy induced Autism. Thank you for giving me my children back. And an extra thank you, to you, from my son, Jack, for in his own words 'stopping my head and tummy from hurting'.

To my two tiny food critics, Luke and Jack, thank you for your invaluable contributions of 'delicious', 'more now!', 'yuckky', 'disgusting', 'can I have some more please' when testing the results of my new 'experiments'.

Disclaimer

Every effort has been made to ensure that the information contained in this book is correct, but mistakes happen! Please ensure that you check through each recipe used carefully to make sure that it is suitable for the individual it is intented for. The author does not take responsibility for any decision taken as a result of the information contained in this book.

The author does not endorse, approve of or assume responsibility for any recipe, product, brand or company. The presence (or absence) of a product does not constitute approval (or disapproval) by the author.

None of the information contained in this book is designed to be taken as medical advice. Always consult a qualified medical practitioner before implementing any dietary intervention.

AiA Information and Acknowledgements

AiA would like to extend their thanks to everyone who has contributed recipes to this book.

We would also like to thank you for purchasing this book. All proceeds from the sale of this book go to AiA, to help us to continue our work helping families implement the gluten free, dairy free, DGa free and artificial sugar free diet with their children.

All the recipes contained in this book are free from gluten, casein, monosodium glutamate, DGa and aspartame.

AiA recognises that many of the children following the traditional gf/cf diet have additional food allergies and intolerances. In order to help you as much as possible to select the recipes that are suitable for your child, each recipe contains an additional code system. This code will indicate those recipes that are also free from other common intolerances/allergies.

The codes:

CF = Corn Free***
EF = Egg Free
FF = Fruit Free
SF = Soya Free
SGF = Sugar Free
TF = Tomato Free
YF = Yeast Free**

* next to a code means that it can easily be converted to being free of the item, if a substitute ingredient is used.

** yeast free here refers only to the type of yeast used in baking and not the wider term of fermented products that may be unsuitable for those who suffer from candida.

*** for those following the recipes outside the UK, the recipes marked as corn free but containing xanthan gum, are not a typing error or a statement of ignorance! In the UK it is possible to get non-corn derived xanthan gum.

Brand names of products, which appear in the ingredients list of a recipe, are the suggestion of the individual contributor, and not a recommendation or an endorsement by AiA or the editor.

Allergy induced Autism (AiA)

Website: www.AutismMedical.com

Please Read Before Starting to Cook

- All the cup measurements used in this book are American measuring cups (250ml), not British measuring cups. British cup measurements are smaller and the recipes will not work with these. American measuring cups are readily available throughout the UK, but if you have problems getting them contact Barbara's Kitchen (details in directory).

- Please use American measuring spoons and not the spoons from your cutlery drawer – these are not the same at all and will drastically affect the result of your cooking. 1 US tablespoon = 15ml; 1 US teaspoon = 5ml.

- All cup, teaspoon and tablespoon measurements are level, unless otherwise stated.

- Please do not swap between cup, metric or imperial measurements.

- All the dairy free milk in the recipes is in liquid form, unless otherwise stated.

- It really isn't worth trying to convert cups to ounces or grams, as cups are a measurement of volume and not weight. I have tried to do this and it is a disaster. For example, 1 cup of white rice flour weighs 4½ oz. So you would expect 1 cup of tapioca flour or potato starch flour to weigh the same, but they don't. One cup of potato starch flour weighs 4 oz and 1 cup of tapioca flour weighs 6 oz.

- All cooking times given in the recipes assume that the oven has been pre-heated to the specific temperature.

- As the temperature of ovens vary, please check towards the end of the given cooking time if dish is cooked.

- In the UK, do not use potato flour instead of the required potato starch flour. Potato flour is a much heavier flour than potato starch flour and this will affect the outcome of your baking.

- The gf flour mix used in the recipes is stated below. If you are using a shop-bought ready mixed gf flour, the results will vary, as they will contain different gf flours, in varying ratios, to the stated gf flour mix. Some commercial mixes also contain various raising agents. The recipes below have raising agents as part of the ingredients, when they are needed. If you are using a commercial gf flour mix that contains raising agents, you will need to omit or reduce the raising agents listed in the recipe. As this can be tricky, and the end product may be significantly different from the desired result, I would recommend that until you feel you have mastered gf/cf baking, to stick with the gf flour mix formula given below

Gluten Free Flour Mix

Those recipes in this book that call for a gf flour mix refer to the following flour mixture (unless otherwise stated):

> 4 cups white rice flour
> 1 cup potato starch flour
> 1 cup tapioca starch flour

It is advisable to make up a huge batch of this flour and store it in an airtight container, so that when you need to bake, you do not have to first mix up the right quantity of the flour before you can get started. When the flour is mixed, put it in the freezer. Flour deteriorates very quickly; by freezing, you will prolong its life. The flour does not freeze whole, it remains free flowing so that you can just measure out what you need for each recipe. There is no need to bring the flour to room temperature except when it is being used for bread recipes.

Converting Traditional Baking Recipes

If you wish to convert traditional baking recipes to gluten and dairy free baking, then the following can be used as a guide, but only when using the basic gf flour mix given above.

Plain flour mix

(2 cups or approx 8 oz)

Ingredients

2 cups gf flour mix
2 tsp xanthan gum

Self-raising flour

Ingredients

2 cups gf flour mix
2 tsp xanthan gum
2 tsp gf baking powder

(2 cups or approx 8oz)

Other tips

For some recipe conversions, it may be necessary to add an extra ½ tsp of gf baking powder, to the amount given in the original recipe, for every 2 cups of gf flour mix (8oz) used, to get the result you desire. It really is a case of experimenting. For recipes where large amounts of flour are being used, you may also need to increase the number of eggs that you are using.

Dairy free margarine can be slightly oilier than traditional dairy margarines and the amount can be slightly reduced when converting normal recipes. For those wishing to reduce the amount of refined sugar in their child's diet, one third of the sugar can easily be omitted from a recipe (especially biscuit recipes), with very little difference being made to the final appearance and taste.

Marilyn Le Breton © Copyright 2001

Egg Substitution Suggestions

To replace each large egg, choose *one* of the following:

- ½ tsp gf baking powder + ½ tsp xanthan gum + 3 tbsp water
- 3 tbsp tapioca starch flour + 3 tbsp water
- ¼ cup blended plain soft tofu
- 1 tbsp ground flaxseed soaked in 3 tbsp water
- ¼ cup pureed fruit
- 1 heaped tsp gf baking powder + 1 tbsp oil
- 1 heaped tsp gf baking powder + 1 tbsp cider vinegar + 1 tbsp warm water

Barbara Powell © Copyright Barbara's Kitchen 2000

Dairy Substitutions in Baked Products

The following are equal to 1 cup of the original dairy ingredient:

Double or heavy cream

- ⅔ cup gluten and dairy free milk alternative + ⅓ cup melted dairy free margarine.

Single or light cream

- ¾ cup gluten and dairy free milk alternative + ¼ cup melted dairy free margarine.

Butter milk

- 1 tbsp apple cider vinegar (or lemon juice), topped up to 1 cup with gluten and dairy free milk alternative.

Allow the liquid to stand for 4–6 minutes before adding to a recipe.

Evaporated milk

- Use light cream alternative – as above.

Sweetened condensed milk

- ½ cup Dari-Free + ¾ cup sugar + 2 tbsp dairy free margarine + ½ tsp xanthan gum or guar gum.

Method

- Mix all the ingredients together well.
- Bring ingredients slowly to the boil, over a medium heat, stirring constantly.
- Boil for I minute or until thick and bubbling, stirring constantly.
- Chill liquid before adding to a recipe.

Butter

- 1 cup dairy free margarine + 1½ tbsp water.

Diane Hartman © Copyright 2000

Useful Substitutions I

- 1 oz unsweetened chocolate = 3 tbsp gluten and dairy free cocoa powder + 1 tbsp melted dairy free margarine.
- 1 oz sweetened chocolate = 3 tbsp gluten and dairy free cocoa powder + 1 tbsp melted dairy free margarine + 1 tbsp sugar.
- Baking powder = ½ tsp cream of tartar + ¼ tsp bicarbonate of soda.
- Light corn syrup = 1 cup + 1 tbsp granulated sugar + ¼ cup water.
- Dark corn syrup = 1 cup + 1 tbsp gluten and dairy free brown sugar + ¼ cup water.
- Gluten and dairy free maple syrup or honey can also be used as a corn syrup replacer.

- Icing sugar = 1½ tbsp tapioca or potato starch flour + enough granulated sugar to make up to 1 cup.

Method
- Process these ingredients on the highest speed of a food blender for 45 seconds or until powdered. Store in an airtight container.

Diane Hartman © Copyright 2000

Useful Substitutions II

- Molasses = use black treacle or honey in a straight swap. Or use slightly less golden syrup than the recipe calls for, as this is a little sweeter than molasses.

- 1 cup sugar = ¾ cup of honey + reduce the liquid used in the recipe by ¼ cup; or ⅔ cup of fructose

- Vanilla extract (vanilla sugar) = 1 pod of vanilla (broken into three pieces) placed into 1 lb of caster sugar in an airtight container. Leave for a week. Omit any vanilla extract required in the recipe, as the sugar will carry a better vanilla flavour.

- Ground cinnamon = replace in sweet recipes by making cinnamon sugar: 1 part ground cinnamon to 12 parts sugar. Mix together well and store in an airtight jar.

- 1 tsp arrowroot = 2 tsp of white rice flour or tapioca starch flour or potato starch flour.

- 1 tbsp cornflour = 2 tbsp white rice flour or potato starch flour or tapioca starch flour.

- 1 tsp guar gum = 1 tsp xanthan gum.

- 1 cup margarine = ¾ cup of oil.

- 1 cup vegetable shortening = 1 cup + 2 tbsp margarine.

- Using flours other than cornflour as a thickener: if the flour is being used to thicken a sauce or other liquid, use tapioca starch flour as it does not separate on freezing as rice or potato starch flour are likely to.

Natural Food Dyes

Please note:

Diane uses these to colour Easter eggs. If you intend to use these to colour play dough or icing etc., omit any vinegar that appears in the recipe.

- Yellowish Green = 1 tsp vinegar + 2 tbsp powdered dried spinach + 1 cup boiling water.

- Red or pink = mash down cooked beetroot and strain off the juice through a muslin cloth. The intensity of the colour will depend on how much juice is used; or use strawberry jam or strawberry juice to colour icing.

- Violet-red = boil the skins of red onions in a very little water and then strain off the water through a muslin cloth.

- Yellow = use turmeric. For Easter egg painting, use 1½ tsp turmeric + ½ tsp vinegar + ⅔ cup boiling water.

- Brown = 1 tbsp instant coffee (or 1 tbsp loose tea leaves) + ⅔ cup boiling water + ¾ tsp vinegar.
  For a dark shade of brown use 1 tbsp gf/cf cocoa powder instead of coffee.

- Blue = red cabbage juice.

- Reddish blue = blackberry juice.

- Blue grey = blueberry juice.

- Purple = ½ cup violet blossoms + 1 cup boiling water. Allow to stand for 3 hours and then strain through a muslin cloth.

- Lavender = use method for purple + ⅛ cup lemon juice.

- Green = use method for purple + ¼ tsp bicarbonate of soda.

- Dark yellow/orange = use method for green and leave to stand overnight.

Diane Hartman © Copyright 2000

UK and USA Cooking Terms

UK	USA
Aubergine	Egg-plant
Baking tray	Baking sheet
Beetroot	Beets
Bicarbonate of soda	Baking soda
Broad beans	Fava beans
Caster sugar	Superfine sugar
Chickpeas	Garbanzo beans
Clingfilm	Plastic Wrap
Coriander	Cilantro
Cornflour	Cornstarch
Courgette	Zucchini
Demerara sugar	Brown crystal sugar
Desiccated coconut	Shredded coconut
Fairy cake	Cupcake
Fish fingers	Fish sticks
Flageolet beans	Small navy beans
French beans	Green beans
Glacé cherries	Candied cherries
Gram flour	Garbanzo/besan flour
Green beans	Dwarf beans
Ice lolly	Popsicle
Icing sugar	Confectioners/powdered sugar
Jacket potato	Baked potato
Jam	Jelly
Jelly	Jell-o
Mince meat	Ground meat
Natural yoghurt	Unsweetened yoghurt

Passata	Sieved tomatoes
Peppers	Bell peppers
Pie tin	Pie plate
Plain flour	All-purpose flour
Prawn	Shrimp
Runner beans	String beans
Scone	Biscuit
Spring onions	Scallions/green onions
Stew	Hotpot
Sultanas	Yellow raisins
Swede	Rutabaga
Sweetcorn	Corn kernels
Sweets	Candy
Swiss roll	Jelly roll
Tofu	Bean curd
Tomato puree	Tomato paste
Tomato sauce	Ketchup
Yorkshire pudding	Pop-overs
4 oz margarine	1 stick

Please note:

If you are following the gluten free and casein free (GF/CF) diet, please replace cider vinegar with water.

Recipes

Bakery Goods: Breads, Rolls and Pizza Bases

Our thanks to Barbara Powell of Barbara's Kitchen for her huge contribution to this section.

1 ½ lb Machine bread

CF, FF, SF, TF

Ingredients

2½ cups white rice flour
½ cup potato starch flour
½ cup tapioca starch flour
1 tbsp xanthan gum
2 tbsp sugar
½ tsp freshly crushed sea salt
1 sachet (2¼ tsp) fast action dried yeast

3 large eggs (room temperature and beaten)
¼ cup sunflower oil
1 tsp cider vinegar or cold water
½ cup gluten and dairy free milk alternative
¾ cup of water (hand hot)

Method

- Mix together the flours, xanthan gum, sugar and salt.
- In a separate bowl, mix together the eggs, oil, vinegar/cold water, milk alternative and hot water.
- Place the liquid mix at the bottom of the bread pan.
- Gently spoon the flour mix on top of the liquid.
- Sprinkle the yeast over the top of the flour mix.
- Use the normal bake setting for the machine and choose either the light or dark crust setting. *Do not use the delayed programme setting.*
- It may be necessary to help turn the ingredients over with a wooden spoon or spatula at the start of the programme.
- When the machine has finished baking, remove the bread and place on its side to cool. Wait until bread has cooled before slicing.

Freezes well.

Variations

- *To make a brown loaf: add 1–2 tbsp of treacle or molasses to the wet ingredients.*
- *For a mock granary loaf: add pine nuts, seeds, etc.*
- *For a mock rye bread: add 1 tbsp treacle/molasses to the wet ingredients and 2 tsp of lemon peel and 1 tsp crushed cardamom.*
- *Many other things can be added to this bread: gf dried herbs, gf spices, mashed banana, apricot, almonds, etc.*

Barbara's Kitchen © Copyright 2000

2–2½ lb Machine bread

CF, FF, SF, TF

Ingredients

2⅓ cups white rice flour
½ cup potato starch flour
½ cup tapioca starch flour
⅓ cup of extra potato starch flour or tapioca starch flour (not white rice flour)
1 tbsp xanthan gum
2 tbsp sugar
½ tsp salt

1 sachet (2¼ tsp) fast action dried yeast
2 large eggs (beaten and at room temperature)
1 tsp cider vinegar (if allowed) or cold water
¼ cup sunflower oil
1⅓ cups gluten and dairy free milk alternative

Method

- Gently combine together the flours, xanthan gum, sugar and salt.
- In a separate bowl, mix together the eggs, vinegar/cold water, oil and milk alternative.
- Place the liquid mix in the bottom of the bread pan.
- Gently spoon the flour mix on top of the liquid mixture.
- Sprinkle the yeast over the top of the flour.
- Use the normal bake setting of the machine and choose either the light or dark crust setting. *Do not use the delayed programme setting.*
- When the machine starts mixing, it may be advisable to give the dough a helping hand by using a wet plastic spatula to mix and turn over the ingredients.
- When the baking cycle has finished, turn the bread out onto a wire tray immediately.
- Do not slice the bread until it is completely cold.

Freezes well.

Variations

- *See variations for 1½ lb loaf.*

3– 3½ lb Machine bread

CF, FF, SF, TF

Ingredients

5 cups white rice flour
1 cup potato starch flour
1 cup tapioca starch flour
2 tbsp xanthan gum
1 tsp freshly crushed sea salt
2 tbsp sugar
1 sachet dried yeast (fast action)

4 large eggs (beaten and at room temperature)
½ cup sunflower oil
1 tsp gf vinegar or cold water
2 cups gluten and dairy free milk alternative
1½ cups water (hand hot)

Method

- Mix together the flours, xanthan gum, salt and sugar.
- In a separate bowl, mix together the eggs, oil, vinegar/cold water, milk alternative and hot water.
- Place all the liquid ingredients in the bottom of the bread pan.
- Gently spoon the flour mixture on top of the liquid ingredients.
- Sprinkle the yeast over the top of the flour mix.
- Set the machine on normal bake and choose the light or dark crust setting. *Do not use the delayed programme setting.*
- When the machine has finished its programme, remove the bread from the pan and allow it to cool before slicing.

Freezes well.

Variations

- *See recipe for 1½ lb loaf.*

Barbara's Kitchen © Copyright 2001

White bread by hand

CF, FF, SF, TF

Ingredients

2 cups white rice flour
½ cup potato starch flour
½ cup tapioca starch flour
2½ tsp xanthan gum
1½ tsp salt
1 sachet dried yeast
2 tbsp sugar

2 large eggs (beaten and at
    room temperature)
¼ cup sunflower oil
½ cup gluten and dairy free
    milk alternative
¾ cup water (hand hot)
1 tsp cider or white wine
    vinegar or cold water

Method

- Pre-heat oven to GM6, 400F, 200C.
- In a small bowl, dissolve 2 tsp of the sugar in the warm water. Mix in the yeast. Set to one side so that the yeast has time to become 'active' – a slight froth will form.
- In a large bowl, mix together the flours, xanthan gum, salt and the remaining sugar.
- Slowly, add the oil and the vinegar/cold water and mix in well.
- Using an electric mixer, slowly add the milk until mixed in thoroughly.
- Add the eggs one at a time to the mix. When the eggs are well mixed in, the mixture should feel warm.
- Pour in the yeast mixture and mix at the highest speed for 3–4 minutes.
- Cover the bowl and put in a warm place for approximately one hour. The dough should have risen and doubled in volume.
- Return the dough to the mixer and mix at the highest speed for 5 minutes.
- Place the mixture in a 2 lb loaf tin or divide the mixture between two 1 lb loaf tins.
- Cover the tins and allow the dough to rise in a warm place for approximately 40–60 minutes. The dough needs to have risen to just above the rim of the tins.
- Bake the 2 lb loaf for 1 hour, slightly less for the 1 lb loaves.
- You may need to cover the loaf with silver foil after 10 minutes of baking to prevent the top from overcooking.

- To test if cooked, remove from tin and tap base. It will sound hollow when cooked.
- When cooked, remove from tins immediately and cool on a wire rack.

Freezes well.

Bread rolls by hand

CF, FF, SF, TF

Ingredients

2 cups white rice flour
½ cup potato starch flour
½ cup tapioca starch flour
2½ tsp xanthan gum
1½ tsp salt
1 sachet dried yeast
2 tbsp sugar

2 large eggs (beaten and at room temperature)
¼ cup sunflower oil
½ cup gluten and dairy free milk alternative
¾ cup water (hand hot)
1 tsp cider or white wine vinegar or cold water

Method

- Pre-heat oven to GM6, 400F, 200C.
- In a small bowl, dissolve 2 tsp of the sugar in the warm water. Mix in the yeast. Set to one side so that the yeast has time to become 'active' – a slight froth will form.
- In a large bowl, mix together the flours, xanthan gum, salt and the remaining sugar.
- Slowly, add the oil and the vinegar/cold water and mix in well.
- Using an electric mixer, slowly add the milk until mixed in thoroughly.
- Add the eggs one at a time to the mix. When the eggs are well mixed in, the mixture should feel warm.
- Pour in the yeast mixture and mix at the highest speed for 3–4 minutes.
- Cover the bowl and put in a warm place for approximately one hour. The dough should have risen and doubled in volume.
- Return the dough to the mixer and mix at the highest speed for 5 minutes.
- Place the dough in a strong plastic food bag.

- Cut the corner off the corner of the bag and pipe out the dough to the desired shape of your rolls (remember they will need to rise again, so make them smaller than needed) on a greased baking tray.

- Cover the tray and allow them to rise for 30–40 minutes until they double in size.

- Cook for approximately 25 minutes but this will depend upon the size of the rolls.

- To check they are cooked, tap one roll on the base. When cooked it will sound hollow.

Barbara's Kitchen © Copyright 2001

Miracle rolls

CF, EF*, FF, SF, SGF, TF, YF

Ingredients

1 cup white rice flour
1/4 cup potato starch flour
1/4 cup tapioca starch flour
2 tsp gf baking powder
1 tsp xanthan gum
pinch of freshly crushed sea salt

1 large egg (beaten) or 1/4 cup warm water
2 tsp cider vinegar (optional) or cold water
2 oz/50g dairy free margarine (melted)
1 cup warm water

Method

- Pre-heat oven to GM4, 350F, 190C.
- Mix together the flours, baking powder, xanthan gum and salt.
- In a separate bowl mix together the egg (or warm water), vinegar/cold water, melted margarine and warm water.
- Mix the two together by hand and then using an electric mixer, beat for 2–3 minutes.
- Divide the mixture between four greased individual pie tins.
- Bake for approximately 20 minutes.
- Allow rolls to cool before removing from tins.

Variations

- *To make smaller rolls, use 8–10 muffin tins and decrease cooking time.*
- *Barbara says that this also makes a good pizza base, but to reduce the water content slightly.*

Barbara's Kitchen © Copyright 2001

Editor's note: Instead of melting the margarine, mash it down and add after mixing the rest of the ingredients together. The lumps of margarine will melt to leave small 'pockets' and when split and toasted these resemble crumpets. Freezes well.

Fibre bread

FF, SF, TF

Ingredients

4 oz (125g) maize/corn meal
4 oz (125g) Dietary Specialities Fibre Mix
2 oz (50g) tapioca flour
2 oz (50g) white rice flour
2 tsp xanthan gum
2 tsp sugar

1 sachet of yeast
¾ pint (450ml) warm liquid (½ water and ½ gluten and dairy free milk alternative)
3 tbsp oil
1 large egg (beaten)
1 tsp cider vinegar (optional)

Method

- Pre-heat oven to GM7, 425F, 220C.
- Mix together the maize/corn meal, the DS fibre mix, flours, xanthan gum, sugar and yeast.
- In a separate bowl mix together the egg, oil and vinegar (if using).
- To the flour mix add the milk/water and combine.
- Add the egg mixture and mix using an electric mixer with the dough hook attachments.
- Mix again with a wooden spoon, ensuring that there are no air pockets remaining.
- Place the dough into two 1 lb loaf tins or a 2 lb loaf tin. These need to be well greased and the bottom of the tin lined with greaseproof paper.
- Leave to rise in a warm place for 30 minutes.
- Bake on the middle shelf for 40 minutes for the 1 lb loaves or 1 hour for the 2 lb loaf. If the loaf browns too quickly reduce the heat to GM6, 400F, 200C after 30 minutes.

Freezes well.

Angela Deakin, Fareham © Copyright

Quick French bread

CF, EF, FF, SF, TF

Ingredients

12 oz (350g) IS Pure GF Blended Flour
2 tsp IS Pure Xanthan Gum
1½ tsp granulated sugar
1 tsp salt
2¼ tsp quick rising yeast

10 fl oz (300ml) warm water
1 tsp cider vinegar
2 egg whites (at room
   temperature)

Method

- Pre-heat oven to GM6, 400F, 200C.
- In a large bowl combine together the flour, xanthan, sugar, salt and yeast.
- In a separate bowl, mix together the water, vinegar and egg whites, until they become frothy.
- Add the liquid mixture immediately to the flour and beat together for 3 minutes. The dough is soft and this can be done with a wooden spoon.
- Spoon the dough into a French baguette tin and smooth the top of the dough over with a knife.
- If you do not have a baguette tin, use 2 small loaf tins. Spoon the mixture in so that only half of the bottom of the tin is covered (i.e., keep the mixture to the left of the tin) and push the dough up the side of the tin.
- Cover the dough with a clean tea towel and allow it to rise in a warm place for 15–20 minutes.
- Bake for 1 hour and then reduce the heat to GM4, 350F, 180C for a further 15 minutes.
- Allow bread to cool.

Best served warm.

Once cold, store the bread in an airtight container.

Innovative Solutions (UK) Ltd © Copyright 2000

Quick and easy egg and yeast free bread rolls

CF, EF, FF, SF, SGF, TF, YF

Ingredients

½ cup chickpea flour
⅔ cup tapioca starch flour
⅓ cup potato flour
2 tsp xanthan gum
2 tsp gf baking powder
½ tsp salt

2 tbsp ground flaxseed/linseed
⅓ cup organic sunflower oil
   (Meridian)
7 fl oz (200ml) sparkling water
1 tsp ground flaxseed/linseed
   (soaked for 5 minutes in 2
   tbsp boiling water)

Method

- Pre-heat oven to GM6, 400F, 220C.
- In a 2 pint (1 litre), glass jug, mix together the flours, xanthan gum, baking powder, salt and dry linseed/flaxseed.
- Add the oil, wet flaxseed/ linseed and half the sparkling water and mix thoroughly.
- Add the remaining water and mix in very quickly.
- Spoon out the mixture on to a baking tray covered in baking parchment (it makes 8–9 rolls)
- Bake for 20–25 minutes. The rolls should sound hollow when tapped. The rolls will be hard on removing from oven, but will soften up as they cool.

Freezes well.

Variations

- *Add 1 tsp of gf ground cinnamon to flours, for cinnamon rolls.*
- *Add ¼ cup gf un-sulphated raisins, for fruit rolls.*

McGill Family, UK © Copyright

Microwave white bread

CF, EF, FF, SF, TF

Ingredients

1½ cups gf flour mix
1½ tsp xanthan gum
1 sachet of gf yeast (or 2¼ tsp)
1 tsp unrefined caster sugar

1 tsp salt
9 fl oz (275ml) warm water
1 tbsp organic sunflower oil

Method

- Combine together the flour, xanthan gum, yeast, sugar and salt.
- Mix in water and oil to form a batter.
- Pour into a 1 litre (2 pint) microwaveable container.
- Allow mix to stand for 25 minutes in a warm place, to rise.
- Cook at full power for 8 minutes.
- Allow bread to stand for 5 minutes.
- Turn bread out of the container and place in the oven at gas mark 7 for 5 minutes to brown and crisp the outside.

For this bread to work, you need to use a container that has exactly a 1 litre (2 pint) capacity and is a loaf tin shape. Other shaped containers mean that the bread will be too wide and shallow, so you will have to reduce the cooking time accordingly.

Marilyn Le Breton © Copyright 2001

Soda bread

CF, EF, FF, SF, SGF, TF, YF

Ingredients

2 cups of gf flour mix
1 tsp of xanthan gum
1½ tsp bicarbonate of soda

1½ tsp cream of tartar
1 tbsp organic sunflower oil
⅔ cup gluten and dairy free milk
   alternative

Method

- Pre-heat oven to GM7, 425F, 220C.
- In a large bowl, combine together the flour, xanthan gum, bicarbonate of soda, and cream of tartar.
- Add the oil and rub it in with your fingers.
- Add milk alternative and mix in with a wooden spoon to create a stiff dough.
- Knead the dough into a ball.
- Place on a greased baking sheet.
- Cut a deep cross into the top of the loaf.
- Bake for 20 minutes.

Soda bread does not keep well and needs to be eaten the day it is baked.

Marilyn Le Breton © Copyright 2001

Breakfast cinnamon rolls

CF, EF, FF*, SF, TF, YF

Ingredients

12 oz (350g) IS Pure GF Blended Flour
2 tsp IS Pure Xanthan Gum
2 tbsp granulated sugar
4 tsp gf baking powder
1 tsp salt
5½ oz (165g) dairy free margarine

9 fl oz (275ml) gluten and dairy free milk alternative
8 oz (225g) gluten and dairy free brown sugar
1 tbsp gf ground cinnamon
2 oz (50g) un-sulphated gf sultanas (optional – see editor's note)

Method

- Pre-heat oven to GM6, 400F, 200C.
- In a large bowl, combine together the flour, xanthan, granulated sugar, baking powder and salt.
- Cut in 2½ oz (65g) of the margarine, using a knife, until the mixture resembles breadcrumbs.
- Make a well in the centre of the mixture and pour in the milk alternative. Stir well until the mixture forms a soft dough.
- Place the dough on a large sheet of parchment paper. Place another piece of parchment on top of the dough and roll the dough out into a rectangle that is ½" (1cm) thick. The rectangle should be approximately 10" x 12"(25cm x 30cm).
- Peel off the top layer of parchment paper, cut the rectangle to size if necessary.
- In another bowl, cream together the remaining margarine, brown sugar and cinnamon.
- Into 12 non-stick muffin tins drop 1 tsp of this cinnamon mix.
- Spread the remaining cinnamon mix on top of the dough and then sprinkle the sultanas over the top.
- Using the edge of the parchment, roll up the dough like a swiss roll, peeling back the parchment as you go.
- With a sharp knife, cut the roll into 12 pieces about ½" (1cm) thick.
- Slide the knife under each piece to lift and place one piece into the muffin tins, on its side (swirl side up). Press them down into the tin if necessary.
- Bake for 20 minutes.

- Allow rolls to cool for 5–10 minutes before removing from tin.
- To remove from tin, push down on one side of the roll, with a spatula and flip them out. The gooey bit will now be on the top.

Innovative Solutions (UK) Ltd © Copyright 2000

Editor's note: I have tried this recipe without the sultanas and also by replacing them with 2 oz (50g) of gluten and dairy free chocolate chips. Both tasted great.

Corn Bread

FF, SF, SGF, TF, YF

Ingredients

2 cups stone ground corn meal/maize meal
I tbsp gf baking powder
I egg (beaten)
I cup gluten and dairy free milk alternative
2 tbsp honey or pure maple syrup
¼ cup canola oil

Method

- Pre-heat oven to GM6, 400F, 200C.
- Combine together the corn meal and baking powder.
- In a separate bowl, mix together the egg, milk alternative, honey and oil.
- Mix the liquids into the corn meal mixture. Do not over mix. The batter should be slightly lumpy.
- Transfer the batter to a well-greased 8" (20cm) baking pan.
- Bake for 20 minutes or until a knife inserted into the middle of the bread comes out clean.

Diane Hartman © Copyright 2000

Corn Bread

FF, SF, TF, YF

Ingredients

1½ cups of corn meal
½ cup white rice flour
1 tbsp unrefined caster sugar
3 tsp gf baking powder

½ tsp salt
1 organic egg (beaten)
1¼ cups gluten and dairy free
   milk alternative
1 tbsp organic sunflower oil

Method

- Pre-heat oven to GM7, 425F, 220C.
- Combine together the corn meal, white rice flour, sugar, baking powder and salt in a large bowl.
- In a separate bowl beat together the egg, milk alternative and oil.
- Gradually stir the wet ingredients into the flour mix, to form a smooth batter.
- Grease a 9" (23cm) pie dish and pour in the dough.
- Bake in the top of the oven for 30–35 minutes or until the top of the bread is beginning to brown.

This bread needs to be used on day of baking.

Marilyn Le Breton © Copyright 2001

Pitta Bread

CF, FF, TF

Ingredients

1 lb (450g) gf flour mix
5 fl oz (125ml) gluten and dairy free milk
   alternative
2 tsp dried fast action yeast
2 tsp caster sugar
½ tsp gf baking powder

2 tbsp oil
5 fl oz (150ml) plain soya
   yoghurt (lightly beaten)
1 large egg (lightly beaten)
large pinch of freshly crushed
   sea salt
extra ¼ tsp oil

Method

- In a bowl, stir together the milk alternative, 1 tsp of sugar and 1 tsp of yeast. Leave this mixture for 15–20 minutes for the yeast to dissolve and for the mixture to become frothy.

- In a large bowl, sieve together the flour, salt and baking powder. Stir in the remaining tsp of yeast and sugar, 2 tbsp oil, yoghurt and egg. Mix the contents of both bowls together well until a dough has formed.

- Knead the dough for approximately 10 minutes until it becomes smooth and satiny in appearance.

- Place ¼ tsp of oil in the bowl and knead this gently into the dough. Form the dough into a ball.

- Cover the bowl with clingfilm and place bowl in a warm, draught free place for an hour or until the dough has doubled in size.

- Heat oven to maximum temperature and place a baking tray in it to heat up.

- Punch down the dough and knead it again.

- Divide the dough into 6 equal portions. Roll each of these into a ball.

- Roll out each ball into a pitta bread shape. Cover the dough (both the used dough and the rolled out dough) with a tea towel as they tend to dry out very quickly.

- Remove the hot baking tray from the oven and place the pittas on it.

- Bake at GM7-8 for 3 minutes. They should puff up slightly.

If you wish to eat these immediately, place the pittas under a pre-heated grill, until they have browned slightly.

   These freeze well and can be defrosted either under a grill or in a toaster.

Barbara's Kitchen © Copyright 2000

Chapatis

CF, EF, FF, SF, SGF, TF, YF

Ingredients

4 oz (125g) white rice flour
2 oz (50g) tapioca starch flour
2 oz (50g) potato starch flour
1 tsp xanthan gum
½ tsp gf baking powder
pinch of crushed sea salt
5 fl oz (150ml) water
oil for cooking

Method

- Gently mix together the flours, xanthan gum, baking powder and salt.
- Mix in the water to form a dough.
- Knead the dough on a floured surface until it is soft and elastic.
- Allow the dough to rest for 10 minutes.
- Knead again until the dough softens.
- Divide the dough into pieces and flatten and then roll out to desired shape ready for cooking.
- Grease a frying pan with a little oil and cook like an English pancake.

Barbara's Kitchen © Copyright 2000

Pizza base

CF, FF, SF, TF

Ingredients

1 cup white rice flour
½ cup of potato or tapioca starch flour
1½ tsp gf baking powder
1 tsp sugar
1 tsp xanthan gum

¾ cup lukewarm water
1 tbsp dried yeast
1 large egg (beaten and at room temperature)
1 tbsp oil
pinch of sea salt

Method

- Pre-heat oven to GM7, 425F, 220C.
- Mix together the yeast, sugar and water. Set to one side to allow the yeast to 'activate'.
- Gently mix together the flours, baking powder, xanthan gum and salt.
- With an electric mixer, on its lowest setting, mix the egg and oil into the yeast mixture.
- Gently, add half the flour mixture and combine and then add the other half of the flour, but mix this in with a wooden spoon.
- Pour the mixture into a greased baking sheet or pizza tray.
- Allow pizza dough to rise in a warm place for 10 minutes.
- Add sauce and toppings and bake for 25–30 minutes.

Freezes well.

Barbara's Kitchen © Copyright 2000

Individual pizza base

CF, EF, FF, SF, SGF, TF, YF

Ingredients

½ cup gf flour mix
½ tsp xanthan gum
½ tsp cream of tartar
½ tsp bicarbonate of soda
1 tbsp dairy free margarine
1½ tbsp cold water

Method

- Pre-heat oven to GM7, 425F, 220C.
- Combine together the flour, xanthan gum, cream of tartar and bicarbonate of soda.
- Rub in the margarine, until the mix resembles fine breadcrumbs.
- Mix in the water, a little at a time, until a smooth dough is formed.
- Place dough on a baking tray, lined with greaseproof paper and with the palm of your hand, press out the dough until it is a flat circle.
- Brush the top of the pizza dough with a little sunflower oil.
- Add the topping of your choice and bake at the top of the oven for 15–20 minutes.

Marilyn Le Breton © Copyright 2001

Mini pizza bases

CF, EF, FF, SF, SGF, TF, YF

Ingredients

½ cup chickpea flour
½ cup potato starch flour
½ cup tapioca flour
1 tsp gf baking powder
½ tsp salt
3 tbsp oil
up to ½ cup gluten and dairy free milk alternative

Method

- Pre-heat the oven to GM6, 400F, 200C.
- Mix and sift together the flours, baking powder and salt.
- Stir in the oil and milk alternative to form a fairly liquid dough.
- Spread the dough in small circles on to a baking sheet.
- Add sauce and toppings of choice.
- Bake for 12–15 minutes or until the base is firm.

McGill Family, UK © Copyright

Potato pizza base

CF, EF, FF, SGF, SGF, TF, YF

Ingredients

6 oz (175g) mashed potatoes (cooled)
6 oz (175g) gf flour mix
2 tsp baking powder
1 tsp xanthan gum

½ tsp salt
2 tbsp organic sunflower oil
2 fl oz (50ml) gluten and dairy
  free milk alternative

Method

- Pre-heat oven to GM7, 425F, 220C.

- Mix together the flour, baking powder, xanthan gum and salt.

- Stir in the mashed potato and mix in well.

- Make a well in the centre of the mixture and add the water and oil.

- Combine all the ingredients together until a dough has been formed.

- Knead the dough for 2 minutes.

- Press the mixture down well into an 8" (20cm) round baking tray or sandwich tin.

- Cover with sauce and toppings of choice.

- Bake for 30 minutes.

Marilyn Le Breton © Copyright 2001

Pancakes and Waffles

Egg and sugar free waffles

CF, EF, FF, SF, SGF, TF, YF

Ingredients

¾ cup gf flour mix
I tsp gf baking powder
½ tsp salt
I tsp ground flaxseed/linseed (soaked in 2
    tbsp boiling water for 5 minutes)

½ cup gluten and dairy free
    milk alternative
2 tbsp oil

Method

- Mix together and sift the flour, baking powder and salt.
- Add the flaxseed/linseed, milk alternative and oil and beat together well with a hand mixer.
- Pour ⅓ of the mixture into a pre-heated electric waffle maker and cook for 3–5 minutes.

McGill Family, UK © Copyright

Waffles

CF, FF, SF, SGF, TF, YF

Ingredients

¾ cup gf flour mix
I tsp gf baking powder
½ tsp salt

2 eggs (separated)
½ cup gluten and dairy free
    milk substitute
2 tbsp oil

Method

- Mix together the flour, baking powder and salt.
- Add the egg yolks, milk alternative and oil and mix in well.
- In a separate bowl, whisk the egg whites until they have formed peaks.
- Fold the egg whites into the batter.
- Pour ⅓ of the batter into a pre-heated electric waffle maker

McGill Family, UK © Copyright

Waffles

CF, FF, SF, TF, YF

Ingredients

2½ oz (65g) gf flour mix
1 tsp gf baking powder
½ tsp xanthan gum
½ oz (7g) unrefined caster sugar
1 organic egg (separated)
4 fl oz (125ml) gluten and dairy free milk
    alternative
1 oz melted dairy free margarine
¼ tsp gf vanilla extract

Method

- In a bowl, mix together the flour, baking powder, xanthan gum and caster sugar.
- Mix in the egg yolk, milk alternative, melted margarine and vanilla extract.
- In a separate bowl, with an electric whisk/mixer beat the egg whites until stiff peaks are formed.
- Gently fold the egg whites into the batter.
- Pour ¼ of the mixture into a pre-heated electric waffle maker.

Marilyn Le Breton © Copyright 2001

Editor's note: My thanks to the McGill family who gave me the original idea for these waffles and whose recipe I have altered beyond belief in order to satisfy my fussy sons.

Waffles

CF, FF, SF, SGF, TF, YF

Ingredients

10½ oz (200g) IS Pure GF Blended Flour
1¾ tsp IS Pure Xanthan Gum
1 tbsp gf baking powder
½ tsp salt
2 eggs (separated)
14½ fl oz (425ml) gluten and dairy free
    milk alternative
4 fl oz (125ml) oil

Method

- In a large bowl, combine together well the flour, xanthan gum, baking powder and salt.
- In a separate bowl, beat the egg yolks together with a fork. Add in the oil and the milk and beat together well.
- Add the milk mixture to the flour mix and mix together; do not worry if the batter is a little lumpy.
- In a third bowl, whisk the egg whites until they are stiff.
- Gently fold the egg whites into the batter, until just mixed. Do not over mix.
- Place some of the mixture into a pre-heated electric waffle maker and cook for 3–6 minutes until golden.

Innovative Solutions (UK) Ltd © Copyright 2000

English pancakes

CF, FF, SF, SGF, TF, YF

Ingredients

1 cup gf flour mix
¼ tsp xanthan gum
1 large organic egg (beaten)
½ pint (300ml) gluten and dairy free milk
    alternative

Method

- Mix together the flour and xanthan gum.
- In a separate bowl, mix together the egg and milk.
- Add ½ of the milk mix to the flour mix and beat together until smooth.
- Gradually add the remaining milk, stirring the mix well all the time.
- The batter mixture should be lump free and runny, add more milk if necessary.
- For best results place the mixture in the fridge for 30 minutes before cooking.
- Cook as for normal pancakes.

Marilyn Le Breton © Copyright 2001

American pancakes

CF, FF, SF, TF, YF

Ingredients

2 cups gf flour
1¼ tsp xanthan gum
¼ tsp salt
1½ tsp gf baking powder
2 tbsp unrefined caster sugar

2 large organic eggs (beaten)
1 cup gluten and dairy free milk
    alternative
2 tbsp organic sunflower oil
½ tsp gf vanilla extract

Method

- Combine together the flour, xanthan gum, salt, baking powder and sugar in a large bowl.

- In a separate bowl, beat together the eggs, milk alternative, oil and vanilla extract.

- Gradually add the milk mixture to the flour mix, stirring all the time until lump free. Use a wooden spoon for this, not an electric mixer or hand whisk. Be careful not to over mix the batter.

- This batter should not be runny. It should drop in one piece from a spoon, when the spoon is turned upside down.

- Add more milk, if necessary to get the desired consistency.

- Heat a very little oil in a non-stick frying pan. Cook the pancake until small bubbles begin to form, and then flip it over.

- Do not be alarmed if these pancakes rise and look too high and thick, during cooking. They will 'collapse' when taken out of the pan.

Filling ideas

- *Don't stick to traditional sugar and lemon for these pancakes. Try jam, honey, cooked fruit and ice cream.*

Marilyn Le Breton © Copyright 2001

Buckwheat Pancakes

CF, FF, SF, SGF, TF, YF

Ingredients

½ cup white rice flour
½ cup buckwheat flour
I organic egg (beaten)
½ pint (300ml) gluten and dairy free milk
   alternative

Method

- Mix together the flours.
- In a separate bowl, mix together the egg and milk.
- Add ½ of the milk mix to the flour mix and beat together until smooth.
- Gradually add the remening milk, stirring the mix well all the time.
- The batter mixture should be lump free and runny, add more milk if necessary.
- For best results place the mixture in the fridge for 30 minutes before cooking.
- Cook as for normal pancakes.

Marilyn Le Breton © Copyright 2001

Spicy chickpea pancakes

CF, FF, SF, SGF, TF, YF

Ingredients

1 cup chickpea (gram) flour
1–2 tsp gf medium curry powder
1 large organic egg (beaten)
¼ pint (300ml) gluten and dairy free milk
    alternative
¼ pint (300ml) cold water

Method

- Mix the flour and curry powder together.
- In a separate bowl beat together the egg, water and milk alternative.
- Add ½ the milk mixture to the flour. Stir together with a wooden spoon, until the mixture is smooth and lump free.
- Gradually add the remaining milk mix, stirring all the time.
- Cook as for normal pancakes.

These are particularly good for wrapping up savoury fillings or using instead of pasta to layer between a meat and sauce mixture, like a lasagne.

These are also good to use as a chapati or naan bread substitute.

Marilyn Le Breton © Copyright 2001

Pancakes

CF, FF, SF, SGF, TF, YF,

Ingredients

4 oz (125g) DS All Purpose Flour
pinch of salt
2 medium eggs (beaten)
10 fl oz (300ml) gluten and dairy free milk
     alternative
oil for frying

Method

- Combine the DS flour with the salt.
- Beat together the eggs and half the milk alternative. Add this to the flour and mix together well.
- Add the remaining milk alternative gradually and beat in.
- Lightly coat the base of a frying pan with oil and place on a moderate heat.
- When the fat is hot, pour in sufficient batter to thinly cover the base of the pan.
- Cook until the pancake is set and golden brown, turn and cook the reverse side.
- Repeat with remaining mixture. Makes 6–8 pancakes.

These freeze well. Place a piece of greaseproof paper between each pancake before freezing.

Dietary Specialities © Copyright Nutrition Point 2001

No milk pancakes

CF, SF, SGF, TF, YF

Ingredients

1 cup white rice flour
¼ cup tapioca starch flour
2 tsp gf baking powder
1 tsp bicarbonate of soda
½ tsp salt

2 large eggs
¼ cup oil
15 oz (425g) can peach slices in
    juice

Method

- Drain off the majority of the juice from the tinned peaches and puree the peaches and a little juice in a blender.
- In a large bowl, mix together the flours, baking powder, bicarbonate of soda and salt.
- Into the flour mix, stir in the pureed peaches, eggs and oil. Beat together well to form a smooth batter.
- Cook as for normal pancakes.

Barbara's Kitchen © Copyright 2001

Potato Pancakes

CF, FF, SF, SGF, TF, YF

Ingredients

1 cup grated, raw potato
¼ cup potato starch flour
1 large egg (beaten)
seasoning to taste

Method

- Mix all the ingredients together well.
- Shape the mixture into patties.
- Fry until golden brown.

These freeze well.

Barbara's Kitchen © Copyright 2001

Potato Pancakes

CF, FF, SF, SGF, TF, YF

Ingredients

8 oz (225g) potatoes (boiled and mashed)
1 large organic egg (beaten)
1 organic egg white (whisked into soft peaks)

2 tbsp gluten and dairy free milk alternative
4 tsp gf flour mix
pinch of salt
pinch of gf baking powder

Method

- Whisk together the beaten egg, milk, flour, salt and baking powder to form a smooth batter.
- Stir the mashed potatoes into the batter.
- Carefully fold the whisked egg white into the potato mix.
- Heat a little oil in a frying pan and drop batter into the pan to form small pancakes (about 8).
- Cook each side of the pancake for approximately 2 minutes or until golden brown.

Variations

- *Add any variety of fresh or dried gf herbs or spices to batter.*
- *Add tiny pieces of nitrate free ham or pre-cooked nitrate free bacon.*
- *Add finely chopped spring onions.*

Plain potato pancakes freeze well.

Marilyn Le Breton © Copyright 2001

Drop scones

CF, FF, SF, SGF*, TF, YF

Ingredients

½ cup white rice flour
¼ cup tapioca starch flour
¼ cup potato starch flour
I large egg (beaten)

2 oz (50g) allowed margarine, melted
½ tsp xanthan gum
2 tsp gf baking powder
2½ tbsp sugar (optional)
½ cup gluten and dairy free milk alternative

Method

- Mix together the flours, xanthan gum, baking powder and sugar if using.
- Add the egg and mix in well.
- Slowly add the milk alternative and the margarine, mixing all the time.
- Using a tablespoon, drop the batter into an oiled hot griddle or frying pan.
- Cook until tiny bubbles appear on the top and the underneath is light brown, then flip over and cook until both sides are light brown.

Barbara suggests that you try these with savoury toppings as well as the traditional sweet toppings.

Barbara's Kitchen © Copyright 2001

Biscuits and Cookies

Travis's lemon o's

CF, EF, SF, TF, YF

Ingredients

1 cup dairy free margarine
2 cups gf flour mix
¾ cup caster sugar
⅓ cup liquid Dari-free or gluten and dairy
    free milk substitute
1 tbsp finely shredded lemon peel

Method

- Pre-heat Oven to GM5, 375F, 190C.
- With an electric mixer, beat together the margarine for approximately 25 seconds on the highest speed.
- Add ½ the flour to the margarine and beat together until combined.
- Add the sugar, Dari-free or milk alternative and shredded lemon peel. Beat until combined.
- Add the remaining flour and beat together.
- Drop the mix (teaspoon size) on to an ungreased baking sheet.
- Bake for 8–10 minutes.

Deborah Jusi © Copyright 2001

Biscotti

CF, FF, SF, TF, YF

Ingredients

18 oz (500g) gf flour mix
9 oz (250g) golden caster sugar
9 oz (250g) dairy free margarine (melted)
3 fl oz (75ml) gluten and dairy free milk
   alternative

3 large egg yolks
2 tsp gf baking powder
2 tsp xanthan gum
2 tsp gf vanilla extract

Method

- Pre-heat oven to GM4, 350F, 180C.
- Sift together the flour, sugar, baking powder and xanthan gum. Make a large well in the middle and add the egg yolks, melted margarine, milk and vanilla.
- Stir the mixture gently to bring the dough together and then turn it out onto a lightly floured work surface and knead lightly until smooth.

Then either

- Roll the dough into a fat sausage, wrap in clingfilm and chill for 1 hour.
- Then slice into thin ¼" (½ cm) width discs.

Or

- Place mixture into an icing bag with a medium star-shaped nozzle and pipe the shapes directly on to a baking tray.
- The baking trays should be greased and lightly dusted with rice flour.
- This will need two baking trays to accommodate the amount of biscuits.
- Bake for 20 minutes, then swap the baking tray positions and bake for a further 5 minutes.

If kept in an airtight container these will keep for 2–3 weeks.

Variation

- *Replace 3oz (60g) of the flour mix with 1½ oz (30g) of gf/cf cocoa powder and 1½ oz (30g) of chestnut flour.*

Maddalena Feliciello, Leeds © Copyright

Mason's cookies

CF, FF, SF, TF, YF

Ingredients

⅓ cup dairy free margarine
¼ cup lard or hard dairy free margarine
1 ⅓ cups gf flour mix
½ cup dark brown sugar
1 egg white

½ tsp gf baking powder
½ tsp bicarbonate of soda
1 tsp gf vanilla extract
sugar to dip fork in

Method

- Pre-heat oven to GM5, 375F, 190C.
- In a large mixing bowl, with an electric mixer, beat together margarine and lard for approximately 45 seconds (or until soft).
- Add ½ the flour mix and beat together until thoroughly combined.
- Add brown sugar, egg white, vanilla, baking powder and bicarbonate of soda and mix in thoroughly.
- Add remaining flour and beat together.
- Cover mixture and allow it to cool in the fridge for at least 4 hours (or overnight).
- Shape dough into balls and place on an ungreased baking tray.
- Dip a wet fork into sugar and press it down onto the balls, making a criss-cross shape.
- Bake for 7–9 minutes or until the bottoms of the cookies are lightly browned.

Ginger biscuits

CF, EF, FF, SF, TF, YF

Ingredients

1 cup gf flour mix
1 tsp gf baking powder
½ tsp xanthan gum
1 oz (25g) fructose
1–1½ tsp gf ground ginger (dependant on
    taste)
2 oz (50g) dairy free margarine
2 oz (2 tbsp/50g) golden syrup

Method

- Pre-heat oven to GM4, 350F, 175C
- Sift together all the dry ingredients.
- Rub in the margarine, until the mixture resembles breadcrumbs.
- Add the syrup. Mix it in first with a wooden spoon and then with your hands, to form a smooth ball.
- Divide the mixture into small balls (approximately 12) and place on a baking tray lined with greaseproof paper. Then press the balls flat with your fingers.
- Bake for 10 minutes.

McGill Family, UK © Copyright

Ginger biscuits

CF, EF, FF, SF, YF, TF

Ingredients

4 oz (125g) dairy free margarine
1½ cups gf flour mix
1½ tsp xanthan gum
1½ tsp gf baking powder
1 tsp gf ground ginger
1 tbsp golden syrup
3 oz (90g) unrefined natural dark brown
    sugar (or caster sugar)

Method

- Pre-heat oven to GM5, 375F, 190C.
- Melt syrup and margarine together in a glass bowl, over a pan of hot water, on a low heat.
- Sift all the dry ingredients together and add to the syrup mix.
- Combine first with a wooden spoon and then knead gently with hands, until dough combines together.
- Chill dough for at least an hour in the fridge.
- Use your hands to press the dough flat and cut using the smallest size cookie cutters, approximately 40 biscuits.
- Place on an ungreased baking tray and bake for 12–15 minutes.

Variation

- *Replace the ground ginger with a tsp of gf ground cinnamon.*

Marilyn Le Breton © Copyright 2001

Cinnamon drop biscuits

CF, FF, SF, TF, YF

Ingredients

5 oz (150g) dairy free margarine
8 oz (225g) granulated sugar
1 egg
½ tsp IS Pure Vanilla Extract
9 oz (250g) IS Pure GF Blended Flour
1½ tsp IS Pure Xanthan

¼ tsp bicarbonate of soda
¼ tsp cream of tartar
2 tbsp granulated sugar
1 tsp gf ground cinnamon

Method

- Pre-heat oven to GM5, 375F, 190C.
- With an electric mixer, set on high speed, beat the margarine for 30 seconds. Add the 8 oz (225g) of sugar and beat until fluffy.
- Beat in egg and vanilla.
- In a separate bowl, combine together well, the flour, xanthan, bicarbonate of soda and cream of tartar.
- Add approximately 6oz (175g) of the flour mix to the creamed mixture and combine until smooth.
- Mix in the rest of the flour and cover and chill for one hour.
- In a small bowl, combine together the cinnamon and the 2 tbsp of granulated sugar.
- Once the dough has chilled, shape into 1" (2.5cm) balls and roll each of them in the cinnamon sugar.
- Place the biscuits 1½" (4 cm) apart on an ungreased baking tray.
- Bake for 8–10 minutes for soft gooey biscuits and for 10–12 minutes for crispier biscuits.

Makes approximately 36 biscuits.

Toby's Smartie-like cookies

CF, FF, SF, TF, TF

Ingredients

3 oz (90g) dairy free margarine
3 oz (90g) granulated sugar
3 oz (90g) soft brown sugar
small amount of freshly crushed vanilla pod
1 egg

6 oz (175g) gf flour mix (Doves Farm)
¾ tsp gf baking powder
1 packet of Whizzers gluten and dairy free chocolate beans

Method

- Pre-heat oven to GM4, 350F, 180C.
- Cream together the margarine, sugar and vanilla.
- Add the egg and beat into the margarine mix.
- Fold in the flour and combine together well.
- Stir in the Whizzers.
- Divide the mixture into approximately 20 pieces.
- Place 10 at a time on to a greased baking tray (spread them out well).
- Bake for 10–12 minutes. Allow biscuits to cool slightly before removing from the tray.

Variation

- *The Whizzers can be replaced by gluten and dairy free chocolate chips.*

Gingerbread Men

EF, TF, YF

Ingredients

4 oz (125g) dairy free margarine
½ cup sugar
1 tsp Orgran 'No Egg'
2 cups Orgran Pizza/Pastry Mix
1 tsp bicarbonate of soda

3 tsp gf ground ginger
3 tbsp golden syrup
gf un-sulphated currants, gluten
and dairy free chocolate
chips and a little icing sugar
to decorate

Method

- Pre-heat oven to GM4, 350F, 180C.
- Warm golden syrup, either in a microwave (low setting), for approximately 20 seconds or in a glass bowl above a pan of hot water.
- Cream together the margarine and the sugar.
- Add the 'No Egg' and beat in well.
- Gradually sift in the pizza/pastry mix, bicarbonate of soda and ginger and combine well.
- Add in the golden syrup and mix in well.
- Gently knead the mixture with your hands.
- Roll out the dough to a 3mm thickness and use a gingerman cookie cutter.
- Lift the shapes onto a lightly greased baking tray.
- Use currants for eyes and the nose.
- Bake for 15 minutes and allow to cool slightly before removing from the tray.
- Use chocolate chips as buttons and icing for a mouth.

Orgran © Copyright 2000

Viennese biscuits

CF, FF, SF, TF, YF

Ingredients

7 oz (190g) gf flour mix
3 oz (90g) unrefined caster sugar
3½ oz (115g) dairy free margarine
1 egg (beaten)

½ tsp salt
½ tsp xanthan gum
½ tsp gf baking powder
½ tsp gf almond extract

Method

- Pre-heat oven GM5, 375F, 190C.
- Cream together the sugar and margarine.
- Mix in the egg and the almond extract
- Sift together the flour, salt, xanthan gum, and baking powder.
- Add flour mix to the sugar/margarine mixture and blend together well.

Then either

- Cover and place in fridge for a minimum of 3 hours.
- Roll out until a ¼" (½ cm) thick and cut out with medium size cookie cutter.

Or

- Put mixture in piping bag with a large holed icing nozzle and make swirls on a baking tray.
- Then place in fridge for 3 hours.
- Bake for 8 minutes.

When cold, sandwich two biscuits together with jam and 'butter' icing and dust with icing sugar.

Marilyn Le Breton © Copyright 2001

Chocolate Viennese biscuits

EF, FF, SF, TF, YF

Ingredients

3 oz (90g) gluten and dairy free chocolate
4½ oz (140g) dairy free margarine
3 oz (90g) icing sugar
6 oz (175g) gf flour mix

1½ tsp xanthan gum
1½ tsp gf baking powder
1 oz (25g) cornflour

Method

- Pre-heat oven to GM5, 375F, 190C.
- In a glass bowl above a pan of warm water, melt the chocolate.
- Cream together the margarine and the icing sugar.
- Add the melted chocolate and mix together well.
- Sift in the flours, xanthan gum and baking powder and stir well. It may be necessary to gently knead the mix with your hands to combine it thoroughly.
- Allow the mixture to chill for an hour.
- Press out the dough to a ¼" (½ cm) thick and cut into circles using a medium size cookie cutter.
- Place biscuits on an ungreased baking sheet and bake for 10–12 minutes.
- Allow biscuits to cool slightly before removing from tray.

Marilyn Le Breton © Copyright 2001

Double chocolate chip cookies

CF, FF, SF, TF, YF

Ingredients

1¾ cups gf flour mix
¼ cup gluten and dairy free cocoa powder
2 tsp xanthan gum
½ tsp baking powder
1¼ cups unrefined caster sugar

1 cup dairy free margarine
2 eggs (beaten)
1 tsp gf vanilla extract
2½ oz (75g) gluten and dairy free chocolate chips

Method

- Pre-heat oven to GM5, 375F, 190C.
- Combine the flour, cocoa powder, xanthan gum and baking powder together.
- Cream sugar and margarine together. Beat in the eggs and then add the vanilla.
- Gradually add in the flour mixture and cream together.
- Stir in chocolate chips.
- Roughly mould the mix into small balls between 2 teaspoons or drop a small amount from a spoon. Mixture makes approximately 35 cookies.
- Place balls onto an ungreased baking tray.
- Bake for 12–15 minutes. Remove immediately from tray and allow them to cool.

Variations

- *Omit the cocoa powder and add an extra ¼ cup of gf flour mix, for plain chocolate chip cookies.*
- *Omit the cocoa chips for American style chocolate cookies.*
- *Omit the vanilla extract and replace with 2–3 tsp of grated orange zest for orange flavoured chocolate chip cookies.*

Marilyn Le Breton © Copyright 2001

'Butter' crunch biscuits

CF, EF, FF, SF, TF, YF

Ingredients

6 oz (175g) dairy free margarine
1 tsp xanthan gum
1 tsp gf baking powder
4 oz (125g) unrefined caster sugar
1 tsp gf vanilla extract
8 oz (225g) gf flour mix
4 tbsp unrefined granulated or caster sugar

Method

- Pre-heat oven to GM4, 350F, 180C.
- Cream together the caster sugar and margarine, until fluffy.
- Add the vanilla extract.
- Gradually sift in the flour and xanthan gum and mix to form a stiff dough. Work the dough together with your hands if necessary.
- Chill mixture in the fridge for at least an hour.
- Using the flat of your hand, press out the dough to ¼" (½ cm) thick.
- Cut out using a medium size cookie cutter.
- Dip one side of each cookie into the granulated sugar and place on a baking tray.
- Bake for 12–15 minutes.

Variation

- *Omit the vanilla extract and replace with 2 tsp of grated lemon rind.*

Marilyn Le Breton © Copyright 2001

Fruity crumble bars

CF, SF, TF, YF

Crumble bar

2 cups gf flour mix
2 tsp xanthan gum
6 oz (175g) unrefined caster sugar
6 oz (175g) dairy free margarine
icing sugar to dust

Fruity filling

3 large eggs (beaten)
7 oz (200g) unrefined caster sugar
3 fl oz (90ml) fruit juice of choice
1 oz (25g) gf plain flour

Method

- Pre-heat oven to GM4, 350F, 180C.
- Mix together the flour, xanthan gum, caster sugar and margarine, until it resembles fine breadcrumbs.
- Divide this mixture in half. Place ½ the mix into the bottom of a 7" (18cm) square tin lined with greaseproof paper and press it down hard with the back of a spoon.
- Bake for 15 minutes.

To make the fruity filling

- Whisk the eggs, sugar and fruit juice until smooth.
- Add flour and whisk again, until smooth and lump free.
- Pour fruity filling over the part cooked base and bake for 20 minutes.
- Sprinkle the remaining flour mixture over the fruity topping (do not press it down) and bake for a further 20 minutes.
- Leave to cool before removing from the tin.
- Dust with icing sugar and cut into approximately 30 pieces.

Marilyn Le Breton © Copyright 2001

Blueberry and orange bars

CF, SF, TF, YF

Ingredients

1 sachet DS Juicy Blueberry Muffin Mix
2 medium eggs (beaten)
2 fl oz (50ml) sunflower oil
zest of 1 orange

2½ fl oz (75ml) orange juice (make up with water if necessary)
1 oz (25g) un-sulphated desiccated coconut (optional)

Method

- Pre-heat the oven to GM4, 350F, 180C.
- Mix together the muffin mix, eggs, oil, orange zest and juice.
- Pour the mixture into a 7"(18cm) square tin lined with greaseproof paper.
- Sprinkle the coconut (if using) over the top of the mix.
- Bake for 40 minutes.
- When cold, cut into bars.

These bars freeze well.

Dietary Specialties © Copyright 2001

Rice flour biscuits

EF, FF, SF, TF, YF

Ingredients

4 oz (125g) white rice flour
2 oz (60g) cornflour

4 oz (125g) dairy free margarine
2 oz (60g) caster sugar

Method

- Pre-heat oven to GM3, 325F, 170C.
- Mix together the white rice flour and cornflour.
- Cream together the margarine and sugar.
- Combine the flour and creamed margarine mix.
- Roll out the mixture and cut out using a cookie cutter.
- Bake on a baking tray lined with greaseproof paper for approximately 20 minutes.

Kate Coull, Abergele © Copyright

Orange cookies

CF, SF, TF, YF

Ingredients

2 ⅓ cups gf flour
1 cup caster sugar
¾ cup dairy free margarine
1 egg
2 tsp finely grated orange peel
2 tbsp orange juice

1 tsp gf baking powder
¼ tsp sea salt
½ cup finlely chopped almonds
  (or caster sugar)

Method

- Pre-heat oven to GM5, 375F, 190C.
- Combine all ingredients with a wooden spoon, then beat with an electric mixer at the highest speed for a full 2 minutes.
- Divide the mixture in half and roll each half into a 7" (18cm) long roll.
- Roll dough sausage in the chopped almonds (or sugar).
- Push the mixture on the dough to make it flat and wrap it in greaseproof paper and chill in fridge overnight.
- Cut the dough into ¼" (½ cm) wide slices and place on an ungreased baking tray.
- Bake for 10–12 minutes until lightly browned.

Variation

- *To make these cookies extra special, cover with a light layer of icing.*

Almost sugar free biscuits

CF, EF, SF, TF, YF

Ingredients

6 oz (175g) gf flour mix
1 ½ tsp xanthan gum
6 oz (175g) dairy free margarine
5–6 tsp iced water
a little melted dairy free margarine
2 tbsp unrefined caster sugar

Method

- Pre-heat oven to GM6, 400F, 200C.
- Mix together flour, xanthan gum and margarine.
- Gradually add the iced water. The dough should come away from the sides of the mixing bowl.
- Cover and chill in the fridge for at least an hour.
- Roll out the dough to ⅛" (3mm) thickness.
- Cut out circles, using a large sized cookie cutter (makes approximately 30 circles).
- Brush circles with melted margarine and sprinkle with sugar.
- Bake 10–12 minutes.

Variation

- *When cold, sandwich two biscuits together with jam or jam and 'butter' cream icing.*

Sugar free chickpea biscuits

CF, EF, FF, SF, SGF, TF, YF

Ingredients

2 oz (50g) chickpea flour
2 tbsp potato starch flour or tapioca starch
    flour
1 tbsp ground linseed/flaxseed
½ tsp xanthan gum
1 tsp gf baking powder
¼–½ tsp sea salt
2 tbsp organic sunflower oil
2–3 tbsp water

Method

- Pre-heat oven to GM4, 350F, 180C.
- Sift together the flours, linseed/flaxseed, xanthan gum, baking powder and salt.
- Stir in the water and oil to form a dough. If it is too sticky to handle, add a little more potato or tapioca starch.
- Roll the dough out thinly between 2 sheets of parchment paper to form a rectangle.
- Cut dough into finger shapes, approximately 2"x1" (5cm x 2.5cm).
- Carefully lift biscuits onto a baking tray lined with parchment paper.
- Bake for 10–12 minutes, or until they have a firm but crumbly texture like oatcakes.
- Bake for an extra 2–3 minutes if you require a crunchy texture.

These biscuits do not keep well and are best eaten the day they are baked.

Variation

- *Mix half chickpea flour and brown rice flour for a crunchier texture. These biscuits will keep to the following day.*

McGill Family, UK © Copyright

Jack's birthday biscuits

CF, FF, SF, TF, YF

Ingredients

1 cup cf margarine
1½ cups unrefined caster sugar
1 egg (beaten)
1 tsp gf vanilla extract
2½ cups gf flour mix
½ tsp xanthan gum
½ tsp salt

Method

- Pre-heat oven to GM4, 350F, 180C.
- Cream together the margarine and sugar.
- Add in the egg and vanilla. Beat together well.
- Sift in the flour, xanthan gum and salt.
- Combine the mixture well.
- Chill the dough for at least 3 hours (overnight is better).
- Press the dough flat, either with your hand or roll out with a rolling pin, until it is ¼" (½ cm) thick.
- Using medium size cookie cutters, cut out the biscuits and place on a baking tray lined with greaseproof paper.
- Bake for 8–10 minutes.

Marilyn Le Breton © Copyright 2001

Peanut butter cookies

EF, FF, TF, YF

Ingredients

6 oz (175g) gf flour mix (Doves Farm)
½ tsp bicarbonate of soda
½ tsp salt
4 oz (125g) dairy free margarine (Pure)
5½ oz (160g) caster sugar or natural light
   brown sugar
1 egg (beaten)
1 tsp gf vanilla extract
8 oz (227g) jar of peanut butter

Method

- Pre-heat oven to GM5, 375F, 190C.
- Mix together the flour, bicarbonate of soda, salt and sugar.
- Cream together the margarine and sugar in a separate bowl.
- Add to the creamed mixture the egg and vanilla extract and stir together well.
- Gradually stir in the dry mix until combined well.
- Mix in the peanut butter.
- On a baking tray lined with greaseproof paper, place golf ball sized mixture and press each down slightly with a wet fork.
- Bake for approximately 15 minutes.

Angela Deakin, Fareham © Copyright

Peanut butter cookies

CF, FF, SF, TF, YF

Ingredients

4 oz (125g) dairy free margarine
5 oz (150g) smooth peanut butter
8 oz (225g) unrefined caster sugar
1 egg (beaten)
5 oz (150g) gf flour mix
1 tsp xanthan gum
1 tsp gf baking powder

Method

- Pre-heat oven to GM5, 375F, 190C.
- Cream together the margarine and sugar.
- Add the peanut butter and cream into the mix.
- Add the beaten egg and mix in well.
- Sift in the flour, baking powder and xanthan gum.
- Shape the mixture into balls the size of golf balls.
- Place on a baking tray, leaving plenty of room between each ball, as they will spread out during cooking.
- Using your fingers, flatten the balls slightly.
- Bake for 12–15 minutes or until golden brown and slightly crisp on the rim.
- Allow biscuits to cool completely before removing from the baking tray.

Makes approximately 25 biscuits.

Marilyn Le Breton © Copyright 2001

Chocolate peanut cookies

CF, EF, FF, SF, TF, YF

Ingredients

7 oz (200g) gf flour mix
1 tbsp gluten and dairy free cocoa powder
2 tsp xanthan gum
½ tsp gf baking powder
3 oz (90g) dairy free margarine
4 oz (125g) unrefined caster sugar
1 tsp gf vanilla extract
4 oz (125g) unsalted peanuts (chopped)

Method

- Pre-heat oven to GM4, 350F, 180C.
- Sift together the flour, cocoa, xanthan gum and baking powder.
- In a separate bowl, cream together the sugar and margarine. Stir in the vanilla.
- Gradually add in the flour mix and stir in well until a soft dough is formed.
- Stir in the peanuts.
- Divide the mixture into approximately 25 balls and place on a baking tray, leaving plenty of room for the cookies to spread during cooking.
- Flatten the balls slightly with your fingers.
- Bake for 10–12 minutes.

Vanilla and almond cookies

CF, EF, FF, SF, TF, YF

Ingredients

2 cups gf flour mix
1½ tsp xanthan gum
½ tsp cream of tartar
½ tsp bicarbonate of soda
⅓ cup unrefined caster sugar
6 oz (175g) dairy free margarine (softened)
½ tsp gf almond extract
½ tsp gf vanilla extract

Method

- Pre-heat oven to GM5, 375F, 190C.
- Mix together the flour, xanthan gum, cream of tartar, bicarbonate of soda and sugar.
- Cream in the softened cf margarine, until all the ingredients are combined together well.
- Add the almond and vanilla extract and mix in well.
- Divide the mixture into 25 and shape into rough balls.
- Place the dough balls on a baking tray and squash each of them down slightly.
- Bake for 12–15 minutes.

Shrewsbury Biscuits

CF, SF, TF, YF

Ingredients

4 oz (125g) dairy free margarine
5 oz (150g) unrefined caster sugar
2 egg yolks
8 oz (225g) gf flour mix
2 tsp xanthan gum
finely grated rind of 1 lemon

Method

- Pre-heat oven to GM4, 350F, 180C.
- Cream together the margarine and sugar.
- Stir in the egg yolks and mix together well.
- In a separate bowl, sift together the flour and xanthan gum.
- Into the flour mixture, stir the lemon rind.
- Fold the flour mixture into the margarine mixture, to form a firm dough.
- Knead the dough lightly.
- On a floured surface, roll the dough out until ¼" thick.
- Using a small sized cookie cutter, cut out the biscuits and place on baking tray.
- Bake for approximately 12 minutes, until beginning to turn golden.

Variations

- *2 oz (50g) of gf un-sulphated chopped, dried fruit can be added at the same time as the lemon rind.*
- *The lemon rind can be replaced with the finely grated rind of half an orange.*

Marilyn Le Breton © Copyright 2001

Blueberry and sultana cookies

CF, SF, TF, YF

Ingredients

1 sachet of DS Juicy Blueberry Muffin Mix
4 oz (125g) dairy free margarine
1 medium egg (beaten)
2 oz (50g) gf un-sulphated sultanas

Method

- Pre-heat oven to GM5, 375F, 190C.
- In a large bowl, combine all the ingredients, working them together by hand to form a smooth dough.
- Divide the mixture into 20 walnut sized balls.
- Place the cookie balls onto a baking tray, allowing room for the cookies to spread and then flatten the top of each ball slightly.
- Bake for approximately 15 minutes.

Variation

- *Substitute the sultanas for gf un-sulphated papaya, pear, pineapple or dates.*

Dietary Specialities © Copyright 2001

Cranberry and sultana biscuits

CF, SF, TF, YF

Ingredients

4½ oz (135g) dairy free margarine
4 oz (125g) natural brown sugar
2 oz (50g) granulated sugar
1 tsp IS Pure Vanilla Extract
1 egg (beaten)
6 oz (175g) IS Pure GF Flour Blend
1 tsp IS Pure Xanthan Gum
½ tsp salt
½ tsp bicarbonate of soda
2½ oz (70g) dried gf
  un-sulphated cranberries*
2½ oz (70g) dried gf
  un-sulphated sultanas

If you have trouble obtaining dried cranberries the recipe works well by adding an extra 2½ oz sultanas.

Method

- Pre-heat oven to GM5, 375F, 190C.
- Cream together the margarine and sugar.
- Add the egg and vanilla.
- In a separate bowl, sift together the flour, xanthan gum, salt and bicarbonate of soda.
- Gradually add the flour mix to the creamed mixture, combining each addition well, until smooth.
- Add cranberries and sultanas and stir in well.
- Cover mixture and cool in the fridge for ½ hour.
- Drop biscuit dough from a teaspoon onto an ungreased baking tray. Biscuits should be approximately 1½" in diameter and 1" high.
- Bake for 6–8 minutes or until golden brown.

Coconut melts

CF, EF, FF, SF, TF, YF

Ingredients

4 oz (125g) dairy free margarine
4 oz (125g) creamed coconut (block not
    liquid)
6 oz (175g) gf flour mix
4 oz (125g) unrefined caster sugar
1 ½ tsp xanthan gum
1 ½ tsp gf baking powder

Method

- Pre-heat oven to GM5, 375F, 190C.
- In a glass bowl over a pan of hot water, melt together the margarine and the creamed coconut.
- In a separate bowl, mix together the flour, sugar, xanthan gum and baking powder.
- To the flour mix, add the melted coconut mix. Stir together with a spoon and then work together with your hands, until they are combined into a ball of dough.
- Chill in the fridge for at least 1 hour.
- Using the ball and flat of your hand, press the dough out until ¼" thick.
- Cut into circles using a small sized cookie cutter.
- Place onto an ungreased baking tray and bake for approximately 12 minutes or until just beginning to brown.
- Allow biscuits to cool, before removing from the baking tray with a spatula. These biscuits remain crumbly until completely cold.

Makes approximately 45 biscuits.

Marilyn Le Breton © Copyright 2001

Coconut macaroons

CF, FF, SF, TF, YF

Ingredients

2 egg whites
4 oz (125g) icing sugar
4 oz (125g) ground almonds

¼ tsp gf almond extract
4 oz (125g) un-sulphated,
    desiccated coconut

Method

- Pre-heat oven to GM2, 300F, 150C.
- Whisk the egg white until it is stiff.
- Gently fold in the icing sugar.
- Gently mix in the coconut, ground almonds and almond extract. This will result in a sticky dough.
- Using a teaspoon, divide the mixture into approximately 24 walnut size pieces and place onto a baking tray lined with greaseproof paper.
- Bake for 25 minutes. The macaroons should be just changing colour on the outside, but soft on the inside.

Marilyn Le Breton © Copyright 2001

Almond macaroons

CF, FF, SF, TF, YF

Ingredients

2 egg whites
8 oz (225g) unrefined caster sugar
6 oz (175g) ground almonds

Method

- Pre-heat the oven to GM4, 350F, 180C.
- Whisk egg whites until they are stiff.
- With a spoon, gently fold in the almonds and icing sugar.
- Spoon mixture onto a baking tray, leaving room for the macaroons to spread.
- Bake for 15–18 minutes.
- Allow biscuits to cool before removing from baking tray.

Marilyn Le Breton © Copyright 2001

Apricot rock drops

CF, SF, TF, YF

Ingredients

4 oz (125g) dairy free margarine
7 oz (200g) gf flour mix
2 tsp xanthan gum
2 tsp gf baking powder
3 oz (90g) unrefined caster sugar

3 oz (90g) un-sulphated dried
  apricots (chopped)
1 egg (beaten)
2 tbsp gluten and dairy free milk
  alternative

Method

- Pre-heat oven to GM6, 400F, 200C.
- Sift together the flour, xanthan gum and baking powder.
- Rub in the margarine, until the mixture resembles fine breadcrumbs.
- Stir in the sugar.
- Stir in the chopped apricots.
- Add the beaten egg and mix together well.
- Use as much of the milk as necessary to combine all the mixture. Do not allow it to get too wet.
- Divide the mixture into 12 and using a spoon drop each onto a baking tray.
- Bake for 15–18 minutes or until the biscuit is firm to the touch.

Marilyn Le Breton © Copyright 2001

Chocolate chip biscuits

CF, FF, SF, TF, YF

Ingredients

7 oz (200g) gf flour mix
2 tsp xanthan gum
2 tsp gf baking powder
4 oz (125g) dairy free margarine
4 oz (125g) unrefined caster sugar
1 egg (beaten)
4 oz (125g) gluten and dairy free chocolate
   chips

Method

- Pre-heat oven to GM5, 375F, 190C.
- Cream together the margarine and sugar.
- Add the egg and beat in, to combine.
- Sift flour, baking powder and xanthan gum and add to the creamed mixture. Beat in well.
- Add the chocolate chips and stir in well.
- Place heaped teaspoons of the mixture on a baking tray and bake for 10–12 minutes.

Marilyn Le Breton © Copyright 2001

Shortbread

CF, EF, FF, SF, TF, YF

Ingredients

6 oz (175g) dairy free margarine
3 oz (90g) caster sugar
6 oz (175g) rice flour
3 oz (90g) ground almonds
½ tsp gf vanilla extract

Method

- Pre-heat oven to GM4, 350F, 190C.
- Cream together the margarine, sugar and vanilla essence.
- Stir in the flour and ground almonds.
- Chill in the fridge for approximately 1 hour.
- Roll out the mixture and cut with cookie cutters.
- Bake until golden brown.
- Allow shortbread to cool for approximately 5 minutes, before lifting off tray with a palette knife.

Variation

- *For chocolate flavoured shortbread, reduce the ground almonds to 2 oz (60g) and add 1 oz (30g) gluten and dairy free cocoa powder.*

Alison Steele, Northampton © Copyright

Shortbread

CF, EF, FF, SF, TF, YF

Ingredients

1½ cups white rice flour
4 oz (125g) dairy free margarine (softened)
2 oz (60g) unrefined caster sugar

Method

- Pre-heat oven to GM3, 325F, 170C.
- Mix together the flour and sugar.
- Mix in the margarine by hand until the mixture resembles breadcrumbs.
- Using the back of a wooden spoon, press the mix into an 8" sandwich tin, lined with greaseproof paper. Be brutal when pressing down the mixture or it will crumble when removed from the tray.
- Bake for 40 minutes or until the top of the shortbread turns pale.
- Cut the shortbread while it is still hot, but do not attempt to take it out of the tray until it is completely cold.

Marilyn Le Breton © Copyright 2001

Shortbread

EF, FF, SF, TF, YF

Ingredients

2½ cups Orgran Self-raising Flour
½ cup rice flour

8 oz (220g) dairy free margarine (melted)
1 cup icing sugar (sifted)

Method

- Pre-heat oven to GM2, 300F, 150C.
- Mix together all the ingredients.
- Knead the dough for approximately 1 minute. Add more self-raising flour if the dough is too wet and sticky.
- On a floured surface, roll out the dough until it is 1cm thick.
- Place dough on a baking tray, lined with greaseproof paper and prick the surface with a fork.
- Bake for 15 minutes or until lightly brown.

Orgran © Copyright 2000

Cakes, Brownies, Muffins and Donuts

Butterscotch brownies

CF, FF, SF, TF, YF

Ingredients

1½ cups gf flour mix
1½ tsp xanthan gum
1 tsp gf baking powder
5 oz (150g) dairy free margarine
4 oz (125g) natural unrefined brown sugar

4 oz (125g) unrefined caster sugar
1 tsp gf vanilla essence
2 large eggs (beaten)

Method

- Pre-heat oven GM4, 350F, 180C.
- Mix together flour, xanthan gum and baking powder.
- In a separate bowl, cream together margarine, sugar and vanilla extract.
- Into the margarine mix, add eggs and beat together well.
- Slowly add flour mix and combine together.
- Pour the mixture into a 9" square tin, lined with greaseproof paper.
- Bake for 40 minutes.
- Allow to cake to cool completely before removing from tin.

Variation

For special occasions, convert into a butterscotch brownie with a marble chocolate topping by:

- *Before baking, drizzle over the top of the mixture, 4 oz (125g) of gluten and dairy free melted chocolate.*
- *Run a knife through the chocolate several times to make a marbled effect.*

Marilyn Le Breton © Copyright 2001

Chocolate chip brownies

CF, FF, SF, TF, YF

Ingredients

½ cup dairy free margarine (melted)
½ cup gluten and dairy free cocoa powder
2 eggs (beaten)
I cup caster sugar
I tsp gf vanilla extract
¼ cup brown rice flour
¼ cup potato starch flour
¾ cup gluten and dairy free chocolate
    chips

Method

- Pre-heat oven to GM5, 375F, 190C.
- Combine together the cocoa and melted margarine.
- In a separate bowl, beat together with an electric mixer, the eggs, sugar and vanilla, until light and fluffy.
- Add the cocoa mixture and blend together well.
- Gently fold in the flours.
- Stir in chocolate chips.
- Line an 8"x 8" baking pan with greaseproof paper and carefully pour in the brownie mixture.
- Bake for 25–30 minutes. Do not over-bake the brownie as it will become too dry.
- Allow brownie to cool before removing from tin.

Chocolate brownies

CF, FF, SF, TF, YF

Ingredients

⅔ cup dairy free margarine
5 oz (150g) gluten and dairy free chocolate
2 eggs (beaten)
1 cup unrefined caster sugar
1 cup gf flour mix
1 tsp xanthan gum
½ tsp gf baking powder
1 tsp gf vanilla extract

Method

- Pre-heat oven to GM4, 350F, 180C.
- Melt together the chocolate and margarine, in a glass bowl above a pan of hot water, on a low heat.
- In a separate bowl, mix together the eggs and sugar.
- Combine together the chocolate and egg mix and stir until it thickens.
- In a separate bowl, mix together the flour, xanthan gum, and baking powder.
- Slowly stir the flour mix into the chocolate mix. When combined well, add the vanilla extract.
- Bake for 40–45 minutes in a 9" square tin, lined with greaseproof paper.
- Allow to cool completely before removing from tin.

Marilyn Le Breton © Copyright 2001

Chocolate brownies

CF, FF, SF, TF, YF

Ingredients

2 oz (50g) gf flour mix
¼ tsp xanthan gum
I tsp gf baking powder
¼ tsp salt
4 oz (125g) fructose
2 eggs (beaten)
2 oz (50g) gluten and dairy free chocolate
    (Green and Black's 'Maya Gold')
4 oz (125g) dairy free margarine

Method

- Pre-heat oven to GM3, 325 F, 170C.
- Sift together the flour, xanthan gum, baking powder, salt and fructose.
- Melt together the chocolate and margarine, in a glass bowl over a pan of simmering water. Remove from heat.
- Combine the chocolate and flour mixes well.
- Pour the mixture into an 8" square baking tin lined with greaseproof paper.
- Bake for 25–35 minutes.

Peanut butter brownies

CF, FF, SF, TF, YF

Ingredients

1 sachet DS Brownie Mix
2 medium eggs (beaten)
5 tbsp sunflower oil

3 tbsp crunchy peanut butter
1 tbsp gluten and dairy free milk
   alternative or water

Method

- Pre-heat oven to GM4, 350F, 180C.
- Mix together all ingredients until well combined.
- Pour mixture into an 8" square tin, lined with greaseproof paper and smooth over the surface.
- Bake for approximately 30 minutes, until well risen and firm to the touch.
- Remove from tin whilst still warm and allow brownie to cool before cutting into squares or fingers with a sharp knife.

Dietary Specialities © Copyright 2001

Tutti frutti brownies

CF, SF, TF, YF

Ingredients

1 sachet of DS Brownie Mix
2 medium eggs (beaten)
7 tbsp sunflower oil

2 oz (50g) gf un-sulphated
   raisins
2 oz (50g) gf glacé cherries
   (chopped)

Method

- Pre-heat oven to GM4, 350F, 180C.
- Mix together the brownie mix, eggs and oil.
- Stir in the cherries and raisins.
- Spread the mixture into an 8" square tin, lined with greaseproof paper.
- Bake for approximately 30 minutes, until well risen and firm to the touch.
- Remove cake from tin whilst still warm.
- When cold cut into fingers or squares.

Dietary Specialities © Copyright 2001

Chocolate marble cake

CF, FF, SF, TF, YF

Ingredients

3 oz (90g) gluten and dairy free chocolate (melted)
8 oz (225g) dairy free margarine
8 oz (225g) unrefined caster sugar
4 large eggs (beaten)

8 oz (225g) gf flour mix
2 tsp xanthan gum
2½ tsp gf baking powder
1 tsp vanilla extract
3 tbsp gluten and dairy free milk alternative

Method

- Pre-heat oven to GM4, 350F, 180C.
- Cream together the margarine and sugar. Then add the eggs and beat together well.
- Sift in the flour, xanthan gum and baking powder. Fold together until well mixed.
- Divide the mixture in half.
- To one half, add the vanilla extract and milk, mix in well.
- Into the other half, stir the melted chocolate.
- In a 9" square baking tin, lined with greaseproof paper, place alternate spoonfuls of the two mixtures.
- Swirl a knife through the mixture, many times (and from different directions) to achieve a marbled effect.
- Bake for 30–35 minutes.
- Allow cake to cool completely before removing from tin.

Marilyn Le Breton © Copyright 2001

Chocolate fridge cake

CF, EF, FF, SF, TF, YF

Ingredients

10 oz (300g) crushed gluten and dairy free
      biscuits (or crushed gluten free
      cornflakes/rice puffs, etc.)
3½ oz (115g) dairy free margarine
2 tbsp golden syrup
2 tbsp gluten and dairy free cocoa powder
3½ oz (115g) gluten and dairy free
      chocolate

Method

- Melt margarine, syrup and cocoa powder together over a low heat.
- Stir in the crushed biscuits/cereal.
- Place mixture in an 8" square baking tin, lined with greaseproof paper.
- Allow the mixture to cool for approximately 15 minutes and then place in the fridge for 30 minutes.
- Melt chocolate and spread this over the chilled cake and return to fridge until set.

Variation

- *Reduce the biscuits/cereal mix by 2 oz (50g) and replace with 2 oz (50g) of gf un-sulphated raisins. Add to the mixture, when adding the biscuits/cereal.*

Sarah Oliver, Trowbridge © Copyright

Chocolate puffed rice squares

CF, EF, FF, SF, TF, YF

Ingredients

7 oz (200g) gluten free puffed rice cereal
5 oz (150g) dairy free margarine
8 fl oz (225ml) golden syrup
8 oz (225g) granulated sugar
3½ oz (110g) gluten and dairy free cocoa
    powder
1 tsp gf IS Pure Vanilla Extract

Method

- In a saucepan combine the margarine, golden syrup, cocoa powder and both types of sugar and bring the mixture to the boil.
- Remove from heat and add the vanilla extract.
- Pour the mixture over the puffed rice and stir well until all of the cereal is coated.
- Spoon the mixture into a greased 9" x 11" oblong tin and press the mixture down with the back of a spoon.
- Allow cake to cool and cut into squares with a sharp knife.

Variation

- *Replace the puffed rice with 6 oz (175g) of puffed millet cereal.*

Vanilla Sponge loaf

CF, FF, SF, TF, YF

Ingredients

5 oz (150g) dairy free margarine (melted)
4 large eggs (beaten and at room
    temperature)
8 oz (225g) unrefined caster sugar
8 oz (225g) gf flour mix
2 tsp xanthan gum
1 tsp gf baking powder
1½ tsp gf vanilla extract

Method

- Pre-heat oven to GM4, 350F, 180C.
- Warm a glass bowl and whisk together the eggs and sugar until the mixture is thick (the whisk should leave a trail when lifted). This takes 4–5 minutes with an electric whisk.
- Slowly add in the cooled, melted margarine, whisking all the time, at the lowest speed. The mixture should now be very thick.
- In a separate bowl, sift together the flour, xanthan gum and baking powder.
- Gently fold the flour into the egg mix, until it is combined.
- Stir in the vanilla extract.
- Gently spoon the mixture into a 2 lb loaf tin, lined with greaseproof paper.
- Bake for 1 hour and 10 minutes.

This cake keeps for approximately 4 days and freezes well, for one month.
Marilyn Le Breton © Copyright 2001

Sponge cake

CF, FF, SF, TF, YF

Ingredients

1 cup white rice flour
1 cup tapioca starch flour
¼ cup potato starch flour
1¼ cups sugar
2 tsp gf baking powder
1 tsp xanthan gum

pinch of finely crushed sea salt
3 large eggs
1 egg white
2 tsp gf vanilla extract
½ cup allowed milk
4 oz (125g) dairy free margarine

Method

- Pre-heat oven to GM4, 350F, 180C.
- In a large bowl mix together the flours, sugar, baking powder, xanthan gum and salt.
- In a separate bowl, using an electric mixer, whisk together the eggs, egg white, vanilla extract, milk and margarine.
- Slowly add the flour to the margarine mixture, stirring all the time. Mix for 3–4 minutes until well combined.
- Divide the mixture between 2 greased and lined 7" sponge tins and cook for 20–25 minutes.
- Or cook all mixture in a greased and lined 7" cake tin for 60–90 minutes.

Barbara's Kitchen © Copyright 2001

Egg free white cake

CF, EF, FF, SF, TF, YF

Ingredients

2 cups gf flour mixture (i.e., Bette Hagman
    Flour Mixture)
1¼ cups granulated sugar
2½ tsp gf baking powder
2 tsp xanthan gum (optional)
½ cup dairy free margarine or shortening
¾ cup gluten and dairy free milk
    alternative (reduce by 1 tsp if using rice
    milk)

Egg replacer

⅓ cup water
3½ tsp flaxseed meal (i.e., Bob's
    Red Mill)
3 tsp gf baking powder
3 tsp oil

Method

- Pre heat oven to GM5, 375F, 190C.
- Whisk together all the ingredients of the egg replacement and allow to stand for 5 minutes before using.
- Combine together the flour, sugar, baking powder and xanthan gum (if using).
- Into the flour mixture, cut the margarine or shortening and add the milk.
- Add the flaxseed mixture and beat whole together for approximately 2 minutes or until the mixture is thick and creamy.
- Divide the mixture between 2 well greased 8" sandwhich tins or lined cup cake trays.
- Bake the cake for 25–30 minutes. Bake the cupcakes for 18–22 minutes.

Diane Hartman © Copyright 2001

Strawberry shortcake

EF, SF, TF, YF

Ingredients

6½ oz (190g) Orgran Pizza/Pastry
   Multi-Mix
2½ oz (60g) dairy free margarine
2 tbsp icing sugar
4 fl oz (90 ml) water

1 punnet of strawberries
   (washed, drained and cut
   into halves)
½ cup strawberry jam
2 tsp water

Method

- Pre-heat oven to GM4, 350F, 180C.
- Mix together the multi-mix and the sugar.
- Rub in the margarine until the mixture resembles fine breadcrumbs.
- Add water and using your hands, knead the mixture into a dough.
- Allow dough to stand in a warm place for 15 minutes and then knead again.
- Press into a lightly greased 20cm sandwich tin.
- Bake for 15–20 minutes.
- Allow the shortbread to cool slightly and then remove from tin.
- Arrange the strawberry halves over the warm shortbread.
- Mix together the jam and 2 tsp of water, stir over a low heat, then strain this through a sieve.
- Allow jam mix to cool slightly then brush the mixture over the strawberries.
- Cool and serve.

Orgran © Copyright 2000

Rock cakes

SF, TF, YF

Ingredients

2 cups Orgran Self-raising Flour (sifted)
3 oz (90g) dairy free margarine
½ cup caster sugar
½ cup gf un-sulphated dried fruit of choice
I tbsp chopped mixed nuts
½ tsp gf ground ginger
I egg (beaten)
I tbsp gluten and dairy free milk alternative

Method

- Pre-heat oven to GM6, 400F, 200C.
- Rub together the flour and margarine until the mixture is fine and crumbly.
- Mix in the fruit, sugar, nuts and ginger.
- Whisk together the egg and milk and add this to the flour mixture. Mix until you have a stiff dough.
- Spoon mixture onto a well greased baking tray into approximately 20 small cakes.
- Bake for 15 minutes or until golden brown.

Orgran © Copyright 2000

Egg free plain scones

CF, EF, FF, SF, TF, YF

Ingredients

1 cup white rice flour
½ cup tapioca starch flour
½ tsp xanthan gum
2 tsp gf baking powder
4 tbsp sugar
4 oz (125g) dairy free margarine
2–3 oz (50–75ml) gluten and dairy free
    milk alternative

Method

- Pre-heat oven to GM6, 400F, 190C.
- Mix together the flours, xanthan gum and baking powder.
- Rub in the margarine until the mixture resembles breadcrumbs.
- Add enough of the milk alternative to form a dough.
- On a floured surface, roll out the dough to required thickness.
- Cut into circles using a small sized cookie cutter.
- Bake on a greased baking tray for 10–12 minutes.

Variation

- *Add dried un-sulphated gf fruit for fruit scones.*

Freezes well.

Scones

FF*, TF, YF

Ingredients

5 oz (150g) gf flour mix (Doves Farm)
3 oz (90g) corn/maize meal
4 oz (125g) dairy free margarine
2 tbsp golden caster sugar
just under 1 level tsp xanthan gum
½ tsp salt
2 tsp gf baking powder

2 oz (50g) un-sulphated dried fruit (optional)
1 large egg (beaten)
gluten and dairy free milk alternative, as necessary

Method

- Pre-heat oven to GM7, 425F, 220C.
- Mix together the flour, corn/maize meal, sugar, xanthan gum, salt and baking powder.
- Add the margarine and rub it in. If using fruit, add this now.
- Add the egg and stir in.
- Add milk little by little until the dough is fairly sticky.
- Roll out the dough on a well-floured board, until ½" thick.
- Cut into circles using a cookie cutter.
- Place scones on a baking tray, lined with greaseproof paper and brush their tops with a little milk substitute.
- Bake for 15–20 minutes until golden.

Judy Saville, Billericay © Copyright

Scones II

FF, TF, SF

Ingredients

2 oz (50g) sweet rice flour
2 oz (50g) gram flour
2 oz (50g) potato flour
2 oz flour mix (Doves Farm)
2 tsp gf baking powder
¼ tsp salt
3 oz (90g) caster sugar (or 2 tbsp honey)

3 oz (90g) dairy free margarine (Pure)
2 eggs (beaten)
¼ pint (150ml) (approx) gluten and dairy free milk alternative

Method

- Pre-heat oven to GM8, 450F, 230C.
- Mix together the dry ingredients and then rub in the margarine.
- Stir in the beaten eggs.
- Stir in enough milk to make a sticky dough.
- Roll out on a well-floured board to about ½ " thickness.
- Cut into circles with a cookie cutter.
- Place on a baking tray lined with greaseproof paper.
- Brush tops of scones with milk substitute.
- Bake for 10 minutes at GM8, 450F, 230C and then reduce oven temperature to GM7, 425F, 220C and continue to bake for a further 10 minutes.
- Allow scones to cool.

Variation

- *Make these into fruit scones by adding 3 oz (90g) of gf un-sulphated dried fruit and reducing the sugar to 1 oz (25g).*

Judy Saville, Billericay © Copyright

Banana scones

CF, EF, SF, TF, YF

Ingredients

12 oz (350g) IS Pure GF Blended Flour
2 tsp IS Pure Xanthan Gum
2 tbsp granulated sugar
2 tsp gf baking powder
½ tsp bicarbonate of soda
½ tsp salt
2½ oz (75g) dairy free
  margarine
1 large ripe banana (mashed)
6 fl oz (175ml) gluten and dairy
  free milk alternative

Method

- Pre-heat oven to GM6, 400F, 200C.
- Combine together the flour, xanthan gum, sugar, baking powder, bicarbonate of soda and salt.
- Cut the margarine into small pieces, add to the flour mix and mix in with a knife until it is crumbly.
- In a separate bowl mix the mashed banana and milk alternative.
- Add the banana mixture to the flour mix and stir just long enough to combine together. Do not over mix.
- Drop large spoonfuls of this mixture onto a greased baking tray. It makes 16 scones.
- Bake for 14 minutes.

Variation

- *To make a softer scone, add either 2–3 tsp of orange peel or 2 oz (50g) of marmalade.*

Innovative Solutions (UK) Ltd © Copyright 2000

Very rich and yummy chocolate cake

CF, FF, SF, TF, YF

Ingredients

5 oz (150g) gluten and dairy free chocolate
7 fl oz (200g) gluten and dairy free milk
    alternative
10 oz (280g) unrefined brown sugar
4 oz (125g) dairy free margarine
3 eggs (beaten)
8 oz (225g) gf flour mix
2 tsp xanthan gum
1 tsp bicarbonate of soda

Method

- Pre-heat oven to GM4, 350F, 180C.
- In a glass bowl, above a pan of warm water on a gentle heat, melt together the chocolate, milk and 3 oz (90g) of the sugar.
- In a separate bowl, cream together the remaining sugar and the margarine, then mix in the eggs.
- Stir in the chocolate mix.
- Sift together the flour, xanthan gum and bicarbonate of soda.
- Pour mixture into a 9" sandwich tin, lined with greaseproof paper.
- Bake for 1 hour.

Marilyn Le Breton © Copyright 2001

Egg free chocolate cake

CF, EF, FF, TF, YF

Ingredients

½ cup white rice flour
½ cup tapioca starch flour
¼ cup potato starch flour
½ cup gluten and dairy free cocoa powder
¾ cup sugar (either caster or unrefined brown)
¼ cup dairy free margarine
½ cup silken tofu
2½ tsp gf baking powder
¼ tsp crushed sea salt
2 tsp gf vanilla extract
½ tsp xanthan gum
⅔ cup of boiling water

Method

- Pre-heat the oven to GM4, 350F, 180C.
- Sift together the flours, cocoa powder, baking powder, salt and xanthan gum.
- In a separate bowl, cream together the sugar, margarine, tofu and vanilla extract, until smooth.
- Add the boiling water and blend together, until it has combined well.
- Using an electric mixer or blender set on the lowest speed, slowly add the flour mix, until the resulting mixture is smooth.
- Line a sandwich tin with greaseproof paper and pour in the cake mix.
- Bake for 25–30 minutes.

Variations

- *Plain sponge: omit the cocoa powder and replace with either ½ cup of potato or tapioca starch flour.*
- *Individual cup cakes: reduce cooking time to 20–25 minutes.*

Barbara Powell © Copyright 2000

Chocolate cake with chocolate 'butter-cream' topping

FF, SF, TF, YF

Cake

1¼ cups Orgran Self-raising Flour
4 oz (125g) dairy free margarine
½ cup caster sugar
⅓ cup icing sugar (sifted)
2 eggs (beaten)
1 tsp gf vanilla extract
½ cup gluten and dairy free cocoa powder
1 tsp bicarbonate of soda
1 cup gluten and dairy free milk substitute

Chocolate 'butter-cream' topping

2oz (50g) gluten and dairy free chocolate (finely chopped)
1 oz (25g) dairy free margarine
4 tsp soya cream alternative
¼ cup icing sugar (sifted)

Method

- Pre-heat oven to GM4, 350F, 180C.
- Cream together the margarine, caster sugar and icing sugar with an electric mixer, until the mixture is light and creamy.
- Gradually add eggs, beating all the time.
- Add the vanilla extract.
- In a separate bowl, mix together the flour, cocoa powder and bicarbonate of soda.
- Using a metal spoon, alternate folding in the flour, with the milk to the margarine mixture. Stir until the mixture has just combined and is almost smooth.
- Pour mixture into a deep 20cm square cake tin, lined with greaseproof paper and smooth over the surface of the cake.
- Bake for approximately 35 minutes.

To make the chocolate 'butter-cream' topping

- Combine together the chopped chocolate, margarine, soya cream and icing sugar in a pan.
- Stir over a low heat until the mixture is smooth and glossy.
- Spread the topping over the cold cake.

Orgran © Copyright 2000

Indian carrot cake

CF, SF, TF, YF

Ingredients

1½ tsp vegetable oil
2 oz (50g) buckwheat flour
2 oz (50g) white rice flour
1 tsp bicarbonate of soda
¼ tsp salt
2 large eggs (beaten)
¼ tsp gf ground cardamon seeds

8 oz (225g) granulated sugar
2 oz (50g) dairy free margarine
8 oz (225g) grated carrot
2 tbsp chopped pistachio nuts
2 tbsp chopped blanched
    almonds
2 tbsp gf un-sulphated raisins

Method

- Pre-heat oven to GM4, 350F, 180C.
- Mix together the flour, bicarbonate of soda and salt.
- In a separate bowl, cream together the eggs, cardamon, sugar and margarine.
- Add the flour mix to the margarine mix.
- Fold in the carrots, pistachios, almonds and raisins.
- Place mixture in a 9" square tin, lined with greaseproof paper. Bake for 40 minutes.

Alison suggests that this can double as a posh pudding and be served with soya cream.

Alison Steele, Northampton © Copyright

Carrot cake with a 'cream cheese' topping

TF, YF

Ingredients

3 eggs (beaten)
1 cup of oil
1¼ cups soft unrefined brown sugar
1½ cups of Orgran Self-raising Flour
1 tsp bicarbonate of soda
pinch of salt
2 tsp gf ground ginger
¾ cup chopped pecan nuts
1⅔ cups of grated carrot

'Cream cheese' topping

4 oz (125g) gluten and dairy free cream cheese (softened)
1 oz (30g) dairy free margarine
1 cup icing sugar (sifted)
2 tsp orange juice

Method

- Pre-heat oven to GM4, 350F, 180C.
- Combine together the eggs, oil and brown sugar.
- In a separate bowl sift together the flour, bicarbonate of soda, salt and cinnamon.
- Stir together the flour and egg mixtures and combine with an electric mixer until smooth.
- Add the nuts and carrots to the mixture and stir in well.
- Pour the mixture into a deep 23cm square cake tin lined with greaseproof paper.
- Bake for 45 minutes.
- Leave to cool before removing from tin.

To make the 'cream cheese' topping

- Mix all ingredients together and beat together well, until the mixture has softened enough to be spread over the cake.
- Spread over the cake and sprinkle with extra chopped pecans if desired.

Orgran © Copyright 2000

Carrot cake

CF, FF, SF, TF, YF

Ingredients

12 oz (350g) IS Pure Blended Flour
2 tsp IS Pure Xanthan Gum
1½ tsp gf ground cinnamon
1 tsp bicarbonate of soda
½ tsp salt
¼ tsp gf ground ginger
12 oz (350g) granulated sugar

9 fl oz (275ml) sunflower oil
3 eggs
1 tsp IS Pure Vanilla Extract
12 oz (350g) grated carrot
4 oz (125g) coarsely chopped
    mixed nuts

Method

- Pre-heat oven to GM4, 350F, 180C.
- Combine together the flour, xanthan gum, cinnamon, bicarbonate of soda, salt and ginger.
- In a separate bowl, mix together the sugar, oil, eggs and vanilla and beat until blended.
- Stir the flour mix into the liquid mix and beat together for 1 minute.
- Stir in the carrot and nuts, mixing well.
- Spoon the cake mixture into a 9"x 13" cake tin (greased and sprinkled with gf flour).
- Bake for 45–60 minutes.

This tastes even better if iced when cool.

Innovative Solutions (UK) Ltd © Copyright 2000

Gingerbread

CF, FF, SF, TF, YF

Ingredients

5 oz (150g) golden syrup
5 oz (150g) black treacle
4 oz (125g) unrefined brown sugar
4 oz (125g) dairy free margarine
1 cup white rice flour
¼ cup potato starch flour

¼ cup tapioca starch flour
1 tsp xanthan gum
1 tsp gf ground ginger
1 tsp gf mixed spice
2 eggs (beaten)
2 tbsp gluten and dairy free milk
  alternative

Method

- Pre-heat oven to GM3, 325F, 170C.
- In a saucepan, mix together the syrup, treacle, sugar and margarine. Heat gently until the margarine has melted.
- Remove the pan from the heat and allow to cool a little before stirring in the flours, xanthan gum, ginger and mixed spice.
- Add in the eggs and combine well.
- Pour mixture into a 12" x 9" baking tray lined with greaseproof paper and bake for approximately 40 minutes.

Kate Coull, Abergele © Copyright

Ginger cake

CF, FF, SF, TF, YF

Ingredients
9 oz (250g) IS Pure GF Blended Flour
1½ tsp IS Pure Xanthan Gum
¾ tsp bicarbonate of soda
1½ tsp gf ground ginger
3 oz (90g) unrefined brown sugar
2 eggs (beaten)
2½ oz (75g) lard (melted)
4 fl oz (120ml) boiling water
4 fl oz (120ml) molasses

Method
- Pre-heat oven to GM4, 350F, 180C.
- Combine together the blended flour, xanthan gum, bicarbonate of soda, ground ginger and brown sugar.
- In a separate bowl, beat together the eggs and melted lard.
- In a third bowl, mix together the boiling water and molasses, until well blended.
- Combine the molasses and egg mixtures.
- Mix in the flour and blend together well.
- Pour mixture into a greased 9" x 13" cake tin and bake for 20–25 minutes.

Sand cake

FF, SF, TF, YF

Ingredients

6 oz (175g) dairy free margarine
6 oz (175g) caster sugar
3 eggs (beaten)
6 oz (175g) cornflour
2 oz (50g) gf flour mix
2 tsp gf baking powder

Method

- Pre-heat oven to GM3, 325F, 170C.
- Cream together the margarine and sugar.
- Stir in eggs and mix well.
- In a separate bowl, mix together the sifted cornflour, flour and baking powder.
- Stir the flour mix into the margarine mix and combine well.
- Pour mixture into a 7" sandwich tin lined with greaseproof paper.
- Bake for 1 hour, reduce the temperature to GM2, 300F, 160C, and then bake for a further 30 minutes.

Marilyn Le Breton © Copyright 2001

Lemon fudge cake

CF, EF, SF, TF, YF

Ingredients

1¼ cups caster sugar

1 cup gf flour mix (Alison uses 6 parts rice flour, 2 parts potato flour and 1 part tapioca flour)

7 tbsp gluten and dairy free cocoa powder

2 tsp gf baking powder

¼ tsp salt

½ gluten and dairy free milk alternative

⅓ cup dairy free margarine

1½ tsp gf vanilla extract

½ cup light brown sugar

1¼ cups water (hot, not boiling)

finely grated rind of 1 lemon

1 tsp of lemon juice

7 tbsp ground almonds

Method

- Pre-heat oven to GM4, 350F, 180C.
- Mix together the flour, ¾ cup of the sugar, baking powder, 3 tbsp of the almonds and salt.
- In a separate bowl, mix together the milk substitute, vanilla extract and margarine.
- Combine the two mixtures well.
- Place the mix in a 9" tin or divide between 6 ramakin dishes.
- Mix together the remaining caster sugar, brown sugar, 4 tbsp ground almonds and lemon rind. Sprinkle this over the cake.
- Mix together the hot water and lemon juice and carefully pour over the top of the cake. The cake cooks up through the water, making a sauce that is dispersed throughout the cake.
- Bake for 35 minutes.

Variations

- *For a plain fudge cake: leave out the lemon juice and rind.*
- *For a chocolate fudge cake: replace the ground almonds with gf/cf cocoa powder.*

Alison says that this freezes well and doubles as a great pudding, served with either custard or soya cream.

Alison Steele, Northampton © Copyright

Banana bread

CF, SF, TF, YF

Ingredients

10½ oz (300g) IS Pure GF Blended Flour
1¾ tsp IS Pure Xanthan Gum
2 tsp gf baking powder
¼ tsp bicarbonate of soda
½ tsp salt

3 oz (90g) dairy free margarine
5 oz (150g) granulated sugar
2 eggs (beaten)
1 tsp IS Pure Vanilla Extract
2–3 ripe bananas (mashed)

Method

- Pre-heat oven to GM4, 350F, 180C.
- Mix together the flour, xanthan gum, baking powder, bicarbonate of soda and salt.
- In a separate bowl, cream together the margarine and sugar.
- Add eggs and vanilla extract to the creamed mixture and blend together well.
- Alternate adding the flour mix and the mashed bananas to the creamed mix, beginning and ending with the flour mix (3 additions of flour and 2 of banana).
- Spoon the dough into a greased and sugared loaf tin and bake for 55 minutes.

Banana cake

SF, TF, YF

Ingredients

4 oz (125g) caster sugar
8 oz (250g) Orgran Self-raising Flour
4 oz (125g) dairy free margarine (softened)
2 eggs
½ tsp bicarbonate of soda
1 tbsp gluten and dairy free milk alternative
2–3 ripe bananas (mashed)
a few drops gf vanilla extract

Method

- Pre-heat oven to GM4, 350F, 180C.
- Cream together the margarine and sugar.
- Add the eggs, one at a time, beating well after each.
- In a separate bowl, mix together the milk and the bicarbonate of soda.
- Add the bananas to the milk mixture.
- Combine the banana and the margarine mixtures.
- Fold in the flour.
- Spoon mixture into a 2 lb loaf tin lined with greaseproof paper.
- Bake for 45–50 minutes.
- Allow to cool before removing from tin.

Orgran © Copyright 2000

Cinnamon tea cake

FF, SF, TF, YF

Cake

2 oz (60g) dairy free margarine
½ cup caster sugar
I egg (beaten)
I tsp gf vanilla extract
5 oz (150g) Orgran Self-raising Flour
½ cup gluten and dairy free milk
    alternative

Topping

I oz (20g) dairy free margarine
    (melted)
I tbsp caster sugar
I tsp gf ground cinnamon

Method

- Pre-heat oven to GM4, 350F, 180C.
- Cream together the sugar and margarine.
- Add the egg and combine together.
- Stir in the vanilla extract.
- Alternate folding in the flour and milk, until the mixture is smooth.
- Spoon into a tin, lined with greaseproof paper and smooth over the top.
- Bake for 30 minutes.
- Allow the cake to cool.
- Brush the melted margarine over the top of the cake.
- Sprinkle the caster sugar and ground cinnamon over the top.

Orgran © Copyright 2000

No sugar fruit cake

CF, SF*, SGF, TF, YF

Ingredients

8 oz (225g) gf flour mix
2 tsp gf baking powder
1½ tsp xanthan gum
1 tsp cooked and dried soya bran
    (optional)
1 cinnamon stick
7 fl oz (200ml) water or fruit juice

4 oz (125g) dairy free margarine
1 large egg (beaten)
½ cup pineapple juice
12 oz (350g) gf un-sulphated
    dried fruit of choice (cut
    into even-sized pieces)

Method

- Pre-heat oven to GM3, 325F, 160C.
- Place fruit, water/juice, margarine and cinnamon stick in a saucepan and simmer for 20 minutes.
- Remove the cinnamon stick and leave mixture to cool.
- Mix together the flour, baking powder, xanthan gum and bran (if using).
- Mix in the cooled fruit mix, egg and pineapple juice and stir until well combined.
- Pour into a cake tin lined with greaseproof paper.
- Bake for approximately 1½ hours (check it is cooked through by inserting a skewer; if so, it will come out clean).
- Allow the cake to cool in the tin for 10 minutes before turning out to finish cooling.
- Wrap the cake and leave overnight before cutting and eating.

Maddalena Feliciello, Leeds © Copyright

Guernsey fruit cake

CF, SF, TF, YF

Ingredients

1¼ lb (600g) organic mixed dried fruit
8 oz (225g) dairy free margarine (pure
    sunflower)
8 oz (225g) unrefined soft brown sugar
3 large eggs
¼ cup water or fruit juice
8 oz (225g) white rice flour
2 oz (50g) potato starch flour

2 oz (50g) tapioca starch flour
4 tsp xanthan gum
2 tsp gf baking powder
pinch sea salt
2 tsp gf dried mixed spice
1 orange (juice and finely grated
    rind)

Method

- Pre-heat oven to GM2, 300F, 150C.
- In a large saucepan, place all the fruit, orange juice and water/fruit juice and simmer over a low heat for 5 minutes. Remove from heat.
- Whilst the fruit is still hot, chop in the margarine and stir.
- Add the sugar and mix well.
- Add the eggs one at a time, beating each one in well before adding the next.
- In a separate bowl, mix together the flours, xanthan gum, baking powder, salt and mixed spice.
- Add the flour mix and stir in well.
- Transfer mixture to a lined deep 8" tin and bake for approximately 2 hours.

Sue says that this also makes a good Christmas cake.

Sue Aldwell, Guernsey © Copyright

Rich fruit cake

CF, SF, TF, YF

Ingredients

8 oz (225g) gf un-sulphated mixed dried fruit

1 cup gluten and dairy free milk alternative

2 oz (50g) dairy free margarine (melted)

6 oz (175g) unrefined brown sugar

7 large eggs at room temperature

8 oz (225g) ground almonds

9 oz (250g) white rice flour

4 oz (125g) tapioca starch

4 oz (125g) potato starch flour

20 gf non-sulphated glacé cherries (cut into quarters and rolled in gf flour)

1 to 2 tbsp treacle or molasses

¼ tsp gf ground mixed spice

¼ tsp orange peel

¼ tsp lemon peel

2 oz (50g) grated carrot

1½ tbsp xanthan gum

3 tbsp water

Method

- Pre-heat oven to GM3, 325F, 160C.
- Place the dried, mixed fruit in a saucepan of hot water and bring to the boil. Remove the pan from the heat and strain off the fruit well and allow to cool.
- Mix all of the ingredients together well and place in a deep 7" cake tin, lined with greaseproof paper.
- Bake for approximately 1 hour 45 minutes. Check towards the end of the cooking time to ensure that the top does not start to burn. If it does, cover with silver foil.

Barbara says that this can also be used as a speedy Christmas pudding substitute.

Barbara Powell © Barbara's Kitchen Copyright 2000

Fruit cake

SF, TF, YF

Ingredients

2 cups gf un-sulphated dried mixed fruit
5 oz (150g) dairy free margarine
½ cup unrefined brown sugar
1 tsp gf mixed spice
1 cup orange juice
2 eggs (beaten)
1¾ cups of Orgran Self-raising Flour
2 tsp gf baking powder

Method

- Pre-heat the oven to GM2, 300F, 150C.
- Place in a large saucepan, the mixed fruit, margarine, sugar, mixed spice and orange juice.
- Bring the mixture to boiling point, stirring all the time. Boil for 4 minutes and remove from heat.
- When the fruit mixture has cooled, use a wooden spoon to beat in the eggs, flour and baking powder, until well combined.
- Spoon the mixture into a deep 20cm round cake tin, lined with greaseproof paper.
- Bake for 1 hour to 1hour 15 minutes.

Orgran © Copyright 2000

Marmalade fruit loaf

CF, SF, TF, YF

Ingredients

5 oz (150g) gf un-sulphated dates
1 mug of hot water
3 oz (90g) gf un-sulphated raisins
2 cups gf flour mix
3 tsp xanthan gum

1 tsp gf baking powder
4 oz (125) caster sugar
2 medium eggs (beaten)
2 tbsp fine shred grapefruit
   marmalade
1 tsp gf allspice

Method

- Pre-heat oven to GM4, 350F, 180C.
- Soak the dates and raisins in the water overnight.
- Place the flour, xanthan gum, baking powder, sugar and allspice in a large bowl and mix together well.
- Make a well in the centre of the flour mix. Place the beaten eggs and marmalade in the well and mix in thoroughly with a wooden spoon.
- Add the soaked fruit and water to the flour mix and combine gently.
- Place the mixture in a lined 2 lb loaf tin and cook for 60 minutes.

Jean Miles, Poole © Copyright

Cherry Bakewell slice

CF, SF, TF, YF

Pastry

1 sachet DS All Purpose Flour Mix
4 oz (125g) dairy free margarine
1 small egg (beaten)
2 tbsp cold water
2 tbsp strawberry or raspberry jam

Filling

1 sachet of DS Victoria
  Sandwich Mix
2 large eggs (beaten)
5¼ fl oz (160ml) sunflower oil
4 fl oz (100ml) cold water
¼ tsp gf almond extract
2 oz (50g) gf un-sulphated glacé
  cherries (chopped)
1 oz (25g) ground almonds
1 oz (25g) flaked almonds

Method

- Pre-heat oven to GM5, 375F, 190C.

To make the pastry

- Add margarine to the flour mix and using a fork combine until the mix resembles breadcrumbs.
- Stir in egg and water, until the dough is soft, but not sticky.
- Put the pastry on a well-floured surface and knead with your hands for 1–2 minutes.
- Roll out the pastry to fit a 11" x 7" oblong tin.
- Spread the jam over the pastry.

To make the filling

- Mix together the victoria sponge mix, oil, water, eggs and almond extract, for about 1 minute.
- Mix in the cherries and ground almonds.
- Gently spread the mixture into the jam-lined pastry base.
- Sprinkle the flaked almonds over the top.
- Bake for 30 minutes or until the cake has risen well and is springy to touch.
- Allow cake to cool and cut into fingers.

Variation

- *Replace the flaked almonds with glacé icing when the cake has cooled.*

Dietary Specialities © Copyright 2001

Welsh cakes

CF, SF, TF, YF

Ingredients

8 oz (225g) gf flour mix
1 tsp gf baking powder
1 tsp xanthan gum
5 oz (150g) dairy free margarine
1 egg (beaten)
4 oz (125g) caster sugar
5 oz (150g) gf un-sulphated raisins
¼ tsp gf ground ginger
1 little grated lemon peel

Method

- Mix together the flour, baking powder and xanthan gum.
- Rub the fat into the flour.
- Add the sugar, raisins, lemon peel and ginger.
- Mix in the egg, to form a stiff dough.
- Dust surface with gf flour and roll out the dough until it is ¼" thick.
- Cut dough into rounds.
- Either bake the cakes on a bakestone or dry fry them, turning once.
- Do not over cook them. They should be just brown on the outside and a little 'squidgy' in the middle.
- Sprinkle with sugar, while they are still warm.

Although these cakes do keep, they are best on day of baking.

Joanna Tomlinson, Birmingham © Copyright

Chocolate cake with chocolate 'butter-cream' icing

CF, FF, SF, TF, YF

Cake

4 oz (125g) gluten and dairy free chocolate
4 tbsp gluten and dairy free milk alternative
⅔ cup dairy free margarine
I cup unrefined caster sugar
3 eggs (beaten)
1¾ cups gf flour mix
2 tsp xanthan gum
2 tsp gf baking powder
I tbsp gluten and dairy free cocoa powder

Chocolate 'butter-cream'

6 tbsp dairy free margarine
1½ cups icing sugar
I tbsp gluten and dairy free cocoa powder
½ gf vanilla extract

Method

- Pre-heat oven to GM4, 350F, 180C.
- Melt the chocolate with the milk in a glass bowl, over a pan of warm water on a low heat.
- Cream together the margarine and sugar and beat in the eggs. Stir in the chocolate mixture.
- In a separate bowl, sift together the flour, xanthan gum, baking powder and cocoa powder.
- Slowly stir the flour into the chocolate mixture.
- Divide the mixture in half and pour into two 7" sandwich tins, lined with greaseproof paper.
- Bake for 35 minutes.

To make the chocolate 'butter-cream'

- Combine all ingredients until smooth and lump free. Use to sandwich the cake together. Add jam of choice if desired.

Marilyn Le Breton © Copyright 2001

'Buttery' caramel cake

CF, FF, SF, TF, YF

Cake

4 oz (125g) dairy free margarine
4 oz (125g) unrefined caster sugar
2 eggs (beaten)
4 oz (125g) gf flour mix
1 tsp xanthan gum
1 tsp gf baking powder
1 tsp gf vanilla extract (optional)
2 tbsp gluten and dairy free milk alternative

Caramel topping

1 oz (25g) dairy free margarine
2 oz (50g) caster sugar
1 tbsp gluten and dairy free milk alternative
4 oz (125g) icing sugar

Method

To make the cake

- Pre-heat oven to GM5, 375F, 190C.
- Cream together the margarine and sugar.
- Mix the beaten eggs in well.
- In a separate bowl, sift together the flour, xanthan gum and baking powder.
- Fold the flour into the creamed mixture.
- Stir in the milk and vanilla extract (if using).
- Spoon into a 9" sandwich tin lined with greaseproof paper.
- Bake for 20–25 minutes and allow cake to cool completely before removing.

To make the caramel topping

- In a saucepan, melt the margarine, add the sugar and over a low heat stir until the sugar has dissolved completely.
- Stir in the milk and remove from heat.
- Vigorously beat in the icing sugar, until the mixture is smooth.
- Use immediately to cover cake.

Marilyn Le Breton © Copyright 2001

Vanilla and coconut crumble cake

CF, FF, SF, TF, YF

Cake

6 oz (175g) dairy free margarine
6 oz (175g) unrefined caster sugar
6 oz (175g) gf flour mix
1 ½ tsp xanthan gum
1 ½ tsp gf baking powder
3 eggs (beaten)
1 ½ tsp gf vanilla extract

Crumble topping

3 oz (90g) dairy free margarine
3 oz (90g) unrefined caster sugar
4 oz (125g) gf flour mix
2 oz (60g) un-sulphated desiccated coconut

Method

- Pre-heat the oven to GM4, 350F, 180C.

To make the cake

- Cream together the margarine and sugar.
- Stir in the eggs.
- Sift together the flour, xanthan gum and baking powder and mix into the creamed sugar.
- Mix in the vanilla extract.
- Pour the mixture into a rectangular baking dish measuring 10"x7", lined with greaseproof paper.

To make the crumble topping

- Cream together the sugar and margarine.
- Stir in the flour, until you achieve a rough breadcrumb mix.
- Stir in the coconut.
- Sprinkle the crumble topping over the cake mixture, ensuring that the top of the cake is covered evenly.
- Press the topping down lightly with the back of a spoon.
- Bake for 45–50 minutes.
- Check the cake after 30 minutes; if the topping is getting too brown, cover the cake with foil, before continuing to cook.

Marilyn Le Breton © Copyright 2001

Microwave meringues

CF, FF, SF, TF, TF

Ingredients

10 oz (280g) icing sugar
1 egg white (size 3 egg)

Method

- Mix together the icing sugar and egg white, until completely combined and smooth.
- Roll the mixture into 10 balls using your hands.
- Place on the microwave turntable (cover this with clingfilm).
- Cook for approximately 2 minutes on full power, in a 650 watt machine (see manufacturer's handbook to adjust times for other wattage microwaves).

Barbara's Kitchen © Copyright 2000

Meringues

CF, FF, SF, TF, YF

Ingredients

3 egg whites (at room temperature)
1 tsp IS Pure Vanilla Extract

¼ tsp cream of tartar
pinch of salt
8 oz (225g) granulated sugar

Method

- Pre-heat oven to GM1, 275F, 140C.
- In a large bowl, combine the egg whites, vanilla extract, cream of tartar and salt and beat until the mixture is frothy.
- Gradually add the sugar, a little at a time, continuing to beat until very stiff peaks form and the sugar has dissolved.
- Cover a baking tray with foil and drop the meringue mixture into 12 large spoonfuls onto the tray.
- Bake for 1 hour. Turn off the heat, but keep the meringues in the oven to 'dry out' and cool for 2 hours.

Innovative Solutions (UK) Ltd © Copyright 2000

Meringues

CF, FF, SF, TF, YF

Ingredients

3 egg whites
6 oz (175g) unrefined caster sugar

Method

- Pre-heat oven to GM¼, 225F, 110C.
- Whisk the egg whites, either by hand or with an electric mixer on the lowest setting, until the mixture is very stiff and will stand up in peaks.
- Fold in sugar a little at a time, with a metal spoon.
- Using a piping bag, pipe the mixture into the required shape and size, onto a baking tray lined with greaseproof paper or spoon the mixture onto the tray.
- Bake for 2 hours until they are well dried out.
- Remove from tray and cool on a wire rack.

Eat on their own or sandwich two together with a little jam or pureed fruit.

Marilyn Le Breton © Copyright 2001

Peach cupcakes

CF, SF, TF, YF

Ingredients

4 oz (125g) dairy free margarine
7 oz (200g) unrefined caster sugar
2 eggs (beaten)
8 oz (225g) gf flour mix
14 oz (422g) tin peach slices (rinsed, drained and pureed)

2 tsp xanthan gum
2 tsp gf baking powder
1 tsp gf vanilla extract
1–2 tbsp gluten and dairy free milk alternative

Method

- Pre-heat oven to GM5, 375F, 190C.
- Cream together the margarine and sugar.
- Mix in the beaten egg.
- Stir in the pureed peach and vanilla extract.
- In a separate bowl, mix together well the flour, xanthan gum and baking powder.
- Slowly stir in the flour mix into the peach mixture.
- Add a little of the milk alternative, if the mixture is too stiff.
- Divide the mixture between 20 cupcake cases or 12 muffin cases.
- Bake for 15–18 minutes for cupcakes or 25 minutes for the muffins.

Variations

- *Works equally well with pureed mangoes, pineapple or apricots.*

Marilyn Le Breton © Copyright 2001

Honey nut cupcakes

CF, FF, SF, TF, YF

Ingredients

6 oz (175g) dairy free margarine
3 oz (90g) honey
3 oz (90g) caster sugar
3 eggs (beaten)
6 oz (175g) gf flour mix
2½ tsp gf baking powder
1 tsp xanthan gum
4 oz (125g) crushed nuts
1 tsp gf ground cinnamon

Method

- Pre-heat oven to GM4, 350F, 180C.
- Cream together the honey, sugar and margarine.
- Mix in the eggs.
- Mix in the flour, baking powder, cinnamon and xanthan gum.
- Stir in the crushed nuts.
- Divide the mixture between 18 cupcake cases.
- Bake for approximately 25 minutes or until the cakes spring back when they are pressed.

Joanna Tomlinson, Birmingham © Copyright

Novelty buns

CF, FF, SF, TF, YF

Ingredients

1 sachet DS Victoria Sponge Mix
2 large eggs (beaten)
5¼ fl oz (160ml) sunflower oil
4 fl oz (100ml) cold water

Topping

6 oz (175g) icing sugar
1 tbsp cold water
Jelly Tots or Whizzers

Method

- Pre-heat oven to GM5, 375F, 190C.
- Mix together the victoria sponge mix, eggs, oil and water. Beat vigorously for 1 minute.
- Divide the mixture between 18 bun paper cases, placed inside a bun tin.
- Bake for approximately 18–20 minutes.
- When buns are cool, mix together the icing sugar and water, until the icing is smooth.
- Place a little icing on top of each bun and spread it out to cover the tops evenly.
- Decorate with Jelly Tots, Whizzers etc. (If feeling very brave let children help with this!)

Dietary Specialities © Copyright 2001

Chocolate cupcakes

CF, EF, FF, SF*, TF, YF

Ingredients

5 oz Trufree No.7 flour or gf flour mix and
   1 tsp gf baking powder
3 oz unrefined soft brown sugar
4 oz dairy free margarine (Pure Organic
   Sunflower)
2 tbsp gluten and dairy free (Green and
   Black's Organic Cocoa Powder)
3 tsp egg replacer
4 tbsp warm water

Method

- Pre-heat oven to GM5, 375F, 190C.
- Cream together the margarine and sugar.
- Add in the cocoa powder and flour and beat together well.
- In a separate bowl, sprinkle the egg replacer into the warm water and whisk until fluffy.
- Add the egg mixture to the cake mix and stir in well.
- Divide the mix between 12 paper cake cases in a muffin tray and bake near the top of the oven for 18 minutes.
- Leave to cool for 5 minutes, before removing from the tray to cool.

Amanda Godfrey, London © Copyright

Chocolate chip queen cakes

CF, FF, SF, TF, YF

Ingredients

4 oz (125g) dairy free margarine
4 oz (125g) unrefined caster sugar
2 eggs (beaten)
4 oz (125g) gf flour mix
1 tsp xanthan gum
1 tsp gf baking powder
2 oz (50g) gluten and dairy free chocolate
   chips

Method

- Pre-heat oven to GM5, 375F, 190C.
- Cream together the margarine and butter.
- Stir in the beaten eggs.
- Sift together the flour, xanthan gum and baking powder.
- Mix together the flour and creamed sugar.
- Stir in the chocolate chips.
- Half fill 18 cake cases, inserted into a bun tray.
- Bake for 15–20 minutes.

Marilyn Le Breton © Copyright 2001

Apple and cinnamon muffins

EF, TF, YF

Ingredients

1 cup Orgran Apple and Cinnamon
   Pancake Mix
1 cup white rice flour
½ cup potato starch flour
½ cup cornflour
2 tsp gf baking powder
1 tsp xanthan gum
1 tsp bicarbonate of soda

¾ cup caster sugar
2 tsp Orgran 'No Egg'
7 fl oz (200ml) plain soya
   yoghurt (or 7 fl oz/200ml
   gluten and dairy free milk
   alternative)
¾ cup of boiling water
2 oz (50g) dairy free margarine
   (melted)

Method

- Preheat oven to GM2, 300F, 160C.
- Sift together the pancake mix, flours, baking powder, xanthan gum, bicarbonate of soda and sugar.
- Stir in the melted margarine, egg replacer, yoghurt and boiling water and mix with an electric mixer for 2–3 minutes, until well combined.
- Pour into 12 muffin cases and bake for 12–15 minutes.

Orgran © Copyright 2000

Banana muffins

TF, SF, YF

Ingredients

2 cups Orgran Self-raising Flour (sifted)
3½ oz (100g) linseeds
¾ cup caster sugar
2 eggs (beaten)
¾ cup gluten and dairy free milk
    alternative
2 oz (60g) dairy free margarine (melted)
2 ripe bananas (mashed)

Method

- Pre-heat oven to GM7, 425F, 210C.
- Mix together the flour, linseeds and sugar.
- Make a well in the centre of the mix.
- In a separate bowl mix together the eggs, milk alternative, melted margarine and mashed bananas.
- Pour banana mix into the well of the flour, all in one go.
- Stir together until just mixed (the mixture should be lumpy).
- Spoon the mixture into 12 muffin cases.
- Bake for 15 minutes or until the muffins are puffed and golden.

Banana muffins

CF, TF, YF

Ingredients

4½ oz (140g) dairy free margarine
10 oz (280g) granulated sugar
2 eggs
1 tsp IS Pure Vanilla Extract
10½ oz (300g) IS Pure GF Blended Flour
1¾ tsp IS Pure Xanthan Gum
1 tsp bicarbonate of soda
1 pinch of salt
5 oz (150g) plain soya yoghurt
3 very ripe bananas (mashed)

Method

- Pre-heat oven to GM6, 400F, 200C.
- Cream together the margarine and sugar until fluffy.
- Beat in the eggs and vanilla.
- In a separate bowl, combine together the flour, xanthan gum, bicarbonate of soda and salt.
- Add to the creamed mixture and mix well until blended.
- Add the soya yoghurt and mashed bananas and mix in well.
- Spoon the batter into a greased or lined muffin tray, filling cups just to the top.
- Bake for 25–30 minutes.
- Makes one dozen.

Variation

Banana and Chocolate Muffins

- *Add 3–4 oz (90–125g) of gluten and dairy free chocolate chips to the mixture after the bananas and yoghurt have been blended in.*

Innovative Solutions (UK) Ltd © Copyright 2000

Sugar Free Muffins

CF, SF, SGF, TF, YF

Ingredients

1 cup gf flour mix
½ tsp xanthan gum
2 tsp gf baking powder
1 tsp gf ground cinnamon
½ cup pureed pears
½ cup and 2 tbsp pear juice
2 tbsp oil
1 egg (separated)
1 egg white

Method

- Pre-heat oven to GM4, 350F, 180C.
- Sift together the flour, xanthan gum, baking powder and cinnamon.
- In a separate bowl, mix together the egg yolk, oil, pear puree and pear juice.
- Mix in the flour mixture and combine together well.
- Whisk together the 2 egg whites, until they are stiff and fold them into the batter.
- Spoon the mixture into 12 muffin cases.
- Bake for 12–15 minutes, until firm and light brown.

Carrot and pineapple muffins

CF, SF, TF, YF

Ingredients

2½ cups white rice flour
½ cup tapioca starch flour
½ cup potato starch flour
2 cups finely grated carrot
6 oz (170g) tin pineapple (liquidised)
1 tsp cider vinegar or water
2 tsp gf vanilla extract
1 tsp xanthan gum
2 tsp gf baking powder

½–1 tsp gf ground cinnamon
½–1 tsp gf mixed spice
2 large eggs (at room temperature)
1 tsp bicarbonate of soda
1 cup of organic oil of choice
¾ cup sugar
pinch of crushed sea salt

Method

- Pre-heat oven to GM4-5, 375F, 190C.
- Mix all of the ingredients together in a very large bowl.
- The mixture should look quite 'wet' and be of a consistency to slowly drop off a spoon. If the mixture is too dry, add a little more liquid until the correct consistency has been achieved.
- Spoon the mixture into 16 muffin cases, set inside a deep muffin tray.
- Bake for 20 minutes.

Variations

- *Replace the pineapple with any tolerated fruit or gluten and dairy free chocolate chips.*

Barbara's Kitchen © Copyright 2000

Egg free pumpkin muffins

CF, EF, FF, SF, TF, YF

Ingredients

½ cup dairy free margarine or shortening

1½ cups brown sugar

2 cups gf flour mix

⅓ cup gluten and dairy free milk alternative (reduced by 1 tsp if using rice milk)

1 cup canned mashed pumpkin

2¼ tsp ground flaxseed meal

6 tbsp water

4 tsp gf baking powder

2 tsp oil

1½ tsp gf ground dried ginger

¼ tsp gf ground cloves

Method

- Pre-heat oven to GM5, 375F, 190C.
- In a small bowl, mix together well the flaxseed meal, water, baking powder and oil. Leave to stand for 5 minutes before using.
- In a large bowl, cream together the margarine/shortening and sugar, until light and fluffy.
- Sift together the flour, ginger and cloves.
- Add the flour mix and the flaxseed mix to the creamed mix and combine together well.
- Divide mixture between two 8" sandwich tins or into lined cupcake trays, making sure that the mixture does not exceed the ¾ way mark.
- Bake the cake for approximately 25 minutes or the cupcakes for 18–20 minutes.

Diane Hartman © Copyright 2001

Potato starch free muffins

CF, FF, SF, TF, YF

Ingredients

1 ½ cups white rice flour
1 ½ cups tapioca starch flour
1 cup sugar
1 tsp gf mixed spice
1 tsp gf ground cinnamon
1 tsp bicarbonate of soda
2 tsp gf baking powder

1 tsp xanthan gum
pinch crushed sea salt
3 large eggs (beaten)
¼ cup gluten and dairy free
   milk alternative
1 tsp cider vinegar or water
1 cup organic oil
2 tsp gf vanilla extract

Method

- Pre-heat oven to GM4, 350F, 190C.
- Mix together the flours, sugar, mixed spice, cinnamon, bicarbonate of soda, baking powder, xanthan gum and salt.
- In a separate bowl, mix together the eggs, milk alternative, vinegar/water, oil and vanilla extract.
- Add the egg mixture to the flour mix and stir together by hand. The mixture should be fairly wet.
- Divide the mixture between 12–14 muffin cases, set in a muffin tray.
- Bake for approximately 20 minutes.

Barbara's Kitchen © Copyright 2000

3 by 3 muffins

CF, SF, TF, YF

Ingredients

⅓ cup millet

⅓ cup chickpea flour

⅓ cup tapioca starch flour

½ cup potato starch flour

½ cup unrefined brown sugar

1 ½ tsp xanthan gum

2 tsp gf baking powder

1 tsp gf ground cinnamon

3 egg whites

1 ½ cups blueberries (fresh or frozen)

Method

- Pre-heat oven to GM5, 375F, 190C.
- Sift together the flours, millet, xanthan gum, baking powder and cinnamon.
- Stir in the sugar.
- Add the egg whites. Using an electric mixer, blend together the ingredients.
- Add the blueberries and give the mixture a quick 'swirl'.
- Spoon mixture into 12 muffin cases and bake for 25–35 minutes.

Deborah Jusi © Copyright 2001

Muffins that taste like donuts

CF, FF, SF, TF, YF

Ingredients

10½ oz (300g) IS Pure GF Blended Flour
1¾ tsp IS Pure Xanthan Gum
1½ tsp gf baking powder
½ tsp gf ground cinnamon
3 fl oz (75ml) sunflower oil
6 oz (175g) granulated sugar
1 egg (beaten)
6 fl oz (175ml) gluten and dairy free milk
     alternative

Method

- Pre-heat oven to GM3, 325F, 170C.
- Combine together the flour mix, xanthan gum, baking powder and cinnamon.
- In a separate bowl, combine the oil, sugar, egg and milk alternative and beat until slightly frothy.
- Add oil mix to the flour mix and stir until combined.
- Spoon into muffin cases in muffin tin. The cases should be half to three-quarters full.
- Bake for 20–25 minutes.

Mini donuts

CF, FF, SF, TF, YF

Ingredients

1 cup gf flour mix
1 tsp gf baking powder
1 tsp xanthan gum
1 cup unrefined caster sugar
6 fl oz (175ml) gluten and dairy free milk
    alternative
2 eggs (beaten)
3 tsp organic sunflower oil
1 tsp gf vanilla extract

Method

- Pre-heat oven to GM3, 325F, 170C.
- Mix together the flour, baking powder, xanthan gum and sugar.
- In a separate bowl, combine together well the milk, eggs, oil and vanilla extract.
- Pour half the batter into a mini donut pan (i.e., Lakeland Ltd).
- Bake for 10 minutes.
- Allow them to cool slightly.
- Re-fill pan with remaining mixture and repeat.

Makes 24 mini donuts.
These can be rolled in sugar or iced.

Marilyn Le Breton © Copyright 2001

Mini donuts

CF, FF, SF, TF, YF

Ingredients

2½ oz (70g) gf flour mix (Hagman General
   Purpose)
½ tsp gf baking powder
¼ tsp xanthan gum
¼ tsp salt
2 oz (50g) caster sugar
2¼ fl oz (60ml) gluten and dairy free milk
   alternative
1 tbsp oil
½ tsp gf vanilla extract

Method

- Pre-heat oven to GM3, 325F, 170C.
- Sift together the flour, baking powder, xanthan gum, salt and sugar.
- Whisk together the milk alternative, oil and vanilla extract.
- Combine the flour mix and milk mixtures.
- Pour mixture into a mini donut pan.
- Bake for 8 minutes.

Makes 12 mini donuts.
Suggested toppings: dip in sugar or melted gluten and dairy free chocolate. Spoon jam into donut hole. Ice.

Variation

- *For apple and cinnamon donuts, grate a large, peeled apple and add to the batter with 1 tsp gf ground cinnamon.*

McGill Family, UK © Copyright

Mexican ring donuts

CF, FF, SF, TF, YF

Ingredients

2 cups gf flour mix
2 tsp xanthan gum
1 tsp gf baking powder
1 tbsp unrefined caster sugar
1 large egg (beaten)
⅔ cup gluten and dairy free milk alternative
2 tbsp dairy free margarine (melted)
organic sunflower oil for frying
unrefined caster sugar for dusting

Method

- In a bowl, mix together the flour, baking powder and sugar.
- In a separate bowl, whisk together the milk alternative and egg.
- Into the milk mix, slowly stir the flour.
- Add the melted margarine and mix in well to form a soft dough.
- Divide the mixture evenly into 16 balls.
- Flatten the balls with the palms of your hands, until they are discs, approximately ¾" thick.
- Using the handle of a wooden spoon, poke a hole through the centre of the disc.
- Deep fry the donuts until they have fluffed up and are golden brown on both sides.
- Whilst still hot, roll the donuts in sugar.

Cake Toppings, Icing and Fillings

Chocolate 'butter-cream' topping

CF, EF, FF, TF, YF

Ingredients

2 oz (50g) gluten and dairy free chocolate
    (finely chopped)
1 oz (25g) dairy free margarine
4 tsp soya cream alternative
¼ cup icing sugar (sifted)

Method

- Combine together the chopped chocolate, margarine, soya cream, and icing sugar in a pan.
- Stir over a low heat until the mixture is smooth and glossy.
- Spread the topping over the cold cake.

Orgran © Copyright 2000

'Cream cheese' topping

CF, EF, TF, YF

Ingredients

4 oz (125g) gluten and dairy free cream
    cheese (softened)
1 oz (30g) dairy free margarine
1 cup icing sugar (sifted)
2 tsp orange juice

Method

- Mix all ingredients together and beat well, until the mixture has softened enough to be spread.
- Spread over the cake and sprinkle with extra chopped pecans if desired.

Orgran © Copyright 2000

Coconut crumble cake topping

CF, EF, FF, SF, TF, YF

Ingredients

3 oz (90g) dairy free margarine
3 oz (90g) icing sugar

2 oz (60g) un-sulphated desiccated coconut

Method

- Cream together the sugar and margarine.
- Stir in the coconut.
- Carefully spread the topping over the cake.

Marilyn Le Breton © Copyright 2001

Caramel cake topping

CF, EF, SF, TF, YF

Ingredients

1 oz (25g) dairy free margarine
2 oz (50g) unrefined caster sugar
1 tbsp gluten and dairy free milk alternative
4 oz (125g) icing sugar

Method

- In a saucepan, melt the margarine, add the sugar and over a low heat stir until the sugar has dissolved completely.
- Stir in the milk and remove from heat.
- Vigorously beat in the icing sugar, until the mixture is smooth.
- Use immediately to cover cake.

Marilyn Le Breton © Copyright 2001

Lemon sauce

EF, SF, TF, YF

Ingredients

4 oz (125g) granulated sugar
1 tbsp cornflour
9 fl oz (275ml) boiling water
rind of 1 lemon (finely grated)
2 tbsp dairy free margarine
juice of ½ lemon

Method

- In a medium sized pan, combine the sugar and cornflour together well.
- Add the boiling water and lemon rind to the sugar solution and bring to the boil over a medium heat.
- Continue to boil the mixture for 5 minutes, stirring constantly.
- Add the margarine and lemon juice and stir in until well combined.
- Serve warm over cake.

Especially good over ginger cake.

Marzipan

CF, SF, TF, YF

Ingredients

4 oz (125g) ground almonds
2 oz (60g) unrefined caster sugar
2 oz (60g) icing sugar
¼ tsp IS GF Almond Extract
1 tsp water
1 tsp lemon juice
1 egg white

Method

- Mix together the ground almonds and caster sugar.
- Sift in the icing sugar.
- In a separate bowl, mix together the almond extract, water and egg white. Whisk this mixture together lightly.
- To the egg mix, add the almond mix and combine together well.
- Using your hands, knead the mix together for 2 minutes.
- Wrap in clingfilm and place inside an airtight container and store in the fridge until ready to use.

Marilyn Le Breton © Copyright 2001

Chocolate 'butter-cream'

CF, EF, FF, SF, TF, YF

Ingredients

6 tbsp dairy free margarine (softened)
1½ oz (40g) icing sugar
1 tbsp gluten and dairy free cocoa powder
½ tsp gf vanilla extract

Method

- Sift together the icing sugar and the cocoa powder.
- Add the margarine and cream together.
- Add the vanilla extract and stir in well.

Marilyn Le Breton © Copyright 2001

Super 'butter-cream'

EF, FF, SF, TF, YF

Ingredients

1 oz (25g) cornflour
8 oz (225g) unrefined caster sugar
12 fl oz (350ml) gluten and dairy free milk
    alternative (hot)
12 oz (350g) dairy free margarine
1½ tsp gf vanilla extract

Method

- Blend together the cornflour with 3 oz of the sugar and 2 tbsp of the hot milk alternative. Mix until a smooth paste is formed.
- Stir in the remaining hot milk. Bring the mixture to the boil, stirring constantly with a whisk. Allow mix to cook at boiling point for 1 minute.
- Pour the mixture through a sieve to remove any lumps and allow it to cool completely.
- Cream together the margarine and remaining 5 oz of sugar.
- Very slowly, add the milk sauce to the sugar and margarine mixture, stirring all the time.
- Add the vanilla extract and stir in well.

Marilyn Le Breton © Copyright 2001

Fudge candy icing

CF, EF, FF SF, TF, YF

Ingredients

4 oz (125g) dairy free margarine
6 oz (175g) gluten and dairy free dark
    chocolate (roughly chopped)
6 oz (175g) unrefined caster sugar
2 tbsp glucose syrup
4 fl oz (100ml) boiling water
11 oz (375g) icing sugar
1½ tsp gf vanilla extract

Method

- In a saucepan, melt the margarine and chocolate together.
- Add the water, caster sugar and glucose syrup and bring the mixture to the boil.
- Reduce the heat and simmer the mixture for 3 minutes, stirring all the time.
- Remove the pan from the heat and then whisk in the icing sugar, until smooth and lump free.
- Stir in the vanilla extract and then beat the mixture until it takes on a shiny appearance.
- Set the pan in a bowl or larger pan of ice cold water and stir continuously, until it has thickened, but is still warm. Do not allow the icing to get cold.
- Spread the icing whilst it is still warm.

Hint: if the icing gets too stiff or cold to work, soften and warm it over a pan of hot water – but do not return to direct heat on the cooker.

Marilyn Le Breton © Copyright 2001

Vanilla icing

CF, EF, FF, SF, TF, YF

Ingredients

2 oz (50g) dairy free margarine
2 tbsp hot water
½ tsp IS Pure Vanilla Extract

7 oz (200g) icing sugar
gluten and dairy free milk
    alternative

Method

- In a bowl, cream the margarine to soften it.
- Blend in the hot water and vanilla extract, mixing until smooth.
- Add the icing sugar and beat in, until the mix is smooth and creamy.
- If the icing is thicker than desired, add a little milk alternative, to thin.
- If the icing is thinner than desired add a little more icing sugar.

Innovative Solutions (UK) Ltd © Copyright 2000

Chocolate fudge sauce

CF, EF, FF, SF, TF, YF

Ingredients

5 tbsp gluten and dairy free milk alternative
I oz (25g) gluten and dairy free cocoa
    powder
4 oz (125g) unrefined caster sugar

6 oz (175g) golden syrup
I oz (25g) dairy free margarine
½ tsp gf vanilla extract

Method

- Mix together all the ingredients (except the vanilla) in a saucepan, over a low heat.
- Slowly bring the mixture up to boiling point, stirring occasionally.
- Boil for 5 minutes.
- Add vanilla and stir well.
- Remove from heat and allow the sauce to cool slightly before serving.

This is a versatile sauce that can be used either as an ice cream sauce or as a cake covering/filling, by reducing the milk to 2 tbsp.

Marilyn Le Breton © Copyright 2001

Desserts and Puddings

Sticky date pudding

CF, TF, SF, YF

Ingredients

2 oz (60g) dairy free margarine
6 oz (175g) caster sugar
2 eggs (beaten)
6 oz (175g) un-sulphated dates (stoned and chopped)
1 tsp bicarbonate of soda

1 cup white rice flour
¼ cup potato starch flour
¼ cup tapioca starch flour
1 tsp xanthan gum
½ tsp gf vanilla extract
¼ pint water

Method

- Pre-heat oven to GM4, 350F, 180C.
- Cream together the sugar and margarine.
- Gradually beat in the eggs.
- Place the dates in a saucepan and cover with ¼ pint of water and bring to the boil.
- Remove from heat and stir in the bicarbonate of soda.
- Mix together the flours and xanthan gum.
- Add the flour mix to the creamed sugar mixture.
- Stir in the date mixture and add the vanilla extract.
- Pour into a 2½ pint (1.4 litre) greased ovenproof dish and bake for 35–40 minutes.

Serve hot or cold.

Kate Coull, Abergele © 2001

Parisian chocolate pudding bake

CF, FF, SF, TF, YF

Ingredients

9 oz (250g) gluten and dairy free chocolate
I cup dairy free margarine
½ cup unrefined caster sugar
5 eggs
I tbsp gf flour mix

Method

- Pre-heat oven to GM4, 350F, 180C.
- Melt together the chocolate, margarine and sugar, in a glass bowl, over a pan of hot water, on a low heat. Allow the mix to cool slightly.
- Beat the eggs together for I minute with an electric mixer.
- Add the flour to the eggs and mix for a further minute.
- Slowly add the chocolate mix.
- Pour mixture into a 9" square tin lined with greaseproof paper.
- Place tin in a roasting tin or similar. Pour boiling water into the roasting tin, until it rises to approximately ¾ of the sides of the square tin.
- Bake for 30 minutes. The mixture should be set, but still soft to touch in the centre.
- Allow cake to cool before removing from tin.

Will keep for 3 days in the fridge.

Marilyn Le Breton © Copyright 2001

Peach and chocolate bake

CF, TF, YF

Ingredients

8 oz (225g) gluten and dairy free chocolate
½ cup dairy free margarine
4 eggs (separated)
½ cup unrefined caster sugar
15 oz can peach slices (drained)

Method

- Pre-heat oven to GM3, 325F, 170C.
- Melt together the chocolate and margarine.
- Whisk in the sugar and egg yolks.
- In a separate bowl, whisk together the egg whites until stiff.
- Fold the egg whites into the chocolate mix.
- Gently fold in the peach slices.
- Gently spoon mixture into a greased ovenproof glass dish or baking tin lined with greaseproof paper.
- Bake 35–40 minutes.

Serve hot or cold.

Marilyn Le Breton © Copyright 2001

Lemon pudding

CF, SF, TF, YF

Ingredients

4 oz (125g) caster sugar
2 oz (50g) dairy free margarine
2 oz (50g) white rice flour
½ tsp xanthan gum
juice and rind of 1 large lemon
2 eggs (separated)
8 fl oz (225g) gluten and dairy milk
    alternative

Method

- Pre-heat oven to GM3½, 340F, 170C.
- Cream together margarine and sugar.
- Stir in the flour, xanthan gum, lemon juice and rind.
- In a separate bowl, whisk together the egg yolks and milk. Add this to the pudding mix a little at a time.
- Beat the egg whites until they are stiff and fold them into the pudding mixture.
- Pour the pudding mix into a greased pie dish and stand it in a roast tin half full of warm water.
- Bake for 45 minutes.

Joanna Tomlinson, Birmingham © Copyright 2001

Microwave sponge pudding

CF, FF, SF, TF, YF

Ingredients

5 oz (150g) dairy free margarine
5 oz (150g) golden syrup
3 eggs (beaten)
6 oz (175g) gluten free flour mix
1 ½ tsp xanthan gum
1 ½ tsp gf baking powder

Method

- Cream together the margarine and golden syrup.
- Mix in the beaten eggs.
- In a separate bowl mix together the flour, xanthan gum and baking powder.
- Sift the flour into the golden syrup mixture and with a wooden spoon combine all the ingredients into a fairly stiff batter,
- Grease a 2 pint (1.1 litres) capacity microwavable pudding basin and pour the mixture in.
- Leaving the basin uncovered, microwave for 5 minutes on high power.
- Leave to stand for 5–6 minutes before turning out.

Variation

- *To make a chocolate sponge pudding, replace 1 oz (25g) of the flour with 1 oz (25g) of gluten and dairy free cocoa powder.*

Marilyn Le Breton © Copyright 2001

Bakewell tart

CF, SF, TF, YF

Ingredients

6 oz (175g) gluten and dairy free
   shortcrust pastry (see Pastry section
   for recipes)
2–3 tbsp strawberry jam
3 oz (90g) dairy free margarine
3 oz (90g) unrefined caster sugar
1 large egg (beaten)
2 oz (50g) ground almonds

2 oz (50g) fresh gluten and
   dairy free breadcrumbs
1 tbsp gluten and dairy free milk
   alternative
½ tsp gf almond extract
1 tsp lemon juice
icing to cover

Method

- Pre-heat oven to GM5, 375F, 190C.
- Line a 7" sandwich tin with the pastry. Prick all over the base of the pastry with a fork and return the pastry case to the fridge to relax.
- Cream together the margarine and sugar, then stir in the egg.
- Add the breadcrumbs, almonds, milk substitute, almond extract and lemon juice.
- Beat the mix together well, ensuring that all of the ingredients have combined together.
- Spread the jam over the pastry base and then carefully spread the almond mix over the jam.
- Bake for 40–45 minutes and allow to cool.
- When cold, either spread icing over the top or sprinkle with approximately 3 tsp of icing sugar.

Marilyn Le Breton © Copyright 2001

Peach with coconut meringue tops

CF, SF, TF, YF

Ingredients

4 tinned peach halves (drained well)
1 egg white
1 oz (25g) caster sugar
1 oz (25g) gf un-sulphated desiccated
    coconut

Method

- Pre-heat oven to GM3, 325F, 170C.
- Place each peach half in an individual pie tin.
- Whisk the egg white until it is stiff.
- Gradually add the sugar to the egg white, whisking the mixture all the time.
- Gently fold in the coconut with a spoon.
- Spoon the coconut meringue on top of the peach halves.
- Bake for 20 minutes or until the meringue is crisp and light brown in colour.

Variation

- *Use well drained tinned pear halves or pineapple slices.*

Marilyn Le Breton © Copyright 2001

Gluten and dairy free crumble topping

EF, SF, TF, YF

Ingredients

4 oz (125g) gf flour mix
4 oz (125g) dairy free margarine
4 oz (125g) unrefined caster sugar

3 oz (90g) crushed Mesa
  Sunrise or other suitable
  cereal

Method

- Pre-heat oven to GM5, 375F, 190C.
- Sift the flour and rub in the margarine to form large breadcrumbs.
- Stir in the sugar and cereal.
- To use, spoon the crumble mix over the fruit filling being used and press it down lightly.
- Bake for approximately 30 minutes or until topping is golden brown and fruit cooked through.

Marilyn Le Breton © Copyright 2001

Fruit crumble

CF, EF, SF, TF

Ingredients

1 lb (450g) fruit suitable for stewing
2 tbsp water
2 tbsp sugar

4 oz (125g) gluten and dairy
  free breadcrumbs
2 oz (125g) gluten and dairy
  free brown sugar

Method

- Pre-heat oven to GM5, 375F, 190C.
- Place fruit in a saucepan with the water and 2 tbsp of sugar. Cook gently until the fruit is just soft.
- Place the fruit in an ovenproof dish.
- Cover the fruit with the breadcrumbs and sprinkle the sugar over the top of the mix.
- Bake in the oven for 20 minutes.

Jean Miles © Copyright

Treacle tart

CF, SF, TF, YF

Ingredients

6 oz (175g) gluten and dairy free pastry
　(see Pastry section for recipes)

3 tbsp fresh gluten and dairy
　free breadcrumbs
4 tbsp golden syrup
juice of ½ lemon

Method

- Pre-heat oven to GM6, 400F, 200C.
- Line a 7" sandwich tin with greaseproof paper.
- Roll out the pastry and line the tin. Place in fridge to chill.
- Mix together the breadcrumbs, golden syrup and lemon juice.
- Spread the treacle mixture into the pastry case.
- Bake for 25 minutes.

Eat hot or cold. Great with either gluten and dairy free custard or gluten and dairy free ice cream.

Marilyn Le Breton © Copyright 2001

Chocolate pudding

CF, EF, FF, TF, YF.

Ingredients

9 oz (250g) plain tofu
½ pint (300ml) organic soya milk
2 oz (50g) unrefined caster sugar
2–3 oz (50–90g) gluten and dairy free
　chocolate

Method

- Blend together the tofu and ¼ pint (150ml) of milk, in an electric blender.
- Over a low heat, warm the remaining milk. Add the chocolate and sugar and stir until melted and mixed together.
- Allow the chocolate mix to cool and then blend into the tofu mix.
- Cool in an airtight container in the fridge for 2–3 hours or until set.

Marilyn Le Breton © Copyright 2001

Manchester tart

CF, SF, TF, YF

Ingredients

6 oz (175g) gluten and dairy free pastry
   (see Pastry section for recipes)
strawberry jam
2 oz (50g) dairy free margarine
2 oz (50g) unrefined caster sugar
1 egg (beaten)
4 oz (125g) gf un-sulphated desiccated
   coconut

Method

- Pre-heat oven to GM5, 375F, 190C.
- Line a 7" sandwich or flan tin with the pastry and allow it to relax in the fridge.
- Cream together the margarine and sugar.
- Beat in the egg.
- Stir in the coconut.
- Spread strawberry jam over the bottom of the pastry case.
- Carefully spoon and then spread the coconut mixture over the top of the jam.
- Bake for 20 minutes and then reduce the oven temperature to GM3, 325F, 170C and cook for a further 20 minutes.

Best served cold.

Marilyn Le Breton © Copyright 2001

Bread and 'butter' pudding

CF, SF, TF, YF

Ingredients

6 thin slices of gluten and dairy free bread
(crusts removed and spread each side
with dairy free margarine)
2 oz (50g) gf un-sulphated currants and
sultanas
2 tbsp unrefined caster sugar
2 eggs (beaten)
1 pint (600ml) gluten and dairy free milk
alternative

Method

- Pre-heat oven to GM4, 350F, 180C.
- Cut bread into quarters.
- In an ovenproof 1½ pint (900ml) capacity dish, layer the bread with fruit and sugar, beginning and ending with a bread layer.
- Beat together the eggs and milk and pour over the contents of the dish.
- Allow the mixture to stand for 20–30 minutes.
- Bake for approximately 40minutes, until it has set and is pale brown.

Marilyn Le Breton © Copyright 2001

Butterscotch pudding

EF, FF, SF, TF, YF

Ingredients

4 oz (125g) unrefined caster sugar
2 tbsp water
2 oz (50g) dairy free margarine
3 tbsp gluten and dairy free custard
    powder
1 pint (600ml) gluten and dairy free milk
    alternative

Method

- Dissolve the sugar in the water and slowly bring to the boil.
- Continue to boil until the sugar solution turns golden brown.
- Remove pan from the heat and wait until the solution stops bubbling, then add the margarine and stir in well, until it has completely melted and mixed in.
- Mix the custard powder with a little milk to form a smooth paste.
- Pour the rest of the milk into the butterscotch, mix well and return to heat.
- When the milk solution is nearly at boiling point, pour in the custard and mix together well.
- Bring custard to the boil stirring all the time.

This can be served hot or cold. If serving cold it is preferable to pour into individual serving dishes, prior to chilling in the fridge.

Marilyn Le Breton © Copyright 2001

Pineapple fritters

CF, SF, SGF, TF, YF

Ingredients

2 tins of pineapple rings (well drained)
4 oz (125g) gf flour mix
1 tbsp organic sunflower oil
¼ pint (150ml) tepid water
2 egg whites
oil to fry

Method

- Sift the flour and make a well in the middle.
- Into the well, pour the oil and the water. Mix together to form a thick batter. Add either a little more flour or water if necessary.
- In a separate bowl, using an electric mixer, whisk the egg whites until stiff.
- Gently fold the egg whites into the batter.
- Heat the oil in a deep fat fryer or a wok. To check if hot enough, put a teaspoon of the batter mixture into the oil. If the batter rises to the surface and begins to colour, the oil is hot enough.
- Dip the pineapple rings into the batter and lightly shake off any surplus batter.
- Place into the hot oil and cook for approximately 5 minutes, turning once, until they are golden brown.
- Drain well and serve.

Rob's spicy pineapple fritters

CF, EF, SGF, SF, TF, YF

Ingredients

1 tin of pineapple rings (well drained)
2 oz (50g) gram flour
1 tsp gf baking powder
3 tbsp water
¼ tsp gf garam masala
¼ tsp gf ground cinnamon
¼ tsp gf ground ginger
oil for frying

Method

- Mix together all of the dry ingredients and then stir in the water.
- Heat the oil as outlined in above recipe.
- Dip the pineapple rings into the batter and gently shake off excess.
- Fry for approximately 2 minutes, turning once.

Tip: if the batter does not cling to the pineapple rings well, pat them dry with kitchen paper.

Marilyn Le Breton © Copyright 2001

Summer pudding

CF, EF, SF, SGF, TF, YF

Ingredients

6 slices gluten and dairy free bread (crusts removed)
large tin tolerated fruit (drained)

Method

- Line the bottom and sides of a pudding basin with some of the bread.
- Place the fruit on top of the bread.
- Cover the fruit with remaining bread.
- Place a circle of greaseproof paper (cut to size) on top of the bread and place a weight on top of the paper.
- Place in the fridge overnight.
- When ready to serve, turn pudding out onto a plate.

Jacqui Jackson © Copyright 2001

Eden pudding

CF, SF, TF, YF

Ingredients
1½ lb (700g) pears (peeled cored and
   sliced)
1 tbsp lemon juice
2 oz (50g) dairy free margarine
2 oz (50g) unrefined caster sugar
1 egg (beaten)
4 oz (125g) gf flour mix

1 tsp xanthan gum
1 tsp gf baking powder
2 tbsp gluten and dairy free milk
   alternative

Method
- Pre-heat the oven to GM4, 350f, 180C.
- Cream together the margarine and sugar.
- Mix in the egg.
- Sift together the flour, xanthan gum and baking powder.
- Mix the flour into the creamed sugar and combine together well.
- Mix in the milk.
- Grease a 1½ pint (900ml) pie dish and place the pear slices on the bottom of it.
- Sprinkle the lemon juice over the pears.
- Gently spoon the pudding mixture over the pears and smooth over.
- Bake for 45 minutes.

Equally good served hot or cold.

Marilyn Le Breton © Copyright 2001

Pear Charlotte

CF, EF, SF, TF, YF

Ingredients

1½ lb (700g) pears (peeled, cored and sliced)
4 oz (125g) fresh gluten and dairy free breadcrumbs
3 oz (90g) unrefined brown sugar
2 oz (60g) dairy free margarine
2 tbsp golden syrup
2 tbsp water
1 tbsp lemon juice

Method

- Pre-heat oven to GM5, 375F, 190C.
- Mix together the breadcrumbs and brown sugar.
- In a 1½ pint (900ml) pie dish alternate layers of pears with the breadcrumb mixture, finishing with the breadcrumbs.
- Press this down well into the dish.
- Melt together the margarine, golden syrup, lemon juice and water.
- Pour this mixture over the top of the breadcrumbs.
- Bake for 30 minutes.

Marilyn Le Breton © Copyright 2001

No bake rice pudding

CF, EF, FF, SF, TF, YF

Ingredients

1 pint (600ml) gluten and dairy free milk alternative
2 oz (50g) sugar
2 oz (50g) pudding rice
1 tsp gf vanilla extract

Method

- Bring the milk and the sugar to the boil.
- Stir in the rice and reduce heat.
- Simmer for approximately 30 minutes until the rice is cooked and nearly all the liquid has been absorbed.
- Stir in the vanilla and serve.

Marilyn Le Breton © Copyright 2001

Almond and apricot flan

EF, SF, TF, YF

Pastry
7 oz (190g) Orgran Pizza/Pastry Multi Mix
9 oz (60g) dairy free margarine
2 tbsp icing sugar
3 fl oz (90ml) water

Filling
2 oz (60g) dairy free margarine
⅓ cup caster sugar
4 tsp Orgran 'No Egg'
¾ 12 oz (350g) ground almonds
1 tbsp cornflour
20 tinned apricot halves well
   drained
apricot jam for glazing

Method
- Pre-heat oven to GM2, 300F, 150C.

To make the pastry
- Mix together the multi mix and sugar.
- Rub in the margarine until the mixture resembles fine breadcrumbs.
- Add the water and with your hands knead the mixture into a dough.
- Allow the dough to stand in a warm place for 15 minutes and then knead again.
- Place the dough between two pieces of greaseproof paper and roll it out until it is large enough to line a 23cm flan case.

To make the filling
- Cream margarine and sugar together until they are just combined.
- Add the egg replacer, one spoonful at a time, beat in well after each addition.
- Fold in the ground almonds and flour.
- Spread the filling into the pastry case.
- Place the apricot halves gently on top of the filling.
- Bake for 45–50 minutes or until golden brown.
- Brush the top of the flan with warm sieved apricot jam.

Chocolate fudge dessert

CF, EF, FF, SF, TF, YF

Batter

1 tbsp dairy free margarine
½ cup caster sugar
½ cup gluten and dairy free milk
   alternative
1 tsp gf vanilla extract
1 cup gf flour mix
1 tsp gf baking powder
¼ tsp salt
1½ tbsp gluten and dairy free cocoa
   powder

Sauce

¼ cup gluten and dairy free
   cocoa powder
½ cup brown sugar
½ cup caster sugar
½ cup chopped nuts
1¼ cups boiling water

Method

- Pre-heat oven to GM4, 350f, 190C.

To make the batter

- Cream together the sugar and margarine.
- Add the milk and vanilla extract and mix in well.
- In a separate bowl mix together the flour, baking powder, salt and cocoa powder.
- Blend together the milk and flour mixtures, until the mix is a smooth, lump free batter.
- Place the mixture in a greased 8" sandwich tin.

To make the sauce

- Mix together all of the sauce ingredients.
- Pour the sauce over the batter.
- Bake for 35 minutes.
- A cake-like topping will form over the top of a thick sauce.

Debby Anglesey © Copyright 2001

Baked banana boats

CF, EF, SF, TF, YF

Ingredients

4 ripe bananas
1 oz (25g) dairy free margarine
1 tbsp unrefined caster sugar

Method

- Leaving the bananas in their skins, cut deep slit lengthways down the banana, but not deep enough to cut right through.
- Pull the slit out slightly.
- Cream together the margarine and sugar.
- Divide the margarine/sugar mix into four and push it down into each banana. Then press the banana back together again.
- Place the bananas in a microwaveable dish, slit side up and bake on high power for 3–4 minutes (the skins should begin to blacken). The banana will be soft and beginning to become translucent.
- Serve immediately, leaving bananas still in their skins.

Warning: do not over fill the bananas. If you do the skins will split open during cooking, depositing this delicious concoction all over the inside of your microwave.

Variations

- *Omit the margarine and sugar mix and substitute, lemon and sugar, honey or gluten and dairy free chocolate.*

Marilyn Le Breton © Copyright 2001

Chinese banana fritters

SF, TF, YF

Ingredients

4 bananas
1 egg (beaten)
bowl of ice cold water
4 tbsp cornflour

4 oz (125g) unrefined caster
 sugar
1 tbsp sesame seeds
3 tbsp organic sunflower oil and
 more for frying

Method

- Cut the bananas in half, lengthways and then cut each piece into 4 widthways.
- Blend the egg and cornflour together, to form a smooth paste.
- Add just enough of the ice cold water to turn the paste into a batter.
- Heat enough oil in a wok to cover the bananas (or set your deep fat fryer to 350F).
- Dip each piece of banana in the batter and deep fry for 2–3 minutes.
- Drain off the excess oil from the banana and pat dry with kitchen paper.
- In a heavy bottomed pan, heat the sugar and 3 tbsp of oil on a low heat for 5 minutes.
- Carefully add 3 tbsp of water to the sugar mix and stir for 2 minutes.
- Stir in the sesame seeds.
- Add the banana fritters and stir slowly and gently, until all the fritters are covered in the sugar solution.
- As soon as the sugar solution begins to caramelise, remove from heat and take out the fritters and plunge them straight into a bowl of ice cold water to harden.

Marilyn Le Breton © Copyright 2001

Pear meringue pie

CF, SF, TF, YF

Ingredients

8 oz (225g) gluten and dairy free pastry
    (see Pastry section for recipes)
1 lb (450g) pears (stewed and pureed)
meringue mix (see recipes in Cakes
    section)

Method

- Pre-heat oven to GM5, 375F, 190C.
- Line a 9" sandwich tin with greaseproof paper.
- Roll out pastry and line the tin with it. Allow it to cool in the fridge for 30–60 minutes.
- The bake the pastry case blind for approximately 20 minutes, until cooked and pale brown.
- Spread the pear puree over the pastry case.
- Spoon the meringue mix on top and pull it up in to small peaks with a knife.
- Bake for 5–10 minutes, or until the meringue is light brown on the peaks.
- Allow pie to cool before serving.

Lemon meringue pie

SF, TF, YF

Ingredients

8 oz (225g) gluten and dairy free pastry
(see Pastry section for recipes)
meringue mix (see recipes in Cakes
section)
2 lemons (juice and grated rinds)

2½ oz (50g) cornflour
3 oz (90g) unrefined caster
sugar
3 egg yolks beaten

Method

- Pre-heat oven to GM5, 375F, 190C.
- Line a 9" sandwich tin with greaseproof paper.
- Roll out pastry and line the tin with it. Allow it to cool in the fridge for 30–60 minutes.
- Then bake the pastry case blind for approximately 20 minutes, until cooked and pale brown.

To make the lemon filling

- Place the lemon rinds and 1 pint of cold water in a saucepan.
- Bring to the boil. Remove from heat and allow mix to stand for 30 minutes.
- Add the lemon juice.
- Take out 4 tbsp of the lemon water and mix it with the cornflour, to form a smooth paste.
- Add the paste to the lemon water and stir well.
- Bring the mix slowly back to the boil, stirring constantly.
- Reduce the heat and cook until thickened. Stir constantly.
- Remove from heat and stir in the sugar.
- Add egg yolks and stir vigorously, until well mixed.
- Pour into pastry case.
- Spoon the meringue mix over the top and pull it up into small peaks with a knife.
- Bake for 5–10 minutes, or until the meringue is light brown on the peaks.
- Allow pie to cool before serving.

Microwave christmas pudding

TF, YF

Ingredients

2 oz (50g) gluten and dairy free vegetable based suet

4 oz (125g) gf flour mix (Doves Farm)

1½ tsp gf baking powder

2 tsp gf mixed spice

2 tsp gf ground nutmeg

good pinch of salt

3 oz (90g) gluten and dairy free breadcrumbs

4 oz (125g) natural dark brown sugar

1 lb 4 oz (600g) mixed gf un-sulphated dried fruit

4 oz (125g) grated carrot

2 large eggs (beaten)

1 tbsp black treacle

½ pint (300ml) soya milk or pineapple juice

Method

- Grease well 2 microwave basins.
- Mix all ingredients together well and then divide the mixture evenly between the 2 basins.
- Place a circle of greaseproof paper on top of the mixture and press it down.
- Cover the basins with clingfilm and pierce it several times.
- Cook each pudding separately on high/full power for 5½ minutes.
- Stand for 5 minutes before serving or cover with an airtight lid (or foil) and store.
- To re-heat: 2 minutes full power.

Judy Saville, Billericay © Copyright 2001

Microwave last minute christmas pudding

CF, EF, SF, TF, YF

Ingredients

3 oz (90g) white rice flour
4 oz (125g) tapioca starch flour
1 oz (25g) potato starch flour
3 tsp xanthan gum
1 rounded tsp gf mixed spice
2 oz (50g) dairy free margarine (melted)
2 large eggs
3 tbsp black treacle/molasses
4 tbsp gluten and dairy free milk alternative

4 oz (125g) sweet mincemeat
  (see recipe)
3 oz (90g) apple sauce
4 oz (125g) gf un-sulphated
  currants
1 lemon (grated zest only)
1 orange (grated zest only)
2 tbsp water

Method

- Mix all of the ingredients together in a large bowl and combine well.
- Divide the mixture between 4–6 microwaveable teacups, well greased or lined with clingfilm. The teacups should only be filled up to halfway.

To microwave: cook one pudding at a time.
  500 watt machine:

- Cook on medium power setting for 3 minutes.
- Turn out the pudding and leave to stand for 2 minutes to continue cooking.

  700 watt machine:

- Cook on the medium power setting for 2 minutes and 20 seconds.
- Turn out the pudding and leave to stand for 2 minutes to continue cooking.

These need to be eaten the day that they are made.

Dairy free organic yoghurt

CF, EF, FF, SGF, TF, YF

Ingredients

3 tbsp organic plain live yoghurt (Provamel
   Organic Yofu)
1 pint (600ml) organic soya milk

Method

- Mix together the yoghurt and milk and leave to stand to reach room temperature.
- Place the liquid in an electric yoghurt maker.
- Follow the guidelines given for your yoghurt maker for time to 'cook'.

Helpful Hints

- The first 3–4 batches of yoghurt made will be a little thin or runny; do not worry, as each batch will get firmer as the 'starter' yoghurt for the following batch gets 'stronger'.
- It is therefore advisable to set aside 3 tbsp of yoghurt from each batch to make the next pint.
- The yoghurt can be strained off either through muslin or a yoghurt strainer to achieve a thicker yoghurt.
- Strain yoghurt for 1–2 hours for a thick set yoghurt.
- Strain yoghurt for 4 hours to get the consistency for 'dips'.
- Strain the yoghurt for 8 hours to get the consistency for cream cheese. It is advisable if straining for this length of time to 'pulse' quickly in a food processor to get a smooth texture.

Variations

- *All sorts can be added to your yoghurt: pureed fruit, sugar, vanilla extract, honey.*

Marilyn Le Breton © Copyright 2001

Lemon sorbet

CF, SF, TF, YF

Ingredients

4 oz (125g) unrefined granulated sugar
½ pint (300ml) water
3 lemons, rind and juice
1 egg white

Method

- In a heavy bottomed saucepan, gently heat the water and sugar, until the sugar dissolves.
- Once all the sugar has dissolved, add the lemon rind and simmer gently for 10 minutes.
- Bring the sugar syrup to the boil and continue to boil for 2 minutes.
- Allow the syrup to cool completely, then strain off the rind.
- Stir in the lemon juice.
- Pour the solution into a shallow freezer proof container. Cover the solution and freeze for approximately 3 hours. The mixture should now be 'slushy'.
- Turn the sorbet out into a bowl and break down the ice crystals gently with the back of a fork.
- In a separate bowl, whisk the egg white until it is very stiff.
- Gently fold the egg white into the sorbet mixture.
- Return mixture to the freezer container, cover and freeze for a further 4 hours.
- Allow the sorbet to soften slightly before serving.

Strawberry sorbet

CF, SF, TF, YF

Ingredients
4 oz (125g) unrefined granulated sugar
½ pint (300ml) water
1 lb (450g) strawberries
2 tbsp lemon juice
2 egg whites

Method

- In a heavy bottomed saucepan, gently heat the water and sugar, until the sugar dissolves.
- Once all the sugar has dissolved, bring to the boil and continue to boil for 2 minutes. Allow the mixture to cool.
- Puree strawberries in a blender and then strain through a sieve.
- Mix strawberry puree with sugar syrup and lemon juice.
- Pour the solution into a shallow freezer proof container. Cover the solution and freeze for approximately 3 hours. The mixture should now be 'slushy'.
- Turn the sorbet out into a bowl and break down the ice crystals gently with the back of a fork.
- In a separate bowl, whisk the egg white until it is very stiff.
- Gently fold the egg white into the sorbet mixture.
- Return mixture to the freezer container, cover and freeze for a further 4 hours.
- Allow the sorbet to soften slightly before serving.

Soups

Minestrone

CF, EF, FF, SF, SGF, YF

Ingredients

1 large onion (chopped)
2 carrots (thinly sliced)
1 leek (sliced)
1 large potato (thinly sliced)
4 oz (125g) nitrate free bacon (Lock's) (diced)
2 oz (50g) dairy free margarine
1 garlic clove (crushed)
2 oz (50g) frozen peas

1½ pints (900ml) homemade beef or vegetable stock (see Stocks section for recipes)
1 tbsp tomato puree
1 tsp dried gf basil or oregano
3 oz (90g) gf spaghetti pasta
1 oz (25g) white rice
14 oz (400g) tin of tomatoes

Method

- Fry the bacon, garlic and onion in the margarine for 5 minutes.
- Stir in the carrots, leeks and peas. Cook for 5minutes.
- Stir in stock, potatoes, tomato puree and herbs. Season and bring to the boil.
- Cover the pan and simmer for 5 minutes.
- Add the pasta, rice and tinned tomatoes and simmer for a further 15 minutes.
- Remove from heat and serve.

Even better re-heated the following day.

Marilyn Le Breton © Copyright 2001

Minestrone soup

CF, EF, FF, SF, SGF, YF

Ingredients

2 slices bacon (finely chopped)
6 medium carrots (finely chopped)
2 leeks (finely chopped)
2 sticks celery (finely chopped)
I large or 2 small courgettes (finely chopped)
2 tomatoes (finely chopped)
I onion (finely chopped)

I clove garlic (crushed)
2–3 tbsp olive oil
2 tsp tomato puree (optional)
2 oz (50g) gf pasta (Glutano spaghetti pasta – contains corn)
2–3 pints (1.1–1.7 l) homemade chicken stock (see Stocks section for recipes)

Method

- In a large pan, heat the oil and cook the bacon for a few minutes.
- Add all the vegetables. Cover the pan and cook on a low heat for 20 minutes, stirring occasionally to prevent sticking.
- Add the stock and simmer gently for at least 30 minutes.
- Break the spaghetti into small pieces and add to the soup.
- Add tomato puree if using and simmer for a further 10 minutes.

Freezes well.

Variation

- *Caroline suggests adding some cooked, chopped chicken at the final stage of the recipe.*

Garden vegetable soup

EF, FF, SGF, YF

Ingredients

3½ pints (2 litres) homemade vegetable
    stock (see Stocks section for recipes)
1 tbsp oil
1 onion (diced)
3 medium potatoes (peeled and diced)
3 celery sticks (sliced)
3 carrots (diced)
¼ cauliflower (cut into small florets)
1¾ lb (880g) canned tomatoes

3½ oz (100g) green peas
3½ oz (100g) sweetcorn
14 oz (440g) can red kidney
    beans (rinsed and drained)
1 packet Orgran Split Pea and
    Soya Pasta Shells
3 tbsp cornflour
8 fl oz (250ml) of extra stock

Method

- In a large stock pot, heat the oil. Add the onion and sauté for 2–3 minutes.
- Add stock, potato, celery, carrot, cauliflower, tomatoes, peas, sweetcorn and kidney beans.
- Cook over a medium heat for 45 minutes.
- Add the Orgran pasta and stir in.
- In a small bowl, mix a little of the extra stock with the cornflour, to form a paste. Then add the remainder of the stock.
- Pour this into the soup and stir until well mixed through.
- Cook for a further 15 minutes.

Orgran © Copyright 2000

Cream of chicken soup

CF*, EF, FF, SF*, SGF, TF, YF

Ingredients

1 cooked chicken carcass (boiled and meat removed from bones)
1 oz (25g) dairy free margarine (Pure)
2 small leeks or 1 small onion (chopped)
2 sticks celery (chopped)
4 oz (125g) potatoes (diced)
2 pints (1.1 litres) homemade chicken stock (see Stocks section for recipes)

½ pint (300ml) gluten and dairy free milk alternative
5 fl oz (175ml) coconut milk or soya cream
1 tbsp potato starch flour or cornflour
seasoning to taste

Method

- Melt margarine in a large pan. Add leeks, celery and potato. Cook on low heat until leeks become transparent.
- Add chicken stock and bring to the boil.
- Simmer until the vegetables are cooked.
- Remove from heat and allow to cool slightly.
- Add chicken, and liquidise at this stage if a smooth soup is required. Then add cream, milk and seasoning and simmer for a few minutes until hot through.
- If a thicker soup is required, add the flour and stir in well and simmer until the soup has thickened.

Angela Deakin, Fareham © Copyright

Leek and potato soup

CF, EF, FF, SF*, SGF, TF, YF

Ingredients

1 oz (30g) dairy free margarine (Pure)
8 oz (225g) leeks (chopped)
8 oz (225g) potatoes (cubed)
1 pint (600ml) homemade chicken stock
    (see Stocks section for recipes)
½ pint (300ml) gluten and dairy free milk
    alternative
seasoning
potato flour for thickening (if required)

Method

- Melt margarine in a large pan. Add leeks and potato. Cook on low heat until leeks become transparent.
- Add chicken stock and bring to the boil.
- Simmer until the vegetables are cooked.
- Remove from heat and allow soup to cool slightly.
- Add milk and seasoning and simmer for a few minutes until hot through.
- If a thicker soup is required, add the flour, stir in well and simmer until the soup has thickened.

Angela Deakin, Fareham © Copyright 2002

Potato soup

EF, FF, SF, SGF, TF, YF

Ingredients

4 potatoes (peeled and cubed)
2 slices of nitrate free bacon *or* 1 gluten and dairy free sausage (cooked and finely chopped)
3 carrots (cubed)
2 celery stalks (chopped)
1 onion (chopped)
14 oz (400g) can sweetcorn

1 summer squash (chopped) – optional
2 cups gluten and dairy free milk alternative
¼ cup gf flour
gf dried rosemary, sage and thyme to taste
seasoning

Method

- Place all the vegetables in a large saucepan and cover with water. Bring the pan to the boil and then simmer until the potatoes are just tender.
- Mix 1 cup of the milk with the flour, until smooth and add to the simmering soup. Stir constantly while the soup thickens.
- Gradually add the remaining milk.
- Add the bacon/sausage pieces, herbs and seasoning. Continue to cook for a few minutes.

Debby Anglesey © Copyright 2000

Cream of celery soup

CF, EF, FF, SF*, SGF, TF, YF

Ingredients

1 oz (30g) dairy free margarine alternative
12 oz (350g) celery (chopped)
4 oz (125g) potatoes (diced)
2 small leeks *or* 1 small onion (chopped)
1 pint (600ml) homemade chicken stock
    (see Stocks section for recipes)
5 fl oz (175ml) soya cream or coconut
    cream
seasoning

Method

- Melt margarine in a large pan. Add leeks, celery and potato. Cook on low heat until leeks become transparent.
- Add chicken stock and bring to the boil.
- Simmer until the vegetables are cooked.
- Remove from heat and allow soup to cool slightly.
- Liquidise at this stage if a smooth soup is required. Then add cream, milk and seasoning and simmer for a few minutes until hot through.

Angela Deakin, Fareham © Copyright

Mixed bean and vegetable soup

CF, EF, FF, SF, SGF, TF, YF

Ingredients

1 onion (chopped)
½ lb (225g) potatoes (diced)
1 carrot (finely sliced)
1 parsnip (finely sliced)
1 pepper (diced)
2 celery sticks (chopped)
1 tbsp sunflower oil
1 garlic clove (crushed)

2 pints (1.1 litres) homemade vegetable stock (see Stocks section for recipes)
15 oz (450g) tin of kidney beans (rinsed and drained)
15 oz (450g) tin of black-eyed beans (rinsed and drained)
1 courgette (sliced)
1 tsp gf mild curry powder (optional)

Method

- Heat oil in a large, heavy based saucepan (a pressure cooker pan is perfect).
- Add all the vegetables except the courgettes and the beans. Cook on a high heat for 5 minutes, stirring constantly.
- Add curry powder and garlic and continue to cook for a further 3 minutes.
- Add the stock. It should cover the vegetables; if it doesn't, then add more.
- Bring to the boil. Reduce heat, cover and simmer for 20 minutes.
- Add beans, continue to cook for a further 10 minutes.
- Remove half of the soup and puree it in the blender.
- Return the puree to the soup and bring the mixture back to the boil.
- Add courgettes and seasoning and then simmer for 4–5 minutes, until the courgettes are tender.
- Add a little water or extra stock if necessary to thin the soup.

Marilyn Le Breton © Copyright 2001

'Instant' vegetable soup

CF*, EF, FF, SF, SGF, TF, YF

Ingredients

½ pint homemade stock of choice (see
    Stocks section for recipes)
3 oz mixed vegetables (frozen or tinned)

Method

- Place all ingredients in a microwaveable jug.
- Cook on full power, for 2 minutes if vegetables are frozen or 1 minute if vegetables are tinned.
- Stand for 2 minutes before serving.

Marylin Le Breton © Copyright 2001

Cream of asparagus soup

CF, EF, FF, SF, SGF, TF, YF

Ingredients

¾ cup of water
½ tsp salt
1 lb (450g) fresh asparagus (cut into small pieces)
1 cup dairy free mock cream (⅔ cup Dari-free to ⅓ cup water)
2 tbsp dairy free margarine

Method

- In a large pan, bring the water and salt to the boil.
- Add asparagus. Cover pan and simmer for 8–10 minutes until the asparagus is tender.
- Cool the liquid and then blend it until smooth.
- Add mock cream and return soup to heat.
- Add margarine and heat through.
- Add a small knob of margarine to each bowl when serving.

Deborah Jusi © Copyright 2001

Cream of leek and potato soup with butter beans and broccoli

CF, EF, FF, SF, TF, YF

Ingredients

1 small leek (roughly chopped)
6 small potatoes (peeled and cooked)
5 oz (150g) broccoli florets
10 oz (280g) tin of butter beans (washed and drained)
2 cloves of garlic (coarsely chopped)
¼ tsp gf dried paprika

¼ tsp gf dried fenugreek
4–5 fl oz (100–150ml) gluten and dairy free milk alternative
2 tsp of dairy free margarine
1 tbsp sunflower oil
1 tsp unrefined granulated sugar
seasoning

Method

- In separate pans, par-boil the potatoes and broccoli. Drain but reserve the water from the broccoli.
- In a large saucepan, gently heat the oil and sauté the leek and garlic.
- Stir in the broccoli and the potatoes and cook for 2 minutes.
- Add all spices and seasoning, cook for a further 2 minutes.
- Add in broccoli water, milk, margarine and sugar. Cover and simmer on a very low heat, for 20–30 minutes, stirring occasionally.
- Remove from heat and allow soup to cool.
- Place soup in a blender and blend until it is of a smooth consistency.

This soup is best made a day in advance of use.
   Can be served cold or re-heated.
   For a chunkier soup there is no need to blend the soup.

Rob Le Breton © Copyright 2001

Lentil soup

CF, EF, FF, SF, SGF, TF, YF

Ingredients

8 oz (225g) lentils
2 pints (1.1 litres) water
2–3 tbsp sunflower oil
6 oz (175g) leeks (chopped)
3 oz (90g) onion (chopped)
1 carrot (chopped)
1 green pepper (chopped)

1 oz (30g) dairy free margarine
3 tbsp white rice flour
4 pints (2.2 litres) of homemade
    vegetable or chicken stock
    (see Stocks section for
    recipes)
2 tsp salt

Method

- In a large pan, bring the water to the boil and add the lentils. Reduce the heat and simmer for 1 hour. Drain and return to pan.
- Heat the sunflower oil and gently cook all of the vegetables for 5 minutes.
- Add the vegetables to the lentils.
- In the pan used to fry the vegetables, melt the margarine and add the white rice flour, stir into paste and cook for 2 minutes.
- Stir in the stock, salt and vinegar (if using) and bring to the boil. Reduce heat slightly and stir until it thickens.
- Pour the stock into the vegetable and lentil mix. Simmer for 30 minutes.

Marilyn Le Breton © Copyright 2001

Lentil soup

CF, EF, FF, SF, SGF, YF

Ingredients

1⅔ cups lentils (rinsed)

1½ quarts of water or homemade vegetable stock (see Stocks section for recipes)

3 stalks celery (chopped)

3 carrots (chopped)

1 tbsp gf dried parsley

1 onion (chopped)

1 tbsp sunflower oil

4 tomatoes (chopped)

1 bay leaf

¼ tsp gf dried thyme

2 cups of chopped spinach or kale

seasoning

1 cup uncooked gf pasta shapes (optional)

Method

- In a large pot simmer together all the ingredients, until the lentils are tender.
- Add the pasta if using and cook for a further 10 minutes.
- Add more water if the soup becomes too thick.

Debby Anglesey © Copyright 2000

Bacon, vegetable and lentil soup

CF, EF, FF, SF, SGF, YF

Ingredients

8 oz (225g) carrots (chopped)

8 oz (225g) parsnips (chopped)

1 lb (450g) leeks (sliced)

4 oz (125g) nitrate free bacon (chopped)

2 tbsp organic sunflower oil

8 oz lentils (yellow or red)

3 pints (1.7 litres) homemade vegetable stock

1 tbsp tomato puree

seasoning

Method

- Heat oil in a large pan and brown off the bacon.
- Add the vegetables and lentils and cook for 2 minutes, stirring occasionally.
- Add the stock, puree and seasoning, mix together well and bring the liquid to the boil.
- Reduce the heat, cover the pan and simmer for 30 minutes until the vegetables and lentils are tender.

Marilyn Le Breton © Copyright 2001

Parsnip, lentil and coconut soup

CF, EF, FF, SF, SGF, TF, YF

Ingredients

1 medium onion (sliced)
1 large leek (sliced)
2 large carrots (chopped)
1 medium parsnip (chopped)
2 medium potatoes (chopped)
2 garlic cloves (crushed)
4 oz (125g) red lentils (rinsed)

2 tsp gf dried coriander
½–1 tsp gf ground cumin
1 tsp salt
¼ pint (150ml) coconut milk
2 tbsp dairy free margarine
2 tbsp sunflower oil
2 pints (1.1 litres) water

Method

- Melt margarine and oil in a large pan over a low heat.
- Sauté the onions for 3 minutes. Add the leek and garlic for 2 minutes.
- Add the carrots and cook for 2 minutes.
- Add parsnips, salt, coriander and cumin, stir in well and cook for 2 minutes stirring constantly.
- Add the potatoes and lentils and stir in well.
- Add the water and bring to the boil.
- Reduce the heat, cover the pan and simmer for 30–40 minutes or until the lentils and vegetables are soft.
- Remove from the heat and allow the soup to cool slightly.
- In a food processor, blend the soup down to a smooth paste.
- Place the soup in a clean pan with the coconut milk and season to taste. Heat through, but do not allow to boil.

Marilyn Le Breton © Copyright 2001

Bacon and vegetable soup

CF, EF, FF, SF, SGF, TF, YF

Ingredients

6 oz (175g) nitrate free bacon (chopped)
1 onion (sliced)
2 carrots (chopped)
1 parsnip (chopped)
2 oz (60g) red lentils (rinsed)
1½ pints (900ml) water
seasoning

Method

- Fry bacon in a little oil, until it is crispy. With a slotted spoon, remove the bacon and reserve.

- In the same pan, fry the onion, carrot and parsnip for 5 minutes (add a little more oil if required), stirring constantly. Do not allow the vegetables to brown.

- Add the lentils and water and stir in well. Bring the water to the boil.

- Cover the pan, reduce heat and simmer for 40 minutes.

- Remove from the heat and cool slightly. Place soup in a food processor and blend down to a smooth paste.

- Return the soup to a clean pan, add the bacon and season to taste, and heat through. Do not allow soup to boil.

Marilyn Le Breton © Copyright 2001

Spicy tomato and lentil soup

CF, EF, FF, SF, SGF, YF

Ingredients

2 tbsp dairy free margarine
2 garlic cloves (crushed)
1 large onion (chopped)
½ tsp gf turmeric
1 tsp gf garam masala
1 tsp gf cumin
1 tsp gf dried coriander

3 tins (total 42 oz/1.2kg) chopped tomato (drained)
6 oz (175g) red lentils
1 pint (300ml) water or homemade gf/cf vegetable stock
½ pint (150ml) coconut milk
seasoning

Method

- Melt the margarine in a large pan and sauté the garlic and onions for 3–4 minutes.
- Add the turmeric, garam masala, cumin and coriander. Stir in well and cook for a further minute.
- Stir in the tomatoes, lentils, and water (or stock if using). Bring the liquid to the boil.
- Reduce the heat and simmer uncovered for 30 minutes (or until the lentils are soft).
- Stir in the coconut milk and season to taste.

Marilyn Le Breton © Copyright 2001

Bacon, lentil and pasta soup

CF, EF, FF, SF, SGF, TF, YF

Ingredients

½ lb (225g) nitrate free bacon (chopped)
1 onion (sliced)
2 cloves garlic (crushed)
2 sticks celery (fine chopped)
1½ oz (40g) small gf pasta (or broken gf
    spaghetti)
3 oz (90g) red lentils (rinsed)
2 pints (1.1 litres) homemade vegetable or
    chicken stock
½ tsp gf dried mixed herbs

Method

- In a large pan mix together the stock and lentils and bring to the boil. Reduce heat, cover the pan and simmer for 30 minutes.
- In another pan, fry the bacon, onion, mixed herbs, garlic and celery together in a little oil, for 5 minutes.
- Add the bacon mix and the pasta to the lentils and stock.
- Bring the soup back to the boil. Reduce heat and simmer for the time needed for the pasta to cook.

Marilyn Le Breton © Copyright 2001

Chinese chicken and sweetcorn soup

EF, FF, SF, SGF, TF, YF

Ingredients

1 lb (450g) filleted chicken breasts (cut into
   thin strips)
2 pints (1.1 litres) homemade chicken
   stock
3 oz (90g) Chinese rice noodles
1 tbsp cornflour
3 tbsp gluten and dairy milk alternative
6 oz (175g) sweetcorn
6 spring onions (finely chopped)
½ tsp gf garlic granules
seasoning

Method

- In a large pan, bring the stock to the boil and add the chicken.
- Reduce the heat and simmer for 20 minutes.
- Add the garlic, onions and seasoning, stir in well.
- Mix together the cornflour and the milk to form a smooth paste. Add to the stock and bring the liquid back to the boil.
- Reduce the heat and stir continuously, until the liquid has thickened a little.
- Add the sweetcorn and rice noodles and cook for a further 3 minutes or until the noodles have cooked through.

Marilyn Le Breton © Copyright 2001

Chickpea, courgette and spinach soup

CF, EF, FF, SF, SGF, YF

Ingredients

2 tbsp oil
2 leeks (sliced)
2 medium courgettes (diced)
2 garlic cloves (crushed)
2 x 14 oz (400g) cans chopped tomatoes
1 tbsp tomato puree
1½ pints (900ml) homemade chicken or
    vegetable stock
14 oz (400g) can chickpeas
8 oz (225g) spinach (rinsed and finely
    chopped)
seasoning

Method

- Heat the oil in a large pan. Add the leeks and garlic and cook for 5 minutes, stirring occasionally.
- Add the courgettes and cook for a further 2 minutes.
- Add tomatoes, tomato puree, stock and chickpeas, stir in well.
- Bring the soup to the boil. Cover and reduce heat and allow to simmer for 5 minutes.
- Add the spinach and cook for a further 2 minutes.

Marilyn Le Breton © Copyright 2001

Carrot, leek and potato soup

CF, EF, FF, SF, SGF, TF, YF

Ingredients

1 tbsp oil
6 oz (175g) leeks (thinly sliced)
2 garlic cloves (crushed)
1½ pints (900ml) homemade vegetable
    stock

¼ tsp gf cumin
6 oz (175g) potatoes (diced)
4 oz carrot (125g) (thinly sliced)
seasoning

Method

- Heat oil in a large pan and sauté the leek and garlic for 2–3 minutes.
- Stir in the cumin well.
- Add the stock, carrots, potatoes and seasoning. Bring to the boil.
- Cover and reduce the heat and simmer for 20 minutes.
- Remove from heat and allow to cool slightly.
- In a food processor, blend the soup down to a smooth puree.
- Return to a clean pan. Season to taste and re-heat.

Marilyn Le Breton © Copyright 2001

Pea and potato soup

CF, EF, FF, SF, SGF, TF, YF

Ingredients

2 tbsp oil
3 large potatoes (diced)
1 large onion (sliced)

3 oz (90g) split green peas
1½ pints (900ml) homemade
    vegetable stock
seasoning

Method

- Heat oil in a large pan. Add the potatoes and onions and sauté over a low heat for 5 minutes, stirring constantly.
- Add the split peas and stir in well.
- Add the vegetable stock and bring to the boil.
- Reduce the heat and cover. Simmer for 20 30 minutes, or until the potatoes are tender and split peas are cooked.
- Season and serve.

Marilyn Le Breton © Copyright 2001

Sweet potato and onion soup

CF, EF, FF, SGF, TF, YF

Ingredients

2 tbsp sunflower oil
2 lb sweet potatoes (diced)
1 carrot (diced)
2 onions (sliced)
2 cloves garlic (crushed)
1½ pints (900ml) water or homemade
    vegetable stock
½ pint (300ml) plain soya yoghurt
2 tsp gf dried coriander *or* 2 tbsp fresh
    coriander (chopped)
seasoning

Method

- Heat the oil in a large pan, add the sweet potatoes, carrots, onions and garlic. Sauté the vegetables for 5 minutes, stirring constantly.
- Add the water or stock and coriander. Bring the liquid to the boil, cover the pan and reduce heat. Simmer for 20 minutes or until the vegetables are tender.
- Remove from heat and allow soup to cool slightly, place in a food processor and blend down to a smooth paste.
- Return the soup to a clean pan and re-heat.
- Take off heat and stir in the yoghurt, immediately before serving.

Marilyn Le Breton © Copyright 2001

Pasta and Pasta Sauces

Fresh pasta

CF*, FF, SF, SGF, TF, YF

Ingredients

3 tbsp potato starch flour
½ cup tapioca starch flour
½ cup cornflour or white rice flour
¾ tsp sea salt
4½ tsp xanthan gum
3 large eggs (room temperature)
1½ tbsp organic oil of choice

Method

- Mix together the flours, salt and xanthan gum.
- In a separate bowl whisk together the eggs and oil.
- Mix the egg mixture into the flour mixture, to form a dough.
- Mould the dough into a ball and knead for a few minutes.
- On a floured surface, roll out the dough very thinly, so that it is almost transparent.
- Slice into very thin strips for spaghetti, slightly wider for noodles, or into rectangles for lasagne.
- If using a pasta machine, roll the dough out a little before placing in the machine. Then follow the instructions.
- Do not use the drying out method given for gluten pasta, as this will not be successful.
- Cook the pasta by adding 1 tbsp oil to boiling salted water for 10–12 minutes, according to size/thickness of pasta.
- Drain and rinse well.

This freezes well either cooked or uncooked.

Barbara's Kitchen © Copyright 2000

Potato noodles

CF, FF, SGF, SF, TF, YF

Ingredients

1 lb (450g) potatoes (cooked, mashed and
 cooled)
8 oz (225g) gf flour mix
2 tsp xanthan gum
1 egg (beaten)
1 tbsp gluten and dairy free milk alternative
1 tsp salt

Method

- Mix all of the ingredients together to form a stiff dough.
- Lightly flour a surface and roll the dough into thin 'sausages'.
- Cut the sausages into 1" lengths.
- Cook the noodles in boiling water for 3–4 minutes. The noodles will rise to the surface when cooked.

Variation

- *These can be flavoured with a variety of herbs and spices.*

Marilyn Le Breton © Copyright 2001

Gnocchi

CF, FF, SF, SGF, TF, YF

Ingredients

2½ lb (1.2kg) potatoes (peeled and diced)
2 oz (60g) dairy free margarine (melted
    and cooled)
1 egg (beaten)
11 oz (310g) gf flour mix
3 tsp xanthan gum
1 tsp salt

Method

- Cook the potatoes in boiling water until tender and drain well.
- Mash the potato and then push through a sieve with the back of a spoon.
- Add the margarine and egg to the potato and mix together well.
- In a separate bowl mix together the flour, xanthan gum and salt.
- Add 6 oz of the flour mix to the potato mixture and stir, until well combined.
- On a lightly floured surface knead the dough, gradually working in the remaining flour as you knead.
- The dough when all the flour has been added should be smooth and soft but still slightly sticky.
- Break off large pieces of the dough and roll into 'sausages' approximately ¾" thick.
- Cut each sausage into pieces ½" long.
- Dip a fork into flour and press down lightly on each piece.
- Bring a pan of salted water to simmer.
- Add small batches of the gnocchi and cook for 3–4 minutes. They rise to the surface when cooked. Do not over-crowd the pan with gnocchi.
- Remove the gnocchi with a slotted spoon.
- Keep each batch warm by placing in a covered dish in a pre-heated oven on a low to moderate heat.

Marilyn Le Breton © Copyright 2001

Spinach gnocchi

CF, EF, FF, SF, SGF, TF, YF

Ingredients

1 lb (450g) potatoes (peeled and chopped)
2 oz (50g) spinach
1 oz (25g) dairy free margarine (melted and cooled)

1 small egg (beaten)
5 oz (150g) gf flour mix
1½ tsp xanthan gum
1 tsp salt

Method

- Cook the potatoes and mash finely, then push through a sieve using the back of a spoon.
- Wilt the spinach in a very little hot water, drain and pat off any excess water using a clean tea towel.
- Chop the spinach finely and mix into the potato well.
- Add the margarine and the egg to the potato mixture and stir in vigorously.
- In a separate bowl mix together the flour, xanthan gum and salt.
- Add 2½ oz of the flour mix to the potato mix and stir in until well combined.
- On a lightly floured surface knead the dough, gradually working in the remaining flour as you knead.
- The dough when all the flour has been added should be smooth and soft but still slightly sticky.
- Break off large pieces of the dough and roll into 'sausages' approximately ¾" thick.
- Cut each sausage into pieces ½" long.
- Dip a fork into flour and press down lightly on each piece.
- Bring a pan of salted water to simmer.
- Add small batches of the gnocchi and cook for 3–4 minutes. They rise to the surface when cooked. Do not over-crowd the pan with gnocchi.
- Remove the gnocchi with a slotted spoon.
- Keep each batch warm by placing in a covered dish in a pre-heated oven on a low to moderate heat.

Marilyn Le Breton © Copyright 2001

Corn and parsley fettuccini with vegetable medley sauce

EF, FF, SGF, YF

Ingredients

I packet of Orgran Corn and Parsley Fettuccini

I small aubergine (peeled and cut into strips 5cm long and Icm thick)

⅓ cup olive oil

I medium courgette (thinly sliced)

I medium onion (thinly sliced)

I medium green pepper (thinly sliced)

I clove garlic (minced)

3 medium tomatoes (peeled and sliced)

I tsp salt

⅓ tsp pepper (coarsely ground)

⅓ tsp fresh, chopped oregano leaves

⅓ tsp fresh, chopped basil leaves

½ tbsp capers

⅓ cup fresh, chopped parsley

Method

- Place ¼ cup of olive oil (from the ⅓ cup) in a saucepan and quickly sauté the aubergine on all sides. Remove the aubergine strips and set aside.
- Add rest of oil to pan and sauté the courgette quickly. Remove and set aside.
- Add garlic, green pepper and onion to the saucepan and sauté for 2–3 minutes.
- Place the tomato slices on top of the garlic mix, cover the pan and cook for 5 minutes.
- Stir in the aubergine, courgette, herbs and capers. Cover the pan and simmer on a low heat for 20 minutes.
- Whilst the sauce is cooking, cook the pasta according to the instructions on the packet.
- Serve hot.

Orgran © Copyright 2000

Creamy celery and ham pasta sauce

CF, EF, FF, SF*, SGF, TF, YF

Ingredients

1 small onion (sliced)
1 small onion (finely chopped)
1 small carrot (sliced)
1 bay leaf
1 ¼ cups gluten and dairy free milk
   alternative
2 tbsp dairy free margarine
4 sticks celery (finely chopped)

¼ cup white rice flour or
   potato starch flour
8 oz (225g) nitrate free ham
   (Lock's) (roughly chopped)
¼ tsp gf dried mixed herbs
½ tsp gf garlic granules
seasoning
2 tbsp soya cream alternative
   (optional)

Method

- In a large saucepan, place the sliced onion, carrot, bay leaf and milk. Bring the mixture slowly to the bowl. Remove from heat.

- Cover and allow it to stand for 30 minutes. Strain the liquid off over a bowl. Keep the flavoured milk and discard the vegetables.

- In another pan, melt the margarine over a low heat. Add the chopped onion and celery and fry gently for 10 minutes, stirring occasionally.

- Stir in the flour and cook for 1 minute stirring constantly. Remove from heat.

- Gradually stir in the flavoured milk and put back on heat.

- Slowly bring to the boil, stirring constantly. Reduce the heat and continue to stir and cook, until the mixture thickens.

- Add ham, herbs, garlic and seasoning. Simmer for 5 minutes.

- Remove from heat. Stir in cream alternative (if using) and serve immediately with pasta of choice.

Marilyn Le Breton © Copyright 2001

Vegetable rice spiral pasta with spicy vegetable stir-fry

CF, EF, FF, SF, SGF, TF, YF

Ingredients

1 packet of Orgran Vegetable Rice Spiral Pasta
½ tsp gf dried thyme
⅓ cup olive oil
1 small onion (sliced)
1 medium green pepper (thinly chopped)
1 small aubergine (chopped)
½ stick celery (sliced)
5 oz (150g) snow peas (sliced)
2 green shallots (chopped)
2 bay leaves
⅔ cup of homemade vegetable stock (see Stocks section for recipes) or water
⅔ cup of pitted black olives

Method

- Heat oil in saucepan and gently fry onion and pepper, stirring constantly, until the onion is soft.
- Stir in aubergine and cook over a low heat for 5 minutes.
- Add celery, stock/water, thyme and bay leaves. Bring to the boil and then simmer uncovered for 10 minutes.
- Stir in peas, olives and shallots. Continue to simmer whilst pasta is cooking.
- Cook pasta according to the instructions on the packet.
- Remove the bay leaves from the sauce, prior to serving.

Orgran © Copyright 2000

Vegetarian Amatriciana

EF, FF, SF, SGF, YF

Ingredients

1 packet Orgran Corn and Vegetable Shells
fresh chilli to taste (de-seeded and
    chopped)
2 medium onions (finely chopped)
1 large tin (1¾ lb/800g) peeled and
    chopped tomatoes
2 cloves of garlic, finely chopped
2 tbsp olive oil
seasoning
5 oz (150g) pitted black olives

Method

- Heat oil in a saucepan and brown the onion, garlic and chilli over a low heat.
- Add the chopped tomatoes and olives. Cover the pan and cook for 20 minutes over a very low heat, stirring occasionally.
- Cook pasta according to the instructions on the packet.
- When pasta is cooked, strain and stir into the tomato sauce, mix thoroughly and serve hot.

Corn spiral pasta with lemon 'butter' sauce

EF, SF, SGF, TF, YF

Ingredients

1 packet Orgran Corn Spiral Pasta
3½ oz (100g) smoked salmon (cut into 1cm strips)
2½ oz (70g) broccoli (broken into small florets)
2½ oz (70g) fine green beans (trimmed and halved)
2½ oz (70g) asparagus tips (trimmed)
2 tsp cornflour
½ tsp finely grated lemon rind
juice of 1 lemon
1½ oz (40g) dairy free margarine
2½ fl oz (55ml) homemade vegetable stock (see Stocks section for recipes) or water
1 tsp honey
3 fl oz (70ml) water

Method

- Cook pasta according to the instructions on the packet. Halfway through the cooking time add all the vegetables.
- Melt margarine in a small saucepan and stir in the stock/water, honey, lemon rind and juice. Cook slowly, until the honey has dissolved.
- Mix the cornflour with the cold water and stir this into the lemon mixture.
- Bring the lemon sauce to the boil, stirring continuously, until the sauce thickens slightly.
- Stir in the salmon strips. Cover the pan and simmer for 2 minutes.
- Drain off pasta and vegetables and then stir in the sauce.

Orgran © Copyright 2000

Corn and spinach rigati pasta with tofu salad and vegetables

EF, FF, SGF, YF

Ingredients

1 packet of Orgran Corn and Spinach
   Rigati Pasta
5 oz (150g) plain, firm tofu (cubed)
3 carrots (grated)
3 small courgettes (grated)
2 sticks celery (chopped)
1 red pepper (chopped)
1 tomato (chopped)

⅔ cup olive oil
2½ tsp cumin seeds
2 tsp white mustard seeds
1 cup plain soya yoghurt
1 small fresh red chilli
   (de-seeded and chopped)
1 medium aubergine (peeled
   and cubed)

Method

- Cook pasta according to the instructions on the packet. Once cooked, rinse with running cold water and drain.
- Place pasta in a bowl and add the carrots, courgette, celery, pepper and tomato. Mix well.
- Heat ⅓ cup of the oil in a pan and gently cook the tofu, stirring, until browned. Remove from oil and drain on kitchen paper. Add tofu to the pasta and vegetable mix.
- Heat a dry pan and add cumin and mustard seeds. Stir continuously, until the seeds pop.
- Add the remaining ⅓ cup of oil, chilli and aubergine. Stir and cook until the aubergine is tender.
- Stir into vegetable mixture.
- Add yoghurt and stir in well.

Cajun chicken fettuccine

EF, FF, SF, SGF, TF, YF

Ingredients

750g Orgran Ris 'O' Mais Fettucine
6 boneless chicken breasts (sliced)
2 tbsp gf ground paprika
2 cloves garlic (crushed)
2 tsp ground black pepper
1 tbsp gf ground cumin
1 tbsp gf ground coriander
½ tsp gf chilli powder
2 tsp sunflower oil

Method

- Mix all spices together in a bowl.
- Add the chicken slices to the spice mix and coat the chicken well.
- Heat the oil in a frying pan, over a medium heat. Add the chicken and cook until it is tender (approximately 5 minutes), stirring continuously.
- Remove chicken from the pan, set aside and keep warm.
- Cook pasta according to the instructions on packet. Drain well.
- Mix together with the chicken.

Orgran © Copyright 2000

Tuna and mixed bean pasta sauce

CF, FF, SGF, TF, YF

Ingredients

¾ cup plain soya yoghurt
½ cup gluten and dairy free mayonnaise
¼ tsp gf garlic granules
¼ tsp gf dried mixed herbs
10 spring onions (finely chopped)

2 sticks celery (finely chopped)
14 oz (400g) can tuna in oil
    (drained and flaked)
14 oz (400g) can cooked, mixed
    beans (rinsed and drained)
seasoning

Method

- In a large bowl, mix together the yoghurt, mayonnaise, garlic, herbs and seasoning.
- To this dressing add the onion, celery, tuna and mixed beans. Mix in well.
- Chill in the fridge, until ready to serve with pasta of choice.

Variations

- *Also goes well with rice.*
- *Substitute the tuna for tinned fish of choice: red or pink salmon, sardines, etc.*

Marilyn Le Breton © Copyright 2001

Spicy vegetable pasta sauce

CF, EF, FF, SF*, SGF, TF, YF

Ingredients

½ pint (300ml) coconut milk
2 onions (thinly sliced)
1 clove garlic (crushed)
2 tbsp gf garam masala
½ pint (300ml) homemade vegetable stock (see Stocks section for recipe) or water
½ cauliflower (cut into florets)
8 oz (225g) courgettes (thickly sliced)
8 oz (225g) broccoli (cut into florets)
4 oz (125g) French beans
4 oz (125g) peas
3 tbsp plain soya yoghurt (optional)
seasoning to taste

Method

- In a large saucepan, fry onions for 5 minutes over a low heat until they have softened.
- Add garlic and garam masala and fry for a further 2 minutes.
- Add the coconut milk and stock and stir in well.
- Add all the remaining vegetables and cook over a medium heat for 15 minutes.
- Just before ready to serve, stir in the soya yoghurt if using.

Marilyn Le Breton © Copyright 2001

Spicy sausage and tomato pasta sauce

CF, EF, FF, SF, SGF, YF

Ingredients

1 lb Lock's AiA sausages (cooked and cut into 1" pieces)
1 tsp organic sunflower oil
1 onion (sliced)
1 clove of garlic (crushed) or ½ tsp gf garlic granules
2 tsp gf garam masala
1 tsp gf turmeric

4 oz (125g) mushrooms (sliced) (optional)
½ cup homemade vegetable stock (see Stocks section for recipes) or water
14 oz (400g) can chopped tomatoes
seasoning

Method

- Heat oil and gently cook onions (and garlic if using fresh) for 5 minutes.
- Stir in turmeric, garam masala, and garlic (if using dried); cook and stir for 1 minute.
- Add sausages, mushrooms (if using), water/stock, tomatoes and seasoning. Mix in and gently bring to the boil.
- Cover and simmer for 20 minutes.
- Add to pasta of choice.

Marilyn Le Breton © Copyright 2001

Tuna and sweetcorn pasta sauce

CF, FF, SGF, TF, YF

Ingredients

4 oz (125g) frozen peas
1 cup plain soya yoghurt
4 tbsp gluten and dairy free mayonnaise
7 oz (200g) sweetcorn (rinsed and drained)
10 spring onions (finely chopped)
7 oz (200g) tin tuna in oil (drained and
    flaked)
seasoning

Method

- Cook peas. Drain and cool.
- In a bowl mix together the yoghurt and mayonnaise.
- To the yoghurt mix, stir in the peas, spring onions, sweetcorn, tuna and seasoning. Mix together gently.
- Serve with pasta of choice.

Variations

- *Replace tuna with gf/cf ham, cooked turkey or chicken, or crispy bacon pieces.*

Salmon and courgette pasta sauce

CF, EF, FF, SF, SGF, TF, TY

Ingredients

2 tbsp dairy free margarine

2 courgettes (cut into very thin slices or matchsticks)

8–10 spring onions (finely chopped)

¼ cup white rice flour or potato starch flour

1¼ cups gluten and dairy free milk alternative

7½ (210g) oz can red or pink salmon in oil (drained and flaked)

seasoning

Method

- Melt margarine over a low heat. Add courgette and cook for 4 minutes.
- Add onion and cook for a further 4 minutes.
- Stir in the flour and cook for 1 minute, stirring continuously. Remove from heat.
- Stir in milk vigorously and return to heat.
- Slowly, bring the mixture to the boil.
- Reduce heat and continue to cook, until the sauce has thickened.
- Add the salmon and seasoning and simmer gently for 5 minutes, stirring occasionally.
- Serve with pasta of choice.

Ham and leek pasta sauce

CF, EF, FF, SF*, SGF, TF, YF

Ingredients

2 tbsp dairy free margarine
1 lb leeks (sliced)
¼ cup white rice flour or potato starch
    flour
1¼ cups gluten and dairy free milk
    alternative

8 oz (225g) nitrate free ham
    (diced)
½ tsp gf dried mixed herbs
½ tsp gf garlic granules
2 tbsp soya cream alternative
    (optional)
seasoning

Method

- Melt margarine over a low heat. Add leeks and cook gently for 8–10 minutes, stirring occasionally.
- Stir in flour and cook for 1 minute, stirring constantly. Remove from heat.
- Stir in milk, return to heat and bring slowly to the boil, stirring constantly.
- Reduce heat and continue to cook until the mix thickens.
- Add ham, herbs, garlic and seasoning. Simmer for 5 minutes, stirring constantly.
- Remove from heat and stir in cream substitute (if using).
- Serve with pasta of choice.

Variations

- *Replace ham with cooked chicken, turkey or bacon.*

Marilyn Le Breton © Copyright 2001

Basic tomato sauce for pasta I

CF, EF, FF, SF, YF

Ingredients

I onion, finely chopped
2 cloves garlic, finely chopped
2 x 14 oz (400g) tins tomatoes
2 tbsp tomato puree
I tsp unrefined caster sugar
½ tsp gf dried mixed herbs/oregano

Method

- Gently fry onion and garlic for 5 minutes.
- Add tomatoes, tomato puree, sugar and herbs.
- Simmer on a low heat for 20 minutes.

Marilyn Le Breton © Copyright 2001

Basic tomato sauce for pasta II

CF, EF, FF, SF, SGF, YF

Ingredients

½ onion (finely chopped)
2 celery sticks (finely chopped)
2 oz (50g) sun dried tomatoes (finely chopped)
2 cloves garlic (crushed)

2 x 14oz (400g) tins chopped tomatoes
2 tbsp gf tomato puree
¼ pint (150ml) homemade vegetable stock (see Stocks section for recipes)

Method

- Very gently fry the onions, celery and garlic for 5 minutes, until soft.
- Add the tinned tomatoes, cover pan and simmer for 3 minutes.
- Add the sun dried tomatoes, tomato puree and stock, stir well and cook for 5 minutes.
- Puree mix in a blender and season to taste.

Marilyn Le Breton © Copyright 2001

Spaghetti Bolognese

CF, EF, FF, SF, SGF*, YF

Ingredients
1 lb (450g) minced beef
homemade tomato sauce (see above for
    recipes)

Method
- Fry the mince on a gentle heat, until browned. Drain off excess oil.
- Add mince to the sauce, cook for a further 20 minutes.

Variations
- *Substitute minced chicken, turkey, bacon or sliced, cooked gluten and dairy free sausages, for the minced beef.*

Marilyn Le Breton © Copyright 2001

Spaghetti Bolognese sauce

CF, EG, FF, SF, YF

Ingredients
1 lb (450g) beef mince
1 small onion
1 glove garlic (crushed)
8 oz (225g) passata or strained tinned
    tomatoes
4 tbsp tomato puree
2 tsp granulated sugar

1 tbsp gf garlic Italian seasoning
$\frac{1}{8}$ tsp gf ground cayenne pepper
$\frac{1}{4}$ tsp gf ground pepper
1–2 carrots (grated)
$\frac{1}{2}$ red pepper (chopped)
$\frac{1}{2}$ green pepper (chopped)
2 oz (50g) mushrooms (sliced)

Method
- Fry mince until cooked thoroughly.
- Add onions, garlic and continue to cook for another 3–5 minutes.
- Add tomato puree, passata, sugar and all spices and herbs and stir together well.
- Add carrots, peppers and mushrooms.
- Allow the sauce to simmer very gently for 30–60 minutes.
- Serve with gf pasta of choice.

Innovative Solutions (UK) Ltd © Copyright 2000

Tomato free pasta sauce

CF*, EF, FF, SF, SGF, TF, YF

Ingredients

2 tbsp cornflour (or white rice or potato
    starch flour)
½ pint (300ml) gluten and dairy free milk
    alternative

1 tbsp dairy free margarine
1 onion (finely chopped)
4 oz (125g) button mushrooms
    (finely sliced) (optional)
½ tsp gf garlic granules

Method

- In a little oil, gently fry the onion for 5 minutes until it has softened.
- Add the mushrooms and garlic granules and gently fry for a further 2–3 minutes.
- Drain off any excess oil and set aside.
- In a cup or small bowl, mix the cornflour (or alternative flour) with 4 tbsp of the milk, into a smooth paste.
- Place the remaining milk in a saucepan and bring to the boil.
- Add the flour paste, stirring or whisking vigorously, to prevent lumps.
- Bring the sauce back up to boiling, stirring continuously, until it thickens.
- Reduce heat, and cook for a further 2–3 minutes.
- Stir in the margarine. When it has melted and the onion and mushroom mix, serve immediately with pasta of your choice.

Marilyn Le Breton © Copyright 2001

White bean pasta sauce

CF, EF, FF, SY, SGF, YF

Ingredients

1 large onion (sliced)
2 garlic cloves (crushed)
½ tsp gf dried mixed herbs
14 oz (400g) tin cooked cannelloni beans
14 oz (400g) tin chopped tomatoes

Method

- Gently fry onions and garlic for 10 minutes.
- Add beans, tomatoes and herbs; cook for 5 minutes.
- Add to cooked pasta of choice and serve.

Marilyn Le Breton © Copyright 2001

Aubergine Bolognese sauce

CF*, EF, FF, SF, SGF, YF

Ingredients

2 aubergines (cubed)
1 red pepper (chopped)
1 yellow pepper (chopped)
2 leeks (sliced)
2 carrots (thinly sliced)
2 cloves garlic (crushed)
5 oz (150g) tin sweetcorn (optional)

4 oz (125g) red lentils
2 x 14 oz (400g) tins tomatoes
1 pint (60ml) homemade
    vegetable stock (see Stocks
    section for recipes)
½ tsp gf dried mixed herbs

Method

- Gently fry the aubergines, peppers, leeks and carrots for 3 minutes
- Add the garlic, sweetcorn (if using), lentils, tomatoes, stock and herbs. Stir in well.
- Bring the mix to the boil. Reduce heat, cover the pan and simmer for 30 minutes.

Marilyn Le Breton © Copyright 2001

Rice Based Dishes

Coconut rice

CF, EF, FF, SF, SGF, TF, YF

Ingredients

8 oz (225g) uncooked long grain or
    basmati rice
1¼ pints (750ml) coconut milk

Method

- Rinse rice thoroughly in cold running water.
- Place rice in a large saucepan and cover with the coconut milk.
- Bring the milk to the boil and reduce to the lowest possible heat.
- Cover pan and cook for 10–12 minutes. Do not remove lid during this time.
- Check that nearly all the liquid has been absorbed. Re-cover, remove from heat and allow to rest for 10 minutes. If liquid hasn't been absorbed, re-cover and allow to cook for another few minutes.

This results in a sticky rice that cannot be fluffed up. It can be moulded into rice balls in your hands.

Marilyn Le Breton © Copyright 2001

Speedy tuna risotto

CF, EF, FF, SF, SGF, TF*, YF

Ingredients

½ onion (finely chopped)
4 oz (125g) rice
4 oz (125g) tin mixed vegetables
1 garlic clove (crushed)
7 oz (200g) tin tuna in oil (drained and
    flaked)
1 pint (600ml) water
4 tsp gluten and dairy free tomato ketchup
    (optional)

Method

- Fry onion until soft.
- Add rice, vegetables, garlic, ketchup (if using) and water.
- Bring to the boil and simmer for 10 minutes.
- Add tuna, stir in well. Heat the tuna through and serve.

Variations

- *Replace the tuna with suitable ham or pre-cooked turkey or chicken.*

This makes two child portions.

Marilyn Le Breton © Copyright 2001

Spinach and bacon risotto

CF, EF, FF, SY, SGF, TF, YF

Ingredients

1 large onion (finely chopped)
1 clove garlic (crushed)
8 oz (225g) rice
1½ pint (900ml) homemade vegetable or
    chicken stock (see Stocks section for
    recipes)
8 oz (225g) nitrate free bacon
4 oz (125g) spinach (washed and shredded)

Method

- Chop and fry the bacon until it is crispy.
- Add the spinach and stir, until the spinach is wilted. Drain off excess oil and put to one side.
- Gently fry the onion until soft, add the garlic.
- Stir in the rice and gradually add the stock. Bring to the boil, then immediately reduce heat to the lowest setting.
- Allow the rice to gently simmer until almost all the liquid has been absorbed. Do not cover the pan and do not stir the rice.
- Add the bacon and spinach. Mix in well and serve immediately.

Marilyn Le Breton © Copyright 2001

Greek risotto

CF, EF, SF, SGF, YF

Ingredients

4 tbsp sunflower oil
I onion (chopped)
I red pepper (chopped)
I green pepper (chopped)
12 oz (350g) rice

8 oz (225g) tin chopped
   tomatoes (drained)
1½ pints 900ml) homemade
   vegetable stock (see Stocks
   section for recipes)
5 oz (150g) frozen peas

Method

- Gently fry onion until soft.
- Add peppers and cook for a further 3 minutes.
- Add the rice and stir in well, until the rice is coated in the oil.
- Add tomatoes and stock.
- Keeping the pan at a low heat, cook until the stock has been absorbed (approximately 20 minutes).
- Add peas and any seasoning. Stir in and wait 2–3 minutes until the peas are cooked.
- Serve immediately.

Marilyn Le Breton © Copyright 2001

Tuna and vegetable rissoles

FF, SF, SGF, TF, YF

Ingredients

4 oz (125g) rice (cooked)

7 oz (200g) tinned tuna in oil (drained and flaked)

1 carrot (peeled and roughly chopped)

1 courgette (roughly chopped)

1 potato (peeled and roughly chopped)

1 onion (peeled and rough chopped)

2 oz (50g) gluten and dairy free breadcrumbs

1 organic egg (beaten)

7 oz (200g) tin creamed sweetcorn

½ tsp gf dried parsley

3 tbsp white rice flour

Method

- Place carrot, courgette, potato and onion into a blender and roughly blend together.
- Mix the tuna, sweetcorn, breadcrumbs, parsley and blended vegetables into the rice.
- Bind the mixture together with the egg.
- Divide the mixture into 12 and using your hands, roll into burger shapes.
- Dip each rissole in flour, coating both sides.
- Fry for 3–4 minutes each side.

Marilyn Le Breton © Copyright 2001

Special fried rice

CF, EF, FF, SF, SGF, TF, YF

Ingredients

8 oz (225g) long grain rice
3 oz (90g) bean sprouts
I large carrot (grated)
4 spring onions (chopped)
2 oz (50g) un-sulphated prawns
I–2 tbsp organic sunflower oil
I–2 cloves garlic (crushed)
3 oz (90g) frozen peas

Method

- Cook the rice until almost tender, drain and rinse through with boiling water. Leave to cool (spreading it out on a plate will speed this up).
- In a wok or large frying pan, heat the oil and cook the carrots and garlic for 2 minutes.
- Add the prawns, peas, bean sprouts and cook for a further minute.
- Add the rice and spring onions, cook for 3 minutes.
- Serve immediately.

Variations

- *The variations for this are almost endless. Any chopped, cooked meats and vegetables can be added.*

Marilyn Le Breton © Copyright 2001

Fast fried rice

CF, FF, SF, SGF, TF, SF

Ingredients

4 cups rice (cooked and cold)
1 lb (450g) frozen mixed vegetables
1 large onion (chopped)
2 cloves garlic (minced)
2 eggs (beaten)
3 tbsp sunflower oil
½ tsp gf Chinese five spice powder
dash of gf cayenne pepper (optional)
seasoning to taste

Method

- Microwave the frozen vegetables until they are tender but still crisp.
- Heat oil in wok and stir-fry the onion until golden.
- Add the garlic and vegetables and fry for a further 3 minutes.
- Push the vegetable mixture to one side of the wok and pour the eggs into the cleared area. Stir the egg gently until it is cooked through.
- Add the rice and seasoning, stir the mixture together thoroughly and continue to cook until the rice is heated through.

Variation

- *Leftover cooked meat can be added at the same stage as the rice.*

Debby Anglesey © Copyright 2000

Egg fried rice

CF, FF, SF, SGF*, TF, YF

Ingredients

12 oz (350g) long grain rice (cooked and cold)

2 organic eggs (beaten)

1 tsp sugar (optional)

1 tsp gf garlic granules (optional)

1–2 tbsp organic sunflower oil

Method

- Heat oil in a wok or large frying pan.
- Pour the egg into the wok in a slow and thin stream, stirring constantly, so that the egg breaks into small pieces as it cooks.
- Add the sugar, garlic (if using) and rice and mix in well.
- Continue to cook until the rice is heated through.
- Add a little extra oil if the rice begins to stick.
- Serve immediately.

Marilyn Le Breton © Copyright 2001

Rainbow rice

CF, EF, FF, SY, SGF, TF, YF

Ingredients

6 oz (175g) (pre-cooked weight) long grain rice (cooked and cooled)

2 tbsp organic sunflower oil

2 medium carrots (diced)

10 spring onions (chopped)

1 medium red pepper (diced)

2 celery sticks (finely chopped)

4 oz (125g) frozen peas

6 oz (175g) nitrate free ham (cut into fine strips)

Method

- Heat the oil in wok until hot.
- Add the carrots and fry for 2 minutes.
- Add the onions, peppers and celery and fry for a further 2 minutes.
- Add peas and ham, fry for 2–3 minutes.
- Add the rice, stir in and cook for approximately 4 minutes or until piping hot throughout.

Marilyn Le Breton © Copyright 2001

Chilli con carne

CF, EF, FF, SF, SGF, YF

Ingredients

1 lb (450g) mince
1 medium onion (chopped)
1 green pepper (chopped)
2 x 14 oz (400g) tins chopped tomatoes
8 oz (225g) passata or sieved tomatoes
1 tsp gf chilli powder
1 tsp salt
⅛ tsp gf cayenne pepper
⅛ tsp gf paprika
8 oz (225g) tin of red kidney beans
    (drained)

Method

- Fry the mince until brown.
- Add onions and peppers. Cook until the onions are soft.
- Add the chopped tomatoes, passata and all spices, stir together well and bring to the boil.
- Reduce heat and simmer for 30 minutes.
- Add kidney beans and cook for a further 10 minutes.
- Serve with rice.

Coconut and coriander rice

CF, EF, FF, SF, SGF, TF, YF

Ingredients

15 fl oz (500ml) basmati rice (uncooked
    weight)
14 fl oz (400ml) can of coconut milk
1 pint (600ml) water
1 tbsp fresh, coriander
1 tbsp chopped lemon grass
½" (1cm) piece root ginger (grated)
1 clove garlic (finely sliced)
3 tbsp sunflower oil
sea salt to taste

Method

- Cover rice with cold water and allow it to soak for 30 minutes. Drain well.
- In a large, heavy based pan, gently heat the oil and sauté the ginger and garlic for 2–3 minutes.
- Add the drained rice and stir well to thoroughly coat with oil. Cook gently for a further 2 minutes.
- Stir in the coconut milk, swill out the can with the water and add the water too.
- Add the coriander, lemon grass and salt.
- Bring to the boil. Reduce to the lowest possible heat and cover pan.
- Allow to cook for 10–12 minutes (do not remove lid during this time).
- Check the water level; if most has been absorbed, replace the lid and turn off heat.
- Allow to stand for 10 minutes then fluff up the rice with a fork.

Freezes well.

Good accompaniment to many dishes, especially using up leftovers.

Maddalena Feliciello, Leeds © Copyright

Mississippi mince

F, EF, FF, SF, SGF, TF, YF

Ingredients

1 lb (450g) steak mince
1 medium leek (finely chopped)
¼ tsp gf ground paprika
¼ tsp gf ground fenugreek
¼ tsp gf turmeric

¼ tsp gf dried mixed herbs
¼ tsp gf cayenne pepper
¼ tsp gf ground cumin
2 cloves garlic (crushed)
seasoning
1 cup boiling water

Method

- Heat a little oil in a pan and gently sauté the leek for 2–3 minutes until it softens.
- Add seasoning and mixed herbs, stir in well.
- Add mince and fry until the mince is brown.
- Add all the remaining spices and continue to cook for a further 2 minutes, stirring constantly.
- Add the water, cover and simmer on a low heat for 20 minutes.
- Remove lid and increase heat slightly. Stir constantly until nearly all the remaining liquid has been absorbed.
- Serve immediately with cooked rice.

Rob Le Breton © Copyright 2001

Stews and Casseroles

Lamb and bean casserole

CF, EF, FF, SF, SGF, YF

Ingredients

1½ lb (700g) lean lamb (cubed)
1 oz (25g) white rice flour
14 oz (400g) tin chopped tomatoes
    (drained)
2 onions (sliced)
½ pint (300ml) homemade vegetable stock
    (see Stocks section for recipes)
1 tsp gf dried thyme or gf mixed herbs
2 x 14 oz (400g) tins gf baked beans

Method

- Coat the lamb in the flour and fry it in sunflower oil until the lamb is brown.
- Add the tomatoes and onions and cook for 2 minutes.
- Add the stock and thyme/mixed herbs and bring the mix up to boiling.
- Reduce the heat to low, cover the pan and simmer for approximately 1 hour or until the lamb is tender.
- Stir in the beans and cook for a further 5 minutes, to heat the beans through.

Jacob's speedy chicken and rice casserole

CF, EF, FF, SF, SGF, TF, YF

Ingredients

6 breasts of chicken
4 celery stalks (leaves included, chopped)
1 large onion (chopped)
4 carrots (cut into ½" circles)
2 cups rice (uncooked)
2 tsp salt

½ tsp gf dried thyme
¼ tsp gf dried sage
¼ tsp gf dried marjoram
¼ tsp gf dried parsley
¼ tsp gf garlic granules
4 cups water

Method

- Pre-heat oven to GM5, 375F, 190C.
- Mix together all of the ingredients but the chicken breasts.
- Spoon this mixture into a large roasting pan and evenly spread out the mix.
- Place chicken pieces on top of the mixture.
- Cover the pan with foil and bake for 1 hour or until the rice is tender and the chicken is cooked through.

Debby Anglesey © Copyright 2000

Moroccan lamb stew

CF, EF, FF, SF, SGF, YF

Ingredients

2 onions (chopped)
1 lb (450g) minced lamb
1 tsp gf ground cinnamon
½ tsp gf allspice
14 oz (400g) tin chickpeas (rinsed and
    drained)
14 oz (400g) tin chopped tomatoes
1 lb (450g) sweet potatoes (peeled and
    cubed)
2 courgettes (sliced)

Method

- Gently fry onions for 3 minutes.
- Add mince and spices and cook for a further 10 minutes.
- Add chickpeas, tomatoes and sweet potatoes and simmer for 20 minutes.
- Add courgettes and simmer for a further 10 minutes.
- Serve with either rice or potatoes.

Marilyn Le Breton © Copyright 2001

Courgette and rice casserole

CF, EF, FF, SF, SGF, YF

Ingredients

1 cup rice (or lentils or Quinoa)
2 cups water
½ tsp salt
1 medium onion (diced)
1 small pepper (diced)
8 oz (225g) mushrooms (sliced)

1 tbsp oil
4 cups tomatoes (chopped)
1 lb (450g) courgette (sliced)
½ cup cashews
1 tsp gf dried oregano
1 tsp gf dried parsley

Method

- Pre-heat oven to GM4, 350F, 180C.
- Bring the rice to the boil in the water and salt. Cover the pan, reduce the heat and simmer for 20 minutes.
- In a separate pan sauté together the onions and pepper in the oil.
- Mix in all the remaining ingredients and stir together well.
- Mix in the cooked rice.
- Place the mixture in a well-greased casserole dish and bake for 20 minutes.

Debby Anglesey © Copyright 2000

Mixed lentil casserole

CF, EF, FF, SF, SGF, TF, YF

Ingredients

½ tsp gf ground cumin
½ tsp gf ground coriander
½ tsp gf ground ginger
¼ tsp gf turmeric
3 onions (sliced)
1 lb (450g) carrots (sliced)
1 lb (450g) leeks (sliced)
8 oz (225g) turnip (sliced)

1 lb (450g) button mushrooms (halved) (optional)
3 tbsp organic sunflower oil
2 garlic cloves (crushed)
6 oz (175g) split orange lentils
2 oz (60g) brown or green lentils
1½ pints (900ml) boiling water

Method

- Pre-heat oven to GM4, 350F, 180C.
- In a very large saucepan, heat the oil and fry the onions, carrots, leeks and turnips for 3 minutes.
- Add the mushrooms, garlic, ginger, turmeric, cumin and coriander. Fry for a further 3 minutes.
- Stir in the lentils and the boiling water. Bring the casserole up to the boil.
- Transfer to a casserole dish. Place in the oven and cook for 45–60 minutes.

This does not freeze.

Marilyn Le Breton © Copyright 2001

Bean and meat hot pot

CF, EF, FF, SF, SGF, YF

Ingredients

8 oz (225g) tinned mixed beans
1 lb (450g) fillet pork (cubed)
1 lb (450g) nitrate free bacon (chopped)
½ lb (225g) gluten, dairy and preservative free sausages (Lock's) (chopped into eighths)
1 lb (450g) onions (sliced)
2 sticks of celery (chopped)

2 tbsp organic sunflower oil
1 oz (25g) dairy free margarine
4 garlic cloves (crushed)
2 tsp gf mixed dried herbs
14 oz (400g) tin chopped tomatoes
½ pint (300ml) water or homemade stock (see Stocks section for recipies)

Method

- Pre-heat oven to GM3, 325F, 170C.
- Heat together the oil and the margarine and brown off the pork, bacon and sausages. Using a slotted spoon, remove the meat and set aside.
- Using the same oil, reduce the heat and sauté the onions, celery and garlic (add a little more oil or margarine if necessary) for 5 minutes or until soft.
- Return the meat to the pan and add the beans, tomatoes, herbs and stock or water and bring the liquid to the boil.
- Transfer the hot pot to a casserole dish and cook for 2 hours.

Marilyn Le Breton © Copyright 2001

Moroccan lamb casserole

CF*, EF, FF, SF, TF, YF

Ingredients

half a leg of lamb
4 large carrots (large slices)
2 large onions (roughly chopped)
2 tsp gf paprika
1 tsp gf fenugreek

2 tsp gf cumin
1 tsp mint sauce
1 pint (600ml) water
3 tsp cornflour or potato starch
    flour
seasoning

Method

- Pre-heat oven to GM5, 375F, 190C.
- Place carrots, onions, paprika, fenugreek, cumin, mint sauce, seasoning and water into a very large casserole dish.
- In a large pan, heat a little oil over a medium high heat and add the lamb. Turn the lamb until all surfaces are sealed.
- Place lamb joint in casserole dish and cover with lid or silver foil.
- Place in middle of oven and cook for 2 hours. Remove after the first hour and stir contents and return. Remove from oven.
- Mix the flour with 2 fl oz (50ml) of cold water until a smooth paste.
- Add the flour mix to the stew and stir in well.
- Return stew to oven and cook for a further 20 minutes. Remove.
- Remove lamb joint from stew. At this stage the meat will be falling off the bone; remove meat fully and discard bone.

Rob Le Breton © Copyright 2001

Snowman casserole

CF, EF, FF, SF, SGF, TF, YF

Ingredients

1 lb (450g) beef mince
2½ cups of mixed vegetables of choice
  (canned or frozen)
½ cup of chopped onion
1½ cups homemade beef or chicken stock
  (see Stocks section for recipes)

1½ tbsp potato starch flour
4–5 medium potatoes (cooked
  and mashed with a little
  dairy free margarine)
peas and slivers of carrot for
  decoration

Method

- Pre-heat oven to GM5, 375F, 190C.
- Heat a little oil in a pan and fry the onions gently until soft.
- Add the mince and cook until browned.
- Add vegetables to the pan. If using frozen
- vegetables, sauté until thawed.
- Transfer mix to a casserole dish.
- Mix together the stock and potato starch until a smooth paste and pour over the casserole.
- Shape the mashed potato into multiple snowman characters and place each one carefully on top of the stew. Allow about 2–3 tbsp of potato for the heads and 4–5 tbsp for the bodies.
- Bake uncovered in the oven for 18–20 minutes.
- Remove from oven and decorate each snowman with peas for eyes and buttons and use a sliver of carrot for the mouth and nose.

Diane Hartman © Copyright 1996

Meat Based Meals

Meat loaf

CF, FF, SF, SGF, TF, YF

Ingredients

12oz (350g) cooked beef or chicken
    (leftovers from roast are ideal)
4 oz (125g) streaky bacon (cooked)
¾ cup gluten and dairy free breadcrumbs
1 large egg (beaten)
seasoning
1–2 tbsp gluten and dairy milk alternative
    or homemade stock (see Stocks
    section for recipes)

Method

- Pre-heat oven to GM4 350F, 180C.
- Put the meat and the bacon through a mincer.
- Add the breadcrumbs, egg, seasoning and just enough milk or stock to soften the mixture.
- Mix together well and pack the mixture firmly into a 2 lb greased loaf tin.
- Cover with greaseproof paper and foil.
- Place loaf tin inside a baking tray or roasting tin containing 1" of boiling water.
- Place in oven and bake for one hour.
- Turn out of tin once cold.

Kate Coull, Abergele © Copyright

Porcupine meatballs

CF, EF, FF, SF, SGF, TF*, YF

Ingredients

1 lb (450g) beef mince

½ cup homemade beef stock (see Stocks section for recipes)

½ cup rice (uncooked long grain)

⅓ cup chopped onion

1 tsp salt

⅛ tsp ground pepper

¼ tsp gf garlic granules

½ tsp gf dried basil

2 cups homemade beef stock *or* 2 cups of gf/cf tomato pasta sauce to cover meatballs prior to baking

Method

- Combine all ingredients together and form into 1" balls.
- Arrange balls in a casserole dish and cover with either stock or pasta sauce.
- Cover dish and cook for 45 minutes.
- Remove lid and bake for an additional 15 minutes.
- Check the centre of one of the meatballs to ensure it is cooked through.

Mincemeat pie

CF, FF, SF, SGF, YF

Ingredients

gluten and dairy free pastry (see Pastry
   section for recipes)
1 lb (450g) beef mince
1 onion (finely chopped)
2 tomatoes (roughly chopped)
3 tbsp tomato puree

1 tsp gf dried mixed herbs
seasoning to taste
a little gluten and dairy free milk
   alternative for sealing and
   glazing pie

Method

- Pre-heat oven to GM7, 425F, 220C.
- Divide pastry in half. Roll out one half and line the bottom of a well-greased 7" pie tin and place in the fridge to chill.
- Gently fry the onion until soft and add the mince and fry until it has browned.
- Add the tomatoes, puree, herbs and seasoning, stir in well and simmer for 5 minutes.
- Allow the mixture to cool slightly and gently spoon onto the pastry.
- Roll out the remaining half of the pastry and cover the pie tin. Seal edges with a little milk and press the edges together with a fork.
- Brush a little milk alternative over the top of the pie.
- Bake for 15 minutes and then reduce the temperature to GM4, 350F, 180C and continue to bake for a further 20–25 minutes.

Marilyn Le Breton © Copyright 2001

Lamb rissoles

CF, FF, SF, SGF, TF, YF

Ingredients

1 oz (25g) dairy free margarine

1 oz (25g) white rice flour

5 fl oz (175ml) gluten and dairy free milk alternative

4 oz (125g) gluten and dairy free breadcrumbs

10 oz (300g) lamb mince (cooked)

¼ tsp gf cayenne pepper

1 tsp gf dried thyme

2 oz (50g) seasoned gf flour

2 organic eggs (beaten)

Method

- Melt margarine. Add the white rice flour and stir until a smooth paste forms.
- Gradually add the milk, stir constantly, until the sauce thickens.
- Stir in half of the breadcrumbs, the lamb, cayenne pepper, thyme and cook for 2 minutes.
- Remove from heat and allow mixture to cool.
- Divide the mix into 8 and shape into small burgers.
- Coat each in the seasoned flour, then the beaten egg and finally the remaining half of the breadcrumbs.
- Place the rissoles in the fridge for 10–15 minutes to chill.
- Deep fry for approximately 5 minutes.

Marilyn Le Breton © Copyright 2001

Hurry up hash

CF, EF, FF, SF, YF

Ingredients

1 lb (450g) minced beef
2 onions (sliced into rings)
5 stalks of celery (chopped)
3½ cups diced tomatoes
1⅔ cups rice (uncooked)
1½ tsp salt
3 tbsp gf chilli powder (or to taste)
1–2 tbsp sugar
2 cloves garlic (minced)
⅛ tsp gf ground pepper
1 cup water

Method

- Pre-heat oven to GM4, 350F, 180C.
- In a large pan, heat a little oil and cook together the mince, onion, garlic and celery until the meat has browned and the vegetables are tender.
- Drain off all the excess oil and fat.
- Stir in all the remaining ingredients and pour into a large casserole dish.
- Bake for 1 hour or until the rice is tender. Add more water if the mixture is too dry.

Variation

- *This works just as well using 1 lb of cooked chicken, finely chopped.*

Debby Anglesey © Copyright 2000

Goulash bake

CF, EF, FF, SF*, SGF, YF

Ingredients

1½ lb (700g) braising steak (cubed)
1 onion (sliced)
2 peppers (sliced)
1 oz (25g) gf flour mix
4 tsp gf paprika
1 pint (600ml) homemade beef stock (see
   Stocks section for recipes)

14 oz (400g) tin chopped
   tomatoes
2 lb (900g) potatoes (thickly
   sliced)
½ pint (300ml) plain soya
   yoghurt (optional)

Method

- Pre-heat the oven to GM3, 325F, 170C.
- In a deep saucepan, fry the beef until it has browned. Remove the beef from the pan, but retain the oil and meat juices.
- In the oil fry the onions and peppers for 5 minutes.
- Add the flour and the paprika and cook for a further minute, stirring well, to stop the flour and paprika sticking to the bottom of the pan.
- Add the stock, tomatoes and meat and bring the liquid to the boil.
- Transfer the contents of the pan to an ovenproof dish and bake for 1½ hours.
- Meanwhile, boil the sliced potatoes for 5 minutes and drain.
- Arrange the potato slices over the goulash and continue to bake for a further 30 minutes, increasing the oven temperature to GM5, 375F, 190C.
- Just prior to serving, pour the soya yoghurt over the goulash bake.

Goulash I

CF, EF, FF, SGF, YF

Ingredients

2 lb (900g) lean beef, pork or lamb (cubed)
3 oz (90g) dairy free margarine
1 onion (sliced)
2 tomatoes (chopped)
1 tsp salt
2 tsp gf ground paprika
2 tbsp tomato puree
1 lb (450g) potatoes (peeled and sliced)
1 green pepper (de-seeded and chopped)
½ pint (300ml) water
¼ pint (150ml) soya cream

Method

- Melt the margarine in a large pan and fry meat and onions until the onions are golden.
- Add the tomatoes, tomato puree, salt and paprika. Stir in well and simmer for 30 minutes.
- Add green pepper and potatoes.
- Add water and stir in. Bring liquid to boiling point, reduce heat to lowest setting and continue to simmer for 1 ½ hours, stirring occasionally, until the meat is very tender. If the goulash gets too dry, top up with a little water.
- Remove from heat and stir in cream just before serving.

Jacqui Jackson © Copyright 2001

Goulash II

CF, EF, FF, SF, SGF, YF

Ingredients

12 oz (350g) potatoes (cooked and sliced)
1 lb (450g) minced lamb
4 tomatoes (skinned and sliced)
fresh chopped parsley
½ pint (300ml) gluten and dairy free white
   sauce (see Sauces section for recipes)

Method

- Pre-heat oven to GM6, 400F, 200C.
- Grease an ovenproof casserole dish and arrange ½ of the potato slices over the bottom of the dish.
- Brown off the mince in a pan and spread over the top of the potatoes.
- Arrange tomato slices over the mince and sprinkle the parsley over the top.
- Arrange the remaining potatoes on the top and then carefully pour over the white sauce.
- Bake for 25 minutes.

Krista's braised pork

CF, EF, SF, TF, YF

Ingredients

4 pork loin chops
seasoned gf flour (for dusting)
4 fresh pears (peeled and halved)
4 tbsp dairy free margarine
4 tbsp sugar

Method

- Poach the pears gently in a pan with the sugar and just enough water to cover them. Poach for 10–15 minutes. Reserve the liquid.
- Lightly dust chops in the seasoned flour and shake off any excess flour.
- Melt margarine in a large frying pan and add 2 tablespoons of the juice from the pear pan and mix together.
- Brown the chops in the mixture on a medium high heat for approximately 1 ½ minutes.
- Remove pan from heat and gently arrange the pears all around the pork chops. Pour the pear juice over the top and return to a medium heat.
- Cover the pan and cook for 30 minutes.

Variation

- *Substitute chicken breasts for the pork.*

Debby Anglesey © Copyright 2000

Pork supreme

CF, EF, FF, SF, SGF, TF, YF

Ingredients

3 oz (90g) dairy free margarine
2 onions (chopped)
2 carrots (sliced)
2 celery stalks (chopped)
1 small green pepper (sliced)

1 lb (450g) pork (cubed)
2 oz (50g) seasoned gf flour
1 pint (600ml) gluten and dairy
   free milk substitute
gf dried herbs to taste

Method

- Melt butter in a saucepan. Add all the vegetables and fry on a moderate heat for 5 minutes.
- Coat the pork in seasoned flour and then add to the vegetables. Fry for a further 8 minutes.
- Gradually add the milk, stirring constantly, until a smooth (but thin) sauce is formed.
- Add the herbs and cover and simmer on a very low heat for 1½ hours.

Marilyn Le Breton © Copyright 2001

Burgers

CF, EF, FF, SF, SGF, TF, YF

Ingredients

8 oz (225g) minced beef
2 thin slices of gf bread, crumbled into
   breadcrumbs *or* ¼ cup cold cooked
   rice *or* ¼ cup of cold mashed potatoes

1 egg (beaten)
1 small onion (finely chopped)
rice flour for coating

Method

- Mix all the ingredients (except the rice flour) together.
- Divide the mixture into 4.
- Using your hands, pat the mixture into burger shapes.
- Sprinkle each side lightly with rice flour.
- Fry in a little sunflower oil, for approximately 4 minutes each side.
- Drain off the excess oil on kitchen paper and serve.

Marilyn Le Breton © Copyright 2001

Italian meatballs

CF, EF, FF, SF, SGF, TF, YF

Ingredients

1 lb (450g) beef mince
1 small onion (finely chopped)
½ tsp gf dried mixed herbs
¼ tsp gf garlic granules

Method

- Mix all the ingredients together.
- Divide the mixture into 20 and form each piece into a small ball.
- Fry for 10 minutes, turning frequently.
- Pat the balls dry with kitchen paper to remove excess oil.

Marilyn Le Breton © Copyright 2001

Spicy lamb meatballs

CF, EF, FF, SF, SGF, TF, YF

Ingredients

1 large onion (grated)
1 lb (450g) minced lamb
1½ tsp gf ground cumin
2 garlic cloves (crushed)
½ tsp salt
½ tsp fresh ground black pepper
1 lemon, juice and grated rind

Method

- Mix together all the ingredients. Cover and refrigerate over night.
- Divide the mixture into 28 and form into balls.
- Brush each lightly with sunflower oil.
- Grill for 10–15 minutes on a high heat, turning and basting frequently.

Marilyn Le Breton © Copyright 2001

Shepherd's pie

CF, EF, FF, SF, SGF, YF

Ingredients

1 large onion (chopped)
2 oz (50g) button mushrooms (sliced)
14 oz (400g) tin of mixed vegetables
14 oz (400g) tin gf baked beans (optional)
1 lb (450g) lean minced beef
1 bay leaf
2 tbsp white rice flour

1 pint (600ml) homemade vegetable or beef stock (see Stocks section for recipes)
1 tbsp tomato puree
1½ lb (700g) potatoes (boiled and mashed)

Method

- Pre-heat oven to GM6, 400F, 200C.
- Gently fry the mince, onions and mushrooms for 10 minutes, stirring frequently.
- Add the flour, stir in well and cook for a further minute.
- Blend in stock and tomato puree, stirring until it has thickened.
- Add a bay leaf.
- Cover the pan and simmer for 20–25 minutes.
- When the mince mix is ready, stir in tinned vegetables (and baked beans, if adding) and transfer to a 3 pint casserole dish. Remove bay leaf.
- Cover the mince mixture with the mashed potato and bake for 20 minutes.

Suitable for freezing.

Marylin Le Breton © Copyright 2001

Lamb and spinach meatballs

CF, SF, SGF, TF, YF

Ingredients

1½ lb (700g) fresh spinach (trimmed of stalks)

1½ lb (700g) minced lamb

gluten and dairy free bread: 2 large or 4 small slices (crusts removed)

2 eggs (beaten)

1 tsp gf allspice

4 tbsp organic sunflower oil

1 lemon (juice only)

2 limes (juice only)

4 fl oz (100ml) water

Method

- Cook spinach, then drain it well and chop into small pieces. Allow to cool and then mix with the minced lamb.
- Soak the bread for 5 minutes in cold water, squeeze out the excess liquid with your hands. Mix the crumbled bread into the lamb mixture.
- Add the eggs, allspice and oil to the mix and combine together well.
- Roll the mixture into small balls (about the size of walnuts).
- Fry the meatballs in 3 tbsp of the oil for 3–4 minutes.
- Remove the meatballs from the oil and pat off the excess oil with kitchen paper.
- In a saucepan, add the water, remaining 1 tbsp of oil, lemon and lime juice.
- Carefully add the meatballs to the liquid and quickly bring the liquid to the boil.
- Reduce the heat, cover the pan and simmer gently 10 minutes. Most of the liquid will have then been absorbed and the meatballs will be very tender.

Marilyn Le Breton © Copyright 2001

Lamb 'shepherd's pie'

CF*, EF, FF, SF, SGF, TF, YF

Ingredients

1 lb (450g) minced lamb
4 tsp cornflour (or potato starch flour)
2 leeks (sliced)
2 large sweet potatoes (boiled and mashed)
2 large onions (chopped)
1 pint (600ml) homemade vegetable stock (see Stocks section for recipes)

14 oz (400g) tin mixed vegetables
3 medium parsnips (boiled and mashed)
1 tsp gf dried mixed herbs *or* gf ground cumin

Method

- Pre-heat oven to GM6, 400F, 200C.
- In a large pan, brown the minced lamb, then add the onion and cook until the onions have softened.
- Stir in the cornflour.
- Add seasoning, herbs, leeks and stock and simmer for 20 minutes.
- Mix together the mashed sweet potato and parsnip.
- Stir the mixed vegetables into the mince mix.
- Transfer the mince mix to a casserole dish and cover with the mashed parsnips and sweet potatoes
- Bake for 15 minutes.

Suitable for freezing.

Mediterranean lamb and potato bake

CF, EF*, FF, SF*, SGF, YF

Ingredients

1 lb (450g) lamb mince
1 large aubergine (diced)
1 onion (chopped)
2 courgettes (sliced)
2 peppers (thinly sliced)
6 medium sized potatoes (peeled and thinly sliced)
8 fl oz (300ml) plain soya yoghurt (optional)

1 large egg (beaten) (optional)
2 garlic cloves (crushed)
14 oz (400g) can chopped tomatoes
2 tbsp tomato puree
2 tsp gf dried oregano
1 tsp cornflour or potato starch flour
seasoning to taste

Method

- Pre-heat the oven to GM5, 375F, 190C.
- Heat a little sunflower oil in a deep sided frying pan and fry the diced aubergine until it is lightly browned.
- Remove the aubergine from the pan and set to one side.
- Add a little more oil to the pan and fry the onion and garlic together for approximately 5 minutes or until the onion has softened.
- Add the minced lamb to the onions and fry over a low heat, stirring all the time, until the meat has browned.
- Add to the pan the oregano, tomatoes, tomato puree, and seasoning.
- Bring the mixture to the boil and then reduce heat, add the courgettes and peppers and simmer gently for approximately 20 minutes, stirring occasionally.
- Add the fried aubergine and mix in well.
- Transfer the mixture to a large ovenproof dish.
- Cook the thinly sliced potatoes in salted boiling water for 6–7 minutes or until just beginning to soften.
- Drain off the potatoes well and arrange the slices over the lamb mixture.
- Beat together the yoghurt, egg and cornflour/potato starch flour and season well.
- Spoon the yoghurt mixture over the top of the potatoes (you can omit the yoghurt mixture).
- Bake for 30–35 minutes.

Marilyn Le Breton © Copyright 2001

Poultry Based Meals

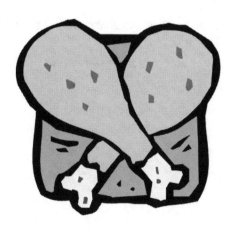

Crispy chicken fingers

CF*, EF, FF, SF*, SGF, TF, YF

Ingredients

4 chicken breasts
I cup plain soya yoghurt *or* rice milk
I cup of corn meal *or* fine gluten and dairy
    free breadcrumbs (*or* a mixture of the
    two)
I tsp gf garlic granules
I tsp gf paprika
½ tsp salt

Method

- Cut chicken into long, I" thick strips and marinate overnight in the yoghurt or milk.
- In zip-lock bag, add and mix together the flour/breadcrumbs, garlic, paprika and salt.
- Add the chicken to the bag and shake until all the chicken pieces are coated in the flour mix.
- Fry the chicken in a little oil for a few minutes until cooked through.

Makes a good finger food for dipping.

Debby Anglesey © Copyright 2000

Crispy honey and mustard baked chicken

EF, FF, SF, SGF, TF, YF

Ingredients

2½ lb (1.2kg) chicken pieces
2 tbsp gf mustard
2 tbsp honey
½ cup gluten and dairy free breadcrumbs
3 tbsp corn meal

3 tbsp gf flour
1–2 tsp salt
¼ tsp gf ground black pepper
1½ tsp gf garlic granules
1 tsp gf dried parsley (optional)
¼–½ tsp gf cayenne pepper

Method

- Pre-heat oven to GM5, 375F, 190C.
- In a large bowl, mix together the mustard and honey. Add the chicken pieces and mix them in, making sure they are well coated on all sides.
- Place all of the remaining ingredients in a zip-lock bag and shake them to mix together well.
- Place 3 pieces of chicken at a time in the bag and shake them, ensuring that the chicken is completely coated.
- Place on an oiled 9" x 13" pan and bake for 45–50 minutes.

Debby Anglesey © Copyright 2000

Shake it, bake it chicken

CF, EF, FF, SF, TF, YF

Ingredients

chicken fillets with skin
2 cups fine gluten and dairy free
  breadcrumbs
¼ cup + 1 tbsp gf flour
3 tbsp gf paprika
1 tbsp salt
2 tbsp sugar

1 tbsp gf onion powder or
  flakes
1 tsp gf dried oregano
1 tsp gf dried thyme
1 tsp gf cayenne pepper
½ tsp gf dried sage
½ tsp gf garlic granules
¼ tsp gf ground black pepper

Method

- Pre-heat the oven to GM5, 350F, 180C.
- Mix all but the chicken together well and place in a zip-lock bag.
- Dip the meat into oil and then into the mixture. Shake the bag until the chicken portion is well covered.
- Place chicken, skin side down on a baking tray and bake for 40–50 minutes, turning once half way through the cooking.

Debby Anglesey © Copyright 2000

Quick coconut chicken curry

CF, EF, FF, SF*, SGF, TF, YF

Ingredients

4 chicken fillets
I large onion (roughly chopped)
2 garlic cloves (crushed)
I oz (25g) cashew nuts
I oz (25g) creamed coconut (roughly chopped)
I oz (25g) dairy free margarine

4 fl oz (100ml) plain soya yoghurt (optional)
4 fl oz (100ml) water
¼ tsp gf ground ginger
¼ tsp gf cayenne pepper
I–2 tsp gf garam masala
I tsp gf dried coriander
½ tsp gf dried turmeric

Method

- Pre-heat oven to GM4, 350F, 180C.
- Place chicken breasts in a greased small roasting tin and bake for 20–30 minutes or until golden and meat juices run clear when skewered.
- In a food processor, place the cashews, creamed coconut, water, ginger, cayenne pepper, garam masala, coriander and turmeric and blend until smooth and well mixed.
- In a pan, melt the margarine and gently fry the onions and garlic until they have softened.
- Add the blended ingredients to the onion mix and cook over a medium heat for 5 minutes, stirring occasionally.
- Remove the curry sauce from the heat, stir in the yoghurt if using and spoon over the chicken and serve.

Marilyn Le Breton © Copyright 2001

Chicken curry

CF, EF, FF, SF, SGF, YF

Ingredients

2 chicken breast fillets (diced)
2 garlic cloves (crushed)
1 onion (finely chopped)
1 tbsp gf garam masala
1 tbsp gf curry powder (mild, medium or hot to suit taste)

1 tsp gf chilli powder
2 tbsp tomato puree
¼ pint (150ml) water
½ pint (300ml) coconut milk
salt to taste
oil for cooking

Method

- Heat the oil in a large pan and fry the onions and garlic until the onions are golden brown.
- Add the chicken cubes, garam masala, curry powder, chilli powder and tomato puree. Stir together thoroughly and continue to cook for 5 minutes.
- Stir in the water and coconut milk and increase heat to bring the mixture to the boil. Reduce heat and simmer for approximately 45 minutes.
- Add salt to taste.

Jacqui Jackson © Copyright 2001

Easy mango and pineapple chicken

CF, EF, SF, TF, YF

Ingredients

½ small jar of gluten free mango chutney
1 clove of garlic (crushed)
1 cup pineapple juice

1 tbsp sunflower oil
4 large chicken breast fillets
seasoning

Method

- Pre-heat oven to GM5, 375F, 190C.
- Make a marinade by mixing together the chutney, garlic, pineapple juice, oil and seasoning.
- Score the chicken breasts a few times and coat well in the marinade. Cover and place in the fridge for at least 30 minutes, overnight is better.
- Place chicken on a grill rack, inside a foil-lined baking dish, reserving the marinade for basting.
- Bake on the middle oven shelf for 40–45 minutes, basting occasionally.

Maddalena Feliciello, Leeds © Copyright

Easy turkey patties

CF, FF, SF, SGF, TF, YF

Ingredients

1 lb (450g) minced turkey
2 oz (50g) gluten free onion and herb stuffing (see Miscellaneous section for recipes)
4 oz (125g) white rice flour

1 egg (beaten)
4 oz (125g) gluten and dairy free breadcrumbs
seasoning to taste

Method

- Mix together the turkey, stuffing and flour.
- Divide the mixture into even sized balls and then press them down into patties about ¾"thick.
- Dip each patty into the beaten egg and then into the breadcrumbs.
- Either fry these or bake at GM6, 400F, 200C for 20 minutes.

Anne Pemberton, Leeds © Copyright

Lemon and pepper turkey steaks

CF, SF, SGF, TF, YF

Ingredients

2 turkey steaks or fillets
I lemon (juice only)
4 oz (125g) gluten and dairy free
    breadcrumbs
I egg (beaten)

2 oz (50g) rice flour
salt to taste
I tbsp freshly ground black
    pepper
olive oil (for frying)

Method

- Marinade turkey steaks in the lemon juice for at least 30 minutes.
- In a shallow dish, mix the breadcrumbs and salt and pepper.
- Coat the turkey in the rice flour.
- Coat the turkey in the beaten egg.
- Finally, coat the turkey in the breadcrumb mix.
- Either fry in a little oil or bake in the oven for 20 minutes on GM5, 375F, 190C.

Anne Pemberton, Leeds © Copyright

Chicken nuggets

CF*, FF, SF, SGF, TF, YF*

Ingredients

1 breast of chicken (filleted and skinned)
1 large egg beaten
breadcrumb mix (see below)

Method

- Either cut the chicken into small, nugget sized pieces or chop the meat into tiny pieces and shape them into nuggets.
- Roll each piece in the egg, and then roll in the breadcrumbs.
- Then each piece again in the egg and breadcrumbs (I find I have to really push the breadcrumbs on the chicken, by enclosing it in my hand).
- Cook under a pre-heated grill on medium heat for 4–5 minutes each side.

Marilyn Le Breton © Copyright 2001

Breadcrumb coating mixes

- 3 oz gluten and dairy free breadcrumbs, 1 oz rice cake crumbled and ¼ tsp gf garlic granules.

Or

- 4 oz gluten and dairy free breadcrumbs and ¼ tsp gf garlic granules or gf celery salt.

Or

- 3 oz gluten and dairy free breadcrumbs and 1 oz suitable crushed cornflakes (Mesa Sunrise).

Or

- 2 oz gluten and dairy free breadcrumbs, 1 oz crushed rice cake and 1 oz suitable cornflakes (Mesa Sunrise).

Marilyn Le Breton © Copyright 2001

Lemon chicken nuggets

EF, SF, SGF, TF, YF

Ingredients

2 chicken breasts (cut into small nugget
    shapes)
2 tbsp cornflour

fine corn meal (for coating)
sunflower oil
1 lemon (juice only)
sunflower oil for frying

Method

- Mix cornflour with a little water to make a fairly runny batter.
- Dip the chicken nuggets into the batter, then roll in the cornflour.
- Shallow fry the nuggets until they are golden brown.
- Turn up the heat and pour the lemon juice over the nuggets, tossing them quickly so that they are all well coated.

Amanda Godfrey, London © Copyright

Kentucky chicken nuggets

CF, EF*, FF, SF, SGF, TF, YF

Ingredients

chicken breast fillets
1 large egg (optional)
¼ cup gluten and dairy free milk
    alternative
¼ cup gf flour mix
1 tsp salt

1 tsp ground pepper
1 pinch gf dried thyme
1 pinch gf dried oregano
3 pinches gf dried basil
3 pinches gf parsley
1 tsp gf garlic salt
1 tsp gf/cf baking powder

Method

- Cut the chicken into pieces of the desired size.
- Into a large bowl mix together all of the ingredients *except* the crisps to form a batter.
- In a separate bowl, crush the crisps as finely as possible.
- Dip the chicken pieces into the batter, coating them completely and then roll them in the crushed crisps.
- Deep fry for approximately 5 minutes (times will very according to the size of the nuggets).

Jacqui Jackson © Copyright 2001

Chicken dippers

FF, SF, SGF, TF, YF

Ingredients

1 chicken breast fillet
¼ cup white rice flour
¼ cup fine maize/corn meal
1 tsp freshly crushed sea salt

1–2 tsp gf garlic granules
1 egg (beaten)
a little gluten and dairy free milk
  alternative

Method

- Cut the chicken fillet into very fine strips, no longer than 2" in length.
- In a zip-lock bag, mix together the flour, meal, salt and garlic granules.
- In a small, shallow dish, mix the egg with a little milk.
- Roll the chicken pieces in the egg and then place them in the bag with the flour mixture. Seal the bag and give it a good shake to coat all the pieces.
- Remove the chicken and cook in a deep fat fryer at 150C for 3 minutes.
- Pat off the excess oil before serving.

These are also good cold, for picnics and packed lunches.

Marilyn Le Breton © Copyright 2001

Jack's dinosaur bones

CF, EF, FF, SF, SGF, TF, YF

Ingredients

2 chicken breast fillets
2 oz (50g) gram flour

1 tsp gf baking powder
4 tbsp water
½ tsp gf garlic granules

Method

- Cut the chicken fillets into very thin strips, the longer the better.
- Mix together the flour, baking powder, garlic granules and water into a thick, smooth batter.
- Dip the chicken in the batter and shake off excess.
- Deep fry the chicken for 2–3 minutes in a deep fat fryer set at 150C.
- Pat off excess oil with kitchen paper.

Rob Le Breton © Copyright 2001

Speedy chicken 'pie'

FF, SF, SGF, TF, YF

Ingredients

1 celery stick or 2 spring onions (finely
    chopped)
2 tbsp sweetcorn
2 tbsp gluten and dairy free mayonnaise
4 oz (125g) cold, cooked chicken (finely
    chopped)
1 packet of gluten, dairy and DGa free plain
    crisps (crushed)

Method

- Mix all the ingredients, except the crisps, together.
- Spoon the mixture evenly between two small pie tins.
- Sprinkle the crisps over the top, when ready to serve.

Variations

- *Substitute the chicken with ham or bacon. Alternatively, top the 'pie' with mashed potato (mash the potatoes with a little dairy free margarine).*

Marilyn Le Breton © Copyright 2001

Jamaican chicken bake

EF, FF, SF, SGF, TF, YF

Ingredients

4 chicken breasts (skinned and filleted)
2 tbsp organic sunflower oil
½ lb (125g) leeks (finely sliced)
1 tsp gf allspice
½ tsp gf cayenne powder
1 oz (30g) polenta
3 tsp coconut milk

Method

- Pre-heat oven to GM6, 400F, 200C.
- Place each chicken breast between 2 pieces of baking parchment and gently hammer the meat out to flatten it, with a rolling pin or meat hammer.
- In a frying pan, heat 1 tbsp of the oil and gently fry the leek, cayenne pepper and allspice, for 5 minutes until the leeks have softened.
- Remove the pan from the heat and stir in the polenta and the coconut milk, mixing together well.
- Spread a little of the mixture onto each chicken breast and roll up the chicken.
- Arrange the chicken rolls in an ovenproof dish and brush the remaining oil over the chicken.
- Bake for 25 minutes. Cut into slices before serving.

Can be served hot or cold.

Marilyn Le Breton © Copyright 2001

Fish and Seafood Based Meals

Crispy crab cakes

CF, FF, SF*, SGF, TF, YF

Ingredients

1 cup fresh gluten and dairy free
   breadcrumbs
2 eggs (beaten)
2 tbsp gluten and dairy free mayonnaise (or
   dairy free milk)
1 tbsp minced onion
1 tbsp minced celery

1 clove garlic (minced)
1 tsp gf dried parsley
1/4 tsp gf cayenne pepper
1/2 tsp salt
1 lb (450g) crab meat
gf flour for coating
2 tbsp sunflower oil

Method

- Combine all the ingredients but the flour and oil.
- Shape the mixture into burger shapes and coat with flour.
- Fry in hot oil until crisp – approximately 5 minutes each side.

Variation

- *Use 1 lb (450g) tinned salmon (in oil) instead of crab meat.*

Debby Anglesey © Copyright 2000

Crab cakes

CF, EF, FF, SF, SGF, TF, YF

Ingredients

1 lb (450g) potatoes (cooked, mashed and
   cooled)
6 oz (175g) tinned crab meat in oil
   (drained and flaked)

4 spring onions (chopped)
3 tbsp gf flour mix
2 tbsp organic sunflower oil
seasoning

Method

- Into the mashed potato, mix the crab meat, spring onions and seasoning.
- Divide the mixture into 8 and shape into cakes.
- Dip each side of the crab cakes into the seasoned flour.
- Heat the oil in a frying pan and cook for 3–4 minutes each side.

Marilyn Le Breton © Copyright 2001

Fish and onion bake

CF, EF, FF, SF, SGF, TF, YF

Ingredients

1 lb (450g) unsmoked, fresh white fish (whiting, cod, etc.)

1 lb (450g) potatoes (peeled and sliced thinly)

2 onions (sliced thinly)

¼ pint (150ml) dairy and gluten free milk alternative

fresh fennel or dill to taste (finely chopped)

fresh parsley to taste (chopped)

1 oz (25g) dairy free margarine (melted)

seasoning

Method

- Pre-heat oven to GM5, 375F, 180C.
- Grease an ovenproof casserole dish.
- Flake the fish.
- In the dish, alternate layers of potatoes, onions and fish, ending with a potato layer.
- Mix together the milk, herbs, melted margarine and seasoning.
- Carefully pour the milk mixture over the top of the potatoes.
- Bake for approximately 30 minutes.

Jacqui Jackson © Copyright 2001

Fish pie

CF, EF, FF, SF, SGF, TF, YF

Ingredients

1 lb (450g) fresh unsmoked fish
1 lb (450g) potatoes (cooked and mashed)
1 bag gluten, dairy, DGa and artificial sugar free crisps (finely crushed)
¼ pint (150ml) gluten and dairy free milk alternative

¼ pint (150ml) gluten and dairy free white sauce (see Sauces section for recipes)
2 bay leaves
whole peppercorns
chopped fresh parsley to taste
salt to taste

Method

- Place the fish, milk, bay leaves, peppercorns and salt in a wide, shallow pan and cook together for approximately 8–10 minutes or until the fish is cooked through. Do not over cook the fish.
- Strain off the fish (reserving the milk to use in the white sauce). Remove and discard the bay leaves and peppercorns.
- Roughly chop the fish and place in an ovenproof dish.
- Cover the fish with the white sauce.
- Mix the mashed potato with the chopped parsley and carefully spread evenly over the top of the fish and white sauce.
- Sprinkle the crushed crisps over the top and place under a hot grill to brown.

Jacqui Jackson © Copyright 2001

Kedgeree

CF, FF, SF, SGF, TF, YF

Ingredients

8 oz (225g) long grain rice (cooked and
    cooled)
1 lb (450g) naturally smoked haddock fillets
2 eggs (hard boiled, cooled and chopped)
6–8 spring onions (finely chopped)

2 oz (50g) dairy free margarine
¼ tsp gf paprika (optional)
seasoning
gluten and dairy free milk
    alternative *or* water for
    poaching fish

Method

- Poach the haddock, by simmering in milk alternative or water for approximately 8–10 minutes over a low heat.
- Drain off the liquid and skin and flake the fish.
- Melt margarine in a large pan and add all of the ingredients.
- Stir continuously over a moderate heat until the kedgeree is hot through.

Marilyn Le Breton © Copyright 2001

Salmon patties

CCF, FF, SF, SGF, TF, YF

Ingredients

16 oz (450g) can salmon in oil (drained and
    flaked)
1 carrot *or* potato *or* courgette (grated)
1 onion (finely chopped)
½ cup fine gluten and dairy free
    breadcrumbs

1 egg (beaten)
seasoning
1 tsp gf dried parsley
¼ tsp gf dried dill (optional)

Method

- Combine all ingredients together well.
- Form into burger shapes.
- Fry in a little oil for 6 minutes each side.

Debby Anglesey © Copyright 2000

Speedy shrimp Creole

CF, EF, FF, YF

Ingredients

2 cups medium un-sulphated shrimps
   (defrosted)
5 cups of cooked rice (hot)
1 tsp gf dried chives
¼ tsp gf celery seeds
1 tsp gf dried parsley

½ tsp gf dried thyme
cayenne pepper to taste
seasoning
2 tsp sugar
4 cups chopped tomatoes
1 cup soya cream or plain soya
   yoghurt

Method

- Pre-heat oven to GM4, 350F, 180C.
- Mix all ingredients except the cream/yoghurt in a casserole dish.
- Bake for 20 minutes or until heated through.
- Just before serving, stir in the yoghurt/cream.

Alternatively, cook in a microwave for 8–10 minutes.

Debby Anglesey © Copyright 2000

Fish fingers

CF, FF, SF, SGF*, TF, YF*

Ingredients

4 oz (125g) potatoes (cooked and mashed)
8 oz (225g) cod (skinned, poached and
    cooled: reserve juices)
seasoning
1 tbsp fresh parsley (chopped)
1 small egg (beaten)
4 oz (125g) gluten and dairy free
    breadcrumbs
DS All Purpose Flour, for dusting

Method

* Combine together the potato, fish, seasoning and parsley. Add some of the reserved fish juice if the mixture seems too dry.
* Divide the mixture into 8 and shape each piece into rectangle 'fingers'.
* Dust each finger with the flour.
* Dip each finger into the beaten egg and then dip into the breadcrumbs, turning several times to make sure that they are well coated with breadcrumbs. (Press the crumbs into the fingers if necessary).
* Heat approximately 1" of oil in a frying pan, until hot.
* Fry fingers for 8–10 minutes turning once.
* Pat off excess oil with kitchen paper and serve immediately.

Dietary Specialities © Copyright 2001

Scampi

CF, EF, FF, SF, SGF, TF, YF

Ingredients

7 oz (200g) un-sulphated prawns
6 oz (175g) gram flour
½ tsp salt
¼ tsp gf baking powder
1 tsp gf cumin

½–1 tsp gf chilli powder
7 oz (200mls) water
1 clove garlic (crushed)
sunflower oil for deepfrying

Method

- In a bowl, mix together well, the flour, salt, baking powder, cumin, chilli powder, garlic and water.
- Leave the batter for 10 minutes to allow the garlic to be infused into the liquid.
- Stir the prawns into the batter, making sure that they are well coated.
- Remove the prawns and deep fry for 3–5 minutes. The batter should have browned.

Anne Pemberton, Leeds © Copyright

Salmon fishcakes

EF, FF, SF, SGF, TF, YT

Ingredients

1¼ lb (600g) floury potatoes (boiled, mashed and cooled)
6 oz (180g) tin pink salmon (drained and flaked)

fine corn meal (for coating)
sunflower oil (for frying)

Method

- Mix together the salmon and mashed potato.
- Take a golf ball sized piece of the mixture and flatten into a patty.
- Coat the fish patties in corn meal and pat off the excess.
- Fry in the oil until golden brown on both sides.

These freeze well and cook best from frozen.

Amanda Godfrey, London © Copyright

Tuna and vegetable rissoles

FF, SF, SGF, TF, YF

Ingredients

4 oz (125g) long grain rice (uncooked weight)

7 oz (200g) tuna in vegetable oil (drained and flaked)

I carrot

I courgette

I potato

I onion

2 oz (50g) gluten and dairy free breadcrumbs

I egg (beaten)

7 oz (200g) tin creamed sweetcorn

½ tsp gf dried parsley

3 tbsp gf flour

Method

- Cook the rice according to the instructions on packet and drain.
- Mix the tuna into the rice.
- In a food processor, blend down the carrot, courgette, potato and onion.
- Mix together the vegetables, parsley, breadcrumbs, sweetcorn and tuna/rice.
- Bind the mixture together with the beaten egg.
- Divide the mixture into 12 and shape into rissoles or burgers.
- Dip in the gf flour, ensuring that all surfaces are coated.
- Fry for 3 minutes each side.

Marilyn Le Breton © Copyright 2001

Sausage Based Meals

Sausage shepherd's pie

CF, EF, FF, SF, YF

Ingredients

2 lb (900g) potatoes (cooked and mashed)
1 lb (450g) Lock's AiA pork and rice
 sausages (cooked)
1 onion (chopped)
14 oz (400g) can gluten free baked beans
2 x 14 oz (400g) can chopped tomatoes
½ tsp gf garlic granules
1 oz (25g) dairy free margarine
½ tsp gluten free Dijon mustard

Method

- Melt margarine in a large saucepan and gently fry the onions until they are soft (but not brown).
- Add the baked beans, tomatoes, garlic granules and Dijon mustard. Stir together and heat through (do not boil).
- Place cooked sausages in the bottom of a casserole dish.
- Spoon the bean and tomato mixture evenly over the top of the sausages.
- Spread the mashed potato over the top of the mixture and flatten down with a fork.
- Either brown the potatoes under a hot grill or keep warm in the oven (pre-heated to GM4, 350F, 180C) for up to 30 minutes.

Lock's Sausages Ltd © Copyright 2001

Toad in the hole

CF, FF, SF, SGF, TF, YF

Ingredients

Barbara's Yorkshire pudding batter mix
  (see Miscellaneous section for recipe)

1 lb (450g) Lock's AiA pork and
  rice sausages
2 tbsp hot sunflower oil

Method

- Pre-heat oven to GM7, 425F, 220C.

- Pour the hot oil into a baking tin.

- Add the sausages and cook for approximately 5 minutes until the sausages have begun to brown.

- Gently pour the batter around the sausages and bake for 35 minutes or until the batter has risen and is golden.

Barbara's Kitchen and Lock's Sausages Ltd © Copyright 2001

Mixed sausage gumbo

EF, FF, SF, SGF, TF, YF

Ingredients

4–6 gluten, dairy and additive free sausages
  (Lock's AiA sausages), mixed varieties
2 lb (900g) new potatoes (boiled and
  roughly chopped)
1 small cauliflower (separated into florets
  and cooked)

1 small tin of sweetcorn (rinsed
  and drained)
½ tsp gf turmeric
½ tsp ground black pepper
1 tbsp sunflower oil
1 tsp gf mint sauce

Method

- Heat the oil and cook the sausages. Remove sausages and roughly chop. Return to pan.

- In a bowl, mix together the cooked cauliflower and the mint sauce.

- To the sausages, add potatoes, sweetcorn, turmeric and pepper and cook for 2 minutes.

- Add the cauliflower and continue to cook for 2 minutes or until heated through thoroughly.

- Serve immediately.

Delicious served with salad.

Rob Le Breton © Copyright 2001

Speedy 'sausage rolls'

CF, EF, FF, SF, SGF*, TF*, YF

Ingredients

sliced gluten and dairy free bread
pre-cooked gluten, dairy and preservative
    free sausages (Lock's AiA pork or
    turkey and rice cocktail sausages)
dairy free margarine
gluten free tomato ketchup (optional)

Method

- Pre-heat oven to GM5, 375F, 190C.
- Cut the off the crusts from the bread, then flatten out, using a rolling pin.
- Cut the bread into long strips, slightly narrower than the cut sausage.
- Spread the bread lightly with tomato ketchup, if using.
- Wrap the bread around the sausage and secure with a cocktail stick.
- Melt the margarine and brush it over the outside of the bread.
- Bake for 10 minutes.

Country sausage

CF, EF, FF, SF, TF, YF

Ingredients

2 lbs (900g) lean pork mince
5 tbsp minced onion
1 tsp gf dried parsley
2 tsp salt
1 tsp gf dried sage

1 tsp gf dried basil
1 tsp gf dried marjoram or
    thyme
1 tsp gf chilli powder
1 tsp gf ground pepper
1 tsp sugar

Method

- Combine all ingredients together well in a bowl.
- Divide the mixture in half and shape each into a log 6"–7" long.
- Wrap in film or foil and place in fridge overnight; this allows the dried herbs to moisten and the flavours blend.
- Slice each log into ½" rounds and fry over a medium heat for 3–4 minutes each side.

The logs may be frozen.

Variations

- *Sausage mixture can be rolled into small balls and frozen. To use, bake at GM4, 350F, 180C for 20–30 minutes.*

These make good hors d' oeuvres or children's party food, especially if served with dips.

Italian sausage

CF, EF, FF, SF, SGF, TF, YF

Ingredients

2 lbs (900g) lean pork mince
2 tsp salt
½ tsp ground black pepper
1 tbsp fennel seed
¼ tsp gf red pepper flakes
¼ tsp gf garlic granules or 1
    clove garlic (minced)
1 tsp gf dried parsley

Method

- Mix all the ingredients together well and place in the fridge for 1 hour.
- Shape mixture into burgers and sauté or grill until well done.

Can be frozen.

Variation

- *Sausage mixture can be rolled into small balls and frozen. To use, bake at GM4, 350F, 180C for 20–30 minutes.*

These make good hors d' oeuvres or children's party food, especially if served with dips.

Debby Anglesey © Copyright 2000

Polish sausage

CF, EF, FF, SF, SGF, TF, YF

Ingredients

2 lbs (900g) lean pork mince
½ tsp gf ground pepper
½ tsp gf dried marjoram
1 tbsp salt
1 clove garlic (minced)

Method

- Mix all of the ingredients together well with your hands.
- Shape into burgers and grill or sauté until well done.

Variation

- *Sausage mixture can be rolled into small balls and frozen. To use, bake at GM4, 350F, 180C for 20–30 minutes.*

These make good hors d' oeuvres or children's party food, especially if served with dips.

Debby Anglesey © Copyright 2000

Scotch eggs

CF, FF, SF, SGF*, TF, YF*

Ingredients

4 eggs (hard boiled and shelled)
8 oz (225g) gluten, dairy and preservative
    free sausage meat
seasoning
½ tsp gf dried mixed herbs (optional)
I small egg (beaten)
4 oz (125g) DS Breadcrumbs
DS All Purpose Flour (for dusting)

Method

* Mix together the sausage meat, seasoning and herbs (if using) and divide into four portions.
* Pat each piece of sausage meat out onto a floured surface and shape roughly into a rectangle 7" x 3".
* Coat each egg with flour.
* Place each egg in the centre of the sausage meat and carefully gather it up to cover the egg completely. Smooth and pat into shape.
* Coat each in beaten egg and then evenly on the breadcrumbs.
* Heat 1½ " of oil in a frying pan or heat a deep fat fryer to 180–190C.
* Fry each egg for 6–8 minutes, turning frequently so that the entire surface is golden brown.

Dietary Specialities © Copyright 2001

Quick sausage and lentil stew

CF, EF, FF, SF, SGF, TF, YF

Ingredients

1 lb (450g) gluten, dairy and preservative
    free sausages (Lock's AiA pork
    sausages)
2 tbsp organic sunflower oil
5 garlic cloves (crushed)
1 onion (sliced)
10 oz (280g) lentils (rinsed)
½ lb (225g) parsnips (rough chopped)
1½ pints (900ml) homemade vegetable or
    chicken stock (see Stocks section for
    recipes)
seasoning

Method

- Cut each sausage into 3 equal pieces and fry in the oil with the onions and garlic for 5 minutes.
- Add the lentils, parsnips and stock and bring the liquid to the boil.
- Reduce the heat and simmer for 20 minutes or until the lentils are tender and most of the liquid has been absorbed. Add more stock or water if the mixture dries out too quickly.
- Season to taste and serve.

Marilyn Le Breton © Copyright 2001

Sausage and bean casserole

CF*, EF, FF, SF, SGF, YF

Ingredients

½ lb (225g) onions (sliced)

½ lb (225g) carrots (sliced)

2 tbsp sunflower oil

1 lb (450g) gluten, dairy and additive free sausages (Lock's AiA pork and chive sausages)

14 oz (400g) can chickpeas

14 oz (400g) can butterbeans

14 oz can (400g) chopped tomatoes

1 tbsp cornflour or potato starch flour

1 pint (600ml) homemade chicken or vegetable stock (see Stocks section for recipes)

2 tbsp tomato puree

seasoning

¼–½ tsp gf paprika

Method

- Pre-heat oven to GM3, 325F, 170C.
- Heat the oil in a pan and brown the sausages for 5 minutes. Remove with a slotted spoon and cut into 4 equal size pieces.
- Reduce the heat in the pan and gently fry the onions and carrots, until they soften, stirring occasionally.
- Return the sausages to the pan and add the chickpeas, butterbeans and tomatoes.
- Blend the cornflour or potato starch flour into a smooth paste with a little of the stock and
- add to the sausage mixture.
- Add the rest of the stock, tomato puree, paprika and seasoning and stir in well.
- Bring the liquid to the boil, stirring constantly.
- Transfer the casserole to an ovenproof dish and bake for at least 1 hour.

Marilyn Le Breton © Copyright 2001

Vegetarian and Vegan Meals

Please note that there are many other vegetarian and vegan recipes in other sections of this book.

Pakoras

CF, EF, FF, SF SGF, TF, YF

Ingredients

8 oz (225g) gram flour
½ tsp gf baking powder
I tsp crushed sea salt
½ tsp gf ground coriander
I tsp gf garam masala
½ tsp gf chilli powder (optional)

½ tsp gf ground cumin
½ pint (300ml) cold water
vegetables of choice (e.g., florets
   of cauliflower, diced
   aubergine, onion slices)
oil for frying

Method

- Mix together the flour, baking powder, salt and spices.
- Add the water, stirring well. The batter should be thick and without lumps.
- Add vegetables to the batter and stir them around until they are completely coated.
- Set the deep fat fryer to 170C (medium hot) and place the mixture into the oil in I tablespoon portions. Be careful not to over fill the pan.
- Cook until golden brown.
- Drain well and serve.

Barbara's Kitchen © Copyright 2001

Traffic-light vegetable puffs

CF, FF, SF, SGF, YF.

Ingredients

1½ lb (700g) potatoes (mashed)
½ lb (225g) sweet potatoes (mashed)
4 oz (125g) spinach (steamed, well drained and finely chopped)
2 oz (50g) dairy free margarine (melted)
4 oz (125g) carrot (finely grated and steamed)
1 tbsp tomato puree

3 large eggs (separated)
2 cloves garlic (finely chopped)
dessert spoon fresh chopped basil
seasoning to taste
2 tsp gluten and dairy free milk alternative
2 tbsp gf flour mix
1 tsp xanthan gum

Method

- Pre-heat oven to GM5, 375F, 190C.
- Mix together the flour, xanthan gum, egg yolks, margarine, seasoning, milk alternative, garlic and mashed potato. Beat this mixture together well, until completely combined and smooth.
- In a separate bowl, whisk the egg whites until they form stiff peaks.
- Fold the egg whites into the potato mix.
- Divide this mixture into 3 equal parts.
- To one mix add the spinach.
- To the second mix, add the mashed sweet potato.
- To the third mix, add the carrot, tomato puree and basil.
- Using a medium nozzle on a meringue bag, pipe small rosettes of each mixture, separately, onto a well-oiled baking tray.
- Bake for 12 minutes and then reduce the oven heat to GM3, 325F, 170C and cook for a further 10 minutes.

These freeze well. Place clingfilm between the puffs for ease of separation on defrosting.

Maddalena Feliciello, Leeds © Copyright

Mini quiches

CF, FF, SF, SGF, TF, YF

Ingredients

8 oz (225g) DS pastry (made earlier, as
    previous recipe)
1 medium onion (finely chopped and sauté)
1 medium egg (beaten)
4 fl oz (150ml) gluten and dairy free milk
    alternative
½ tsp gf dried mixed herbs
seasoning to taste

Method

- Pre-heat oven to GM6, 400F, 200C.
- Roll out the pastry on a floured surface and cut out using a 3" cookie cutter.
- Place the pastry circles in the bottom of a bun tray.
- Place a little of the sautéd onion in the bottom of each pastry case.
- In a bowl mix together the egg, milk alternative, herbs and seasoning and carefully pour the mixture into the pastry cases.
- Bake in the oven for 15–20 minutes.

To freeze, place quiches, uncovered, on a tray in the freezer. Once frozen, place in a freezer bag.

Dietary Specialities © Copyright Nutrition Point 2001

Potato and onion quiche

CF, FF, SF, SGF, TF, YF

Ingredients

8 oz (225g) pastry (see Pastry section for recipe)

1 large onion (sliced)

6 oz (175g) potatoes (cooked, cooled and diced)

2 oz (50g) dairy free margarine

2 organic eggs (beaten)

¼ pint (150ml) gluten and dairy free milk alternative

¼ tsp gf dried mixed herbs

½ tsp gf garlic granules (optional)

Method

- Pre-heat oven to GM5, 375F, 190C.
- Line an 8" flan dish with greaseproof paper and then line with pastry; place in fridge to chill.
- Fry onions and cooked potatoes in the margarine for 5 minutes.
- Remove the onions and potatoes and allow them to cool.
- Beat together the eggs, milk alternative, herbs and garlic granules (if using).
- Place the onions and potatoes to top of the pastry case and spread out evenly.
- Pour the egg mixture over the top of the vegetables, slowly and carefully.
- Bake for 40 minutes or until the filling has set and is golden brown.
- Serve hot or cold.

Potato and onion omelette

CF, FF, SF, SGF, TF, YF

Ingredients

1 ¼ cups oil
6 large potatoes (peeled and sliced)
2 large onions (sliced)
6 large organic eggs (beaten)
seasoning to taste

Method

- Heat all the oil in a large non-stick frying pan.
- Stir in the potatoes and onions. Cover the pan and cook over a gentle heat for approximately 20 minutes or until the potatoes begin to soften.
- Remove the potatoes and onions with a slotted spoon to drain off as much oil as possible.
- Place them in a large bowl with the beaten eggs. Season the mixture and stir together gently.
- Pour off all but 4 tbsp of the oil from the pan and re-heat the oil.
- When the oil is very hot, carefully pour in the mixture.
- Cook for 2–3 minutes or until the egg is nearly set.
- Cover the pan with a plate and very carefully invert the pan.
- Slide the omelette back into the pan and cook for a further 5 minutes.

This is very filling and is delicious served either hot or cold.

Marilyn Le Breton © Copyright 2001

Spicy tofu burgers

CF, EF, FF, SGF, YF

Ingredients

1 large carrot *or* 1 small parsnip (finely grated)

1 large onion (finely chopped)

1 tbsp organic sunflower oil

1 garlic clove (crushed)

1 tbsp tomato puree

1 tsp mild gf curry paste *or* gf ground cumin

8 oz (225g) gf plain tofu (mashed down)

1 oz (25g) gluten and dairy free breadcrumbs

1 oz (25g) finely chopped nuts (optional)

Method

- Heat the oil and fry the carrot/parsnip and onion for 3 minutes, stirring constantly.
- Add the garlic, tomato puree and curry/cumin. Mix them in well and cook for 2 minutes. Remove from heat and place mixture in a bowl.
- Add the tofu and the breadcrumbs to the bowl.
- Mix in all the ingredients well, until they have combined.
- Divide the mixture into 8 and shape into burger patties with well-floured hands.
- Fry the burgers for 4 minutes each side, until golden brown or brush each with oil and grill for 3 minutes each side.
- Pat off the excess oil with kitchen paper and serve hot.

Marilyn Le Breton © Copyright 2001

Falafels

CF, SF, SGF, TF, YF

Ingredients

14 oz (400g) tin chickpeas (drained)
1 tsp gf ground cumin
1 tsp gf ground coriander
1 small onion (finely chopped)
1 tsp gf dried parsley
2 garlic cloves (crushed)
1 tbsp lemon juice

¼ tsp gf chilli powder/cayenne
    pepper (optional)
1 organic egg (beaten)
3 oz (90g) gluten and dairy free
    breadcrumbs
2 oz (60g) white rice flour

Method

- Mash the chickpeas down roughly with a fork.
- Add the cumin, coriander, onion, parsley, garlic, lemon and chilli/cayenne and mix in very well.
- Stir in the egg, breadcrumbs and flour.
- Divide the mixture up and roll into walnut sized pieces.
- Deep fry for 5 minutes and drain well.

Mediterranean chickpeas

CF, EF, FF, SF, SGF, YF

Ingredients

2 x 14 oz (400g) tins of chickpeas
1 onion (chopped)
2 celery stalks (sliced)
2 cloves garlic (crushed)
1 pepper (finely chopped)
½ pint (300ml) sieved tomatoes/passata
2 tbsp tomato puree
½ tsp gf dried parsley
1 oz (25g) black olives (cut in half)
seasoning to taste

Method

Fry together the onion, celery and garlic for 5 minutes.

- Add the diced pepper and fry for a further 3 minutes.
- Add the chickpeas, sieved tomatoes, tomato puree, parsley and seasoning; stir in well and bring to the boil.
- Reduce the heat and simmer for 10 minutes.
- Sprinkle the olives over the dish when served.

Tastes great with rice or salad, or wrapped inside a gf pitta bread or spicy chickpea pancake.

Marilyn Le Breton © Copyright 2001

Potato and lentil bake

FF, SGF, YF

Topping
2 lb (900g) potatoes
2 tbsp dairy free margarine
1 tbsp gluten and dairy free milk alternative
2 oz (50g) sweetcorn
½ tsp gf onion granules

Filling
8 oz (225g) red lentils (rinsed)
2 oz (50g) dairy free margarine
1 leek (sliced)
2 cloves garlic (crushed)
1 celery stick (fine chopped)
4 oz (125g) broccoli florets
6 oz (175g) plain tofu (cubed)
2 tbsp tomato puree
1 oz (30g) frozen peas (thawed)
seasoning

Method

- Pre-heat oven to GM6, 400F, 200C.
- Cook the potatoes and mash with the margarine and milk.
- Stir in the sweetcorn and the onion granules. Set to one side to use as topping.
- In a large pan, cover the lentils with water, bring to the boil, reduce heat and simmer for 25–30 minutes until lentils are cooked.
- Drain off the lentils and rinse under running water. Set these aside.
- Melt the margarine in a pan and sauté the leek, garlic, celery and broccoli for approximately 5 minutes or until the leeks are soft.
- Add the tofu, lentils, tomato puree and peas, mix together well and season.
- Place the lentil mixture in a shallow ovenproof dish.
- Spoon the potato mixture over the lentil mixture and cover the lentils evenly.
- Bake for 20–25 minutes or until the potato topping begins to brown.

Marilyn Le Breton © Copyright 2001

Mild vegetable curry

CF, EF, FF, SF, SGF, TF, YF

Ingredients

2 tbsp organic sunflower oil
I large onion (sliced)
2 garlic cloves (crushed)
2 lb (900g) mixed fresh vegetables (cut to cubes or florets)
¼ tsp gf dried ginger
2 tsp gf turmeric
2 tsp gf dried coriander
2 tsp gf dried cumin
I tsp gf dried fenugreek
I pint (600ml) coconut milk
2 oz (50g) flaked almonds (optional)

Method

- Heat the oil in a large pan and sauté the onion for 5 minutes.
- Add the garlic and cook for a further 2 minutes.
- Add in the ginger, turmeric, coriander, cumin and fenugreek. Mix in very well and cook for a further minute, stirring all the time.
- Add the vegetables and stir in well to coat them in the spices.
- Gradually stir in the coconut milk and bring the liquid to the boil. Reduce the heat, cover and simmer for 45 minutes or until all the vegetables are tender. Stir the mixture occasionally and add a little water if the sauce dries out too much.

Then either serve and sprinkle the almonds over the top or allow to cool slightly and blend down into a smooth paste.
     Serve with rice.

Marilyn Le Breton © Copyright 2001

Vegetarian chilli

CF, EF, FF, SF, SGF, YF

Ingredients

2 tbsp organic sunflower oil
1 large onion (chopped)
2 garlic cloves (crushed)
1 tsp–2 tbsp gf cayenne powder (depends how hot the chilli is required!)
2 tsp gf ground cumin
2 tbsp tomato puree
1 large green pepper (chopped)

2 lb (900g) mixed vegetables (diced or florets)
2 x 14 oz (400g) tins chopped tomatoes
14 oz (400g) tin kidney beans (rinsed)
1 tsp gf dried coriander
seasoning
water

Method

- Heat the oil in a large pan, sauté the onions for 3 minutes, add the garlic and cook for a further 2 minutes.
- Add the cayenne pepper, cumin and coriander, mix in well and cook for a further 2 minutes, stirring constantly.
- Add the tomato puree, stir in well.
- Add the vegetables and cook for 3–4 minutes.
- Add the chopped tomatoes and enough water to cover the vegetables. Bring the liquid to the boil. Cover the pan and reduce heat. Simmer for 40–45 minutes.
- Add the kidney beans and cook for a further 15 minutes.

¼ pint of soya cream, plain soya yoghurt or coconut milk can be stirred in just prior to serving.

Marilyn Le Breton © Copyright 2001

Mixed bean goulash

CF, EF, FF, YF

Ingredients

1 lb (450g) mixed tinned beans
2 tbsp organic sunflower oil
1 large onion (sliced)
1 lb (450g) potatoes (diced)
½ tsp gf dried mixed herbs
1–2 tsp gf paprika
4 tbsp tomato puree

1 tbsp sugar
2 tbsp gf flour
1 pint (600ml) homemade
    vegetable stock or water
½ pint (300ml) plain soya
    yoghurt
seasoning

Method

- Heat oil in a large pan and gently sauté together the potatoes and onions.
- Add the tomato puree, paprika, mixed herbs and sugar and cook for 2 minutes, stirring constantly.
- Add the flour and cook for 1 minute, stirring constantly.
- Gradually add the stock, stirring all the time and bring to the boil.
- Add the beans. Cover pan, reduce heat and simmer for 20–30 minutes.
- Remove from heat and stir in the yoghurt.

Marilyn Le Breton © Copyright 2001

Rich and creamy ratatouille

CF, EF, FF, SF, YF

Ingredients

I large aubergine (cubed)
2 onions (sliced)
I lb (450g) courgettes (sliced)
2 x 14oz (400g) tins chopped tomatoes
I green pepper (sliced)
I red pepper (sliced)
2 fl oz (50ml) organic sunflower oil

4 garlic cloves (crushed)
2 tbsp tomato puree
4 oz (125g) creamed coconut
   (roughly chopped)
½ tsp gf dried mixed herbs
½ tsp gf dried oregano
1–2 tbsp sugar
seasoning

Method

- Soak the aubergines in salted water for I hour and drain well.
- In a large pan, heat the oil and gently fry the onions for 5 minutes until soft.
- Add the garlic, mixed herbs, oregano and peppers and gently fry for a further 5 minutes, stirring constantly.
- Add the aubergines and courgettes and continue to fry for a further 2 minutes.
- Add the tomatoes and puree, stir in well and bring the liquid to the boil.
- Reduce the heat and stir in the creamed coconut.
- Cover the pan and simmer gently for 45–60 minutes, stirring occasionally.
- Add water if the dish dries out.

This also makes a great pasta sauce.

Marilyn Le Breton © Copyright 2001

Spinach dhal

CF, EF, FF, SF, SGF, TF, YF

Ingredients

8 oz (225g) red or orange lentils (rinsed)
1 lb (450g) frozen spinach (thawed and
    chopped)
3 oz (90g) dairy free margarine
1 onion (finely chopped)
1 garlic clove (crushed)
1 tsp gf coriander
1 tsp gf turmeric
¼ 1 tsp gf cayenne pepper
½ pint (300ml) water

Method

- Melt the margarine and gently fry the onion and garlic for 3 minutes.
- Add the spices and lentils, stirring in well and continue to fry for 2 minutes.
- Add the water and bring it to the boil. Cover the pan, reduce the heat and simmer for approximately 30 minutes or until the lentils are tender. Add a little more boiling water if necessary.
- Stir in spinach and increase the heat for 5 minutes, until the spinach is heated through and the excess liquid has evaporated.
- Add salt to taste if required.

Marilyn Le Breton © Copyright 2001

Mini vegetable tureens

CF, FF, SF, SGF, TF, YF

Ingredients

10 oz (280g) potatoes (cooked)
4 oz (125g) swede (cooked)
1 carrot (cooked)
1 lb (450g) spinach (blanched, well drained
    and finely chopped or pureed)
1 tbsp gluten and dairy free milk alternative
1 tbsp dairy free margarine
1 oz (25g) gf flour mix
1 organic egg (beaten)
¼ tsp gf garlic granules (optional)

Method

- Pre-heat oven to GM4, 350F, 180C and grease 4 ½ pint ramekins or individual ½ pint pudding bowls.
- Mash the potato with the milk alternative and margarine and then mix in the egg (garlic granules if using) and flour to a smooth mixture and divide into 3 equal portions.
- In a food processor blend down the swede to a puree and this to ⅓ of the potato and mix in well.
- Clean the food processor and blend down the carrot to a puree and add this to another ⅓ of the potato and mix in well.
- Mix the spinach into the remaining potato mixture.
- Divide all of the 3 mixes into 4 equal portions.
- Into each ramekin place a layer of the swede, carrot and spinach mixture, smoothing each layer flat.
- Cover each ramekin with silver foil and place in a roasting tin, half filled with boiling water.
- Bake for 40 minutes.
- Turn out directly onto serving plates.

Marilyn Le Breton © Copyright 2001

Quick and easy spicy chickpeas

CF, EF, FF*, SF, SGF, YF

Ingredients

2 x 14 oz (400g) tins chickpeas (rinsed and
    drained)
1 onion (chopped)
2 tsp gf turmeric
1 tsp gf cumin
1 tsp gf garlic granules
1 lb (450g) fresh tomatoes (roughly
    chopped)
1 tbsp lemon juice (optional)
4 tbsp fresh coriander (chopped and
    rinsed)

Method

- Fry the onion gently for 8–10 minutes, stirring occasionally.
- Add the turmeric, cumin and garlic granules and cook for a further 2–3 minutes, stirring constantly.
- Add the chickpeas, tomatoes, lemon juice (if using) and coriander, mix in well and cook for another 3–5 minutes, stirring constantly.

This is good with pasta, rice or salad. It also makes a great jacket potato filling or savoury pancake filling.

Marilyn Le Breton © Copyright 2001

Bean and nut rissoles

CF, FF, SF, SGF, TF, YF

Ingredients

4 oz (125g) cashew nuts
2 x 14 oz (400g) cans butter beans
2 oz (60g) gluten and dairy free
    breadcrumbs
1 onion (finely chopped)
1 tbsp cumin seeds

1 oz (30g) dairy free margarine
1 clove garlic (crushed)
1 organic egg (beaten)
1 tsp gf dried parsley
1 tsp sunflower oil
1 tsp gf paprika
seasoning

Method

- In a small saucepan, heat the sunflower oil and stir in the cumin seeds. Cook over a low heat for 2–3 minutes, stirring continuously.
- In a separate pan, melt the margarine and gently fry the onion and garlic for approximately 5 minutes until they have softened.
- Into the cumin seed pan, add the cashews and paprika and cook for 2 minutes.
- Allow the contents of both pans to cool and then place in a food processor.
- To the processor, add the egg, breadcrumbs, seasoning and parsley. Blend them together until smooth.
- Shape the mixture into very small burgers.
- Heat some oil in a frying pan and cook the rissoles for 2–3 minutes each side.
- Pat off the excess oil with kitchen paper.

Serve hot or cold.
Great for lunch boxes.
Suitable for freezing.

Marilyn Le Breton © Copyright 2001

Vegetable hash browns

CF, EF, FF, SF, SGF, TF, YF.

Ingredients

1 lb (450g) potatoes (peeled and grated)
1 carrot (peeled and grated)
1 celery stick (finely diced)
1 small onion (finely chopped)
1 oz (25g) frozen peas (thawed)
2 garlic cloves (crushed)
4 tbsp organic sunflower oil
2 tbsp dairy free margarine

Method

- Cook the potatoes and carrots for 3 minutes in boiling water. Drain and allow to cool.
- Mix in the celery, onion, garlic and peas.
- Add seasoning.
- Divide the mixture into 8 and shape each into a patty or square.
- Heat the oil and margarine together in a frying pan and fry the hash browns for 4–5 minutes each side until they are crisp and golden.

Marilyn Le Breton © Copyright 2001

Spicy potato fritters

CF*, FF, SF, SGF, TF, YF

Ingredients

1 oz (25g) gf flour mix
¼ tsp gf dried coriander
¼ tsp gf cumin
¼ tsp gf turmeric
1 large pinch of salt
1 organic egg (beaten)
1 tbsp gluten and dairy free milk alternative

6 oz (175g) potatoes (peeled)
1 garlic clove (crushed)
4 spring onions (chopped)
1–2 oz (25–50g) sweetcorn
  (optional)
organic sunflower oil for frying

Method

- Grate the raw potatoes and rinse well under running water and allow to drain. Remove excess moisture by placing the grated potato in a clean tea towel and squeezing out.
- In a large bowl, mix the flour, coriander, cumin, turmeric and salt together well.
- Into the seasoned flour, stir the grated potatoes and chopped onion.
- Add to flour and potato mix, the egg and milk and beat together to form a thick batter.
- Stir in the sweetcorn if using.
- Heat enough oil in a frying pan to shallow fry.
- Divide the mixture into 4 and spoon each quarter into the frying pan, flattening it out with the back of the spoon to form a thin patty.
- Fry over a low heat for 2–3 minutes each side or until golden brown and cooked through.
- Remove from pan and drain off any excess oil on kitchen paper.

Marilyn Le Breton © Copyright 2001

Snacks

Deep fried potato skins

CF, EF, FF, SF, SGF, TF, YF

Ingredients

as many potatoes (approx 4 oz in weight
     each) as required, each potato will
     make 4 skins
oil
salt

Method

- Pre-heat oven to GM6, 400F, 200C.
- Scrub potatoes and pat them dry.
- Brush each with a little oil and sprinkle with a little salt (freshly crushed sea salt is best).
- Place each potato directly onto the oven shelf and bake for approximately 50 minutes (or until they are soft when squeezed).
- Cut each potato into quarters.
- Scoop out the potato, leaving about ½" of the flesh next to the skin.
- Heat oil in a deep fat fryer to 190C/375F.
- Deep fry a few skins at a time, for approximately 45 seconds or until brown and crispy.
- Remove and drain well.
- Sprinkle with a little extra salt.
- Serve with dip of choice.

Luke's potato salad

CF*, FF, SF, SGF, TF, YF

Ingredients

1 ½ lb (900ml) very small new potatoes
8 tbsp gluten and dairy free mayonnaise
2 oz (50g) sweetcorn (optional)
4 rashers nitrate free bacon
8 spring onions (finely chopped)
2 organic eggs (hard boiled and shelled)
seasoning to taste

Method

- Scrub the potatoes clean and cook in their skins until tender. Drain and cool the potatoes and cut into little bite sized pieces.
- Fry the bacon until crispy. Cut off the rind and excess fat and cut into small pieces.
- In a bowl, mash down the eggs with a fork and mix in the mayonnaise.
- Add the sweetcorn, bacon pieces, potatoes, onions and seasoning and mix together well.

This is great for picnics and packed lunches.

Marilyn Le Breton © Copyright 2001

Potato waffles

CF, FF, SF, SGF, TF, YF

Ingredients

6 oz (175g) mashed potatoes
2 fl oz (50ml) dairy free milk alternative
    (hot)
6 tsp gf flour mix
2 tbsp oil
2 eggs (beaten)
¼ tsp salt

Method

- Mix the potato, milk, flour and oil together until the mixture is smooth.
- Add the salt to the beaten eggs and stir into the potato mix.
- Place some of the mixture into a pre-heated electric waffle maker and cook for approximately 5 minutes, until it has puffed up and is light brown in colour.

McGill Family, UK © Copyright

Potato cakes

CF, EF, FF, SF, SGF, TF, YF

Ingredients

3 lb (1.35kg) potatoes (mashed and chilled)
1½ oz (40g) dairy free margarine (melted)
seasoning to taste
rice flour for dusting

Method

- Mix together the potatoes, margarine and seasoning.
- Mould the mixture into thick cakes (¼ lb burger size).
- Dip both sides of the cakes in flour.
- Shallow fry until golden brown each side.

Marilyn Le Breton © Copyright 2001

Spicy nut and seed mix

CF, EF, FF, SF, SGF, TF, YF

Ingredients

4 oz (125g) pumpkin seeds
4 oz (125g) sunflower seeds
4 oz (125g) pine nuts
4 oz (125g) peanuts

2 tbsp freshly crushed sea salt
1 tsp gf paprika
1 tsp gf garlic powder

Method

- Spread out all the nuts and seeds evenly on a baking tray.
- Place tray under the grill on a medium heat and cook until they just begin to change colour, stirring occasionally.
- In a large zip-lock bag, mix together the salt, paprika and garlic.
- Add the nuts and seeds to the bag and shake well until they are covered in the salt mix.
- Cool and store in an airtight container.

Marilyn Le Breton © Copyright 2001

Sweet French toast

CF, FF, SF, TF

Ingredients

2 large organic eggs (beaten)
2 tbsp gluten and dairy free milk alternative
1 tsp icing sugar

1 large pinch of gf ground cinnamon (optional)
6 slices of gluten and dairy free bread

Method

- Beat together the eggs, milk, sugar and cinnamon (if using).
- Soak both sides of each slice of bread in mixture.
- Heat a very little oil in a non-stick frying pan, using a low to medium heat setting. Fry each side of the bread, until golden brown.
- Serve immediately, either as is, or with a little jam.

Marilyn Le Breton © Copyright 2001

Microwave potato crisps

CF, EF, FF, SF, SGF, TF, YF

Ingredients

Potato

Method

- Scrub an organic potato. Leave the skin on if you wish to add more fibre to your diet.
- Slice the potato very thinly and pat the slices dry with kitchen paper.
- Place the slices on a suitable microwave dish (ideally a plastic tray, with ridges on the base, for cooking bacon). Do not overlap the potato slices.
- Now promise you will not leave the microwave unattended for any reason at all (e.g. answering the phone or attending to your children, etc.). If you have to leave the microwave, switch it off.
- Place the dish in the microwave and set on high power. Cook for 2 minutes (if you have a 100 watt machine reduce the cooking time).
- Open the door to let out the steam. Microwave again. Keep opening the door to release steam and to check the colour of the crisps. The colour sequence is: pale gold, mid gold, dark brown, catch fire!
- Once you have the desired colour, remove crisps from the microwave. They will harden/crisp up in 1–2 minutes. If they do not, you have not cooked them long enough.

This also works using sweet potato – a very nutritious snack.

Salt, herbs and spices can be sprinkled over the potatoes prior to microwaving if desired.

Barbara's Kitchen © Copyright 2000

Editor's note: I've typed this up as I received it. Even if you don't attempt to make these, this recipe should bring a smile to your face!

Tuna and sweetcorn pancake fillings

FF, SF, SGF, TF, YF

Ingredients

4 pre-cooked pancakes (see recipe in
  Pancakes section)
½ pint (300ml) white sauce (see recipe in
  Sauces section)

4 oz (125g) canned tuna in oil
  (drained)
2 oz (50g) canned sweetcorn
  (drained)

Method

- Pre-heat oven to GM6, 400F, 200C.
- Mix together 2 tbsp of white sauce with the tuna and sweetcorn.
- Divide the mixture equally between 4 pancakes and roll them up.
- Place the pancakes in an ovenproof dish.
- Cover them with the remaining white sauce.
- Bake for 20–25 minutes.
- Serve hot.

Dietary Specialities © Copyright Nutrition Point 2001

Chicken and onion pancake filling

CF, FF, SF, SGF, TF, YF

Ingredients

4 pre-cooked pancakes (see recipe in
  Pancakes section)
½ pint (300ml) white sauce (see recipe in
  Sauces section)

4 oz (125g) cooked chicken
  (diced)
2 oz (50g) finely chopped spring
  onions

Method

- Pre-heat oven to GM6, 400F, 200C.
- Mix together 2 tbsp of white sauce with the chicken and onion.
- Divide the mixture equally between 4 pancakes and roll them up.
- Place the pancakes in an ovenproof dish.
- Cover them with the remaining white sauce.
- Bake for 20–25 minutes.
- Serve hot.

Dietary Specialities © Copyright Nutrition Point 2001

Condiments, Sauces, Marinades, Pâtés and Dips

Creole salt

CF, EF, FF, SF, SGF, TF, YF

Ingredients

⅔ cup ground sea salt
½ tsp gf cayenne pepper
1 tsp gf garlic granules
¼ tsp gf ground black pepper

Method

- Mix all the ingredients together.

Debby Anglesey © Copyright 2000

Lemon pepper

CF, EF, SF, SGF, TF, YF

Ingredients

⅔ cup salt
2 tsp gf ground black pepper
2 tsp gf lemon peel (ground and dried)
pinch of gf dried tarragon *or* dill *or* thyme

Method

- Mix all ingredients together well.

Debby Anglesey © Copyright 2000

Mock soy sauce marinade

CF, EF, SF, TF, YF

Ingredients

juice of 1 lime *or* lemon
3 tbsp oil
3 tbsp water
1 tsp gf five spice powder
¼ cup sugar (white or brown)
¼ tsp gf dried ginger *or* 1 tsp fresh grated ginger
⅛ tsp gf ground black pepper
¼ tsp gf dried red pepper flakes

Method

- Mix all ingredients together.

Debby Anglesey © Copyright 2000

Oriental style sauce

CF, EF, SF, TF, YF

Ingredients

½ lime *or* lemon (juice only)
2 tbsp sugar
⅛ tsp gf dried red pepper flakes
½ tsp gf five spice mix

¼ tsp gf garlic granules
⅛ tsp gf dried ginger
seasoning to taste

Method

- Mix all ingredients together.

Debby Anglesey © Copyright 2000

Caribbean salsa

CF, EF, SF, YF

Ingredients

2 tomatoes (chopped)
2 avocados (chopped)
1 mango *or* papaya (chopped)
¼ cup chopped red onion
1 tsp gf dried parsley
½ red pepper (chopped)

½ yellow pepper (chopped)
juice of 1 lemon *or* lime
1½ tsp sugar
1 tsp gf chilli powder
½ tsp gf cumin
seasoning to taste

Method

- In a large bowl, mix together the tomatoes, avocados, mango, onion, parsley and peppers.
- In a separate bowl or jug mix together the lemon juice, sugar, cumin, chilli and seasoning.
- Pour the dressing over the salad and mix in well.
- Chill until ready to serve.

Debby Anglesey © Copyright 2000

Sweet and sour sauce

CF, EF, SF, SGF, TF, YF

Ingredients

2 tbsp gf vinegar
¼ cup honey
2 tbsp lemon juice
1 tsp gf paprika

Method

- Mix all ingredients together well and then heat through gently.

New England salad dressing

CF, EF, SF, TF, YF

Ingredients

1 tsp fresh lime juice
¼ cup minced onion
½ tsp salt
¼ tsp pepper
½ cup gf oil
¾ cup sugar
¼ cup gf vinegar

Method

- Combine all ingredients together well.

Marinade for meat and poultry

CF, EF, SF, SGF*, TF, YF

Ingredients

¼ cup gf vinegar
3 tbsp sunflower oil
I clove garlic (minced)
dash of gf cayenne pepper (optional)

3 tbsp water
½ tsp salt
¼ tsp gf ground black pepper
2 tsp sugar (optional)

Method

- Combine together all of the ingredients.
- Place the marinade and the meat/poultry in a zip-lock bag.
- Place bag in fridge, turning the meat occasionally.
- Allow meat to marinate for at least 30 minutes.

This makes enough to marinade 2 lb of meat.

Variation

- *The variations on this are almost endless, by adding one or more gf dried herbs or spices.*

Debby Anglesey © Copyright 2000

Ranch style dressing

CF, EF, FF, SGF*, TF, YF

Ingredients

I cup plain soya yoghurt
⅛ tsp gf garlic granules
⅛ tsp gf onion granules or powder
½ tsp gf dried parsley
½ tsp gf dried dill

¼ tsp gf dried thyme
dash gf cayenne pepper
I tsp sunflower oil
½ tsp gf vinegar
a little sugar to taste (optional)
seasoning to taste

Method

- Blend all ingredients together well.

Can be used either as a salad dressing or dip.

Debby Anglesey © Copyright 2000

Green goddess dressing

CF, EG, SF, TF, YF

Ingredients

1 avocado (cut into chunks)
½ lemon (juice only)
1 clove garlic
¼ tsp salt
gf black pepper to taste

½ cup olive oil
¼ tsp gf dried thyme
½ tsp gf dried dill
½–1 tsp sugar
⅓ cup gluten and dairy free milk
    alternative

Method

- Place all ingredients but the milk into a food processor and blend to a smooth paste.
- Gradually add the milk, blending again after every addition.
- More milk can be added until the required consistency is achieved.

Debby Anglesey © Copyright 2000

Mediterranean tomato relish

CF, EF, FF, SF, TF, YF

Ingredients

1 lb (450g) tomatoes (either skinned, fresh tomatoes or drained, chopped, tinned tomatoes)
1 onion (finely chopped)
1 pepper (finely diced)
1 clove garlic (chopped)

4 oz (125g) unrefined sugar
¼ pint (150ml) white wine vinegar
¼ tsp gf dried basil
¼ tsp gf dried thyme
½–1 tsp sea salt

Method

- Mix all ingredients together in a large saucepan.
- Bring to the boil and then simmer for 40 minutes.
- Allow the relish to cool before use.
- Can be stored in the fridge in an airtight container for 3 weeks.

Marilyn Le Breton © Copyright 2001

Tzaziki dip

CF, EF, FF, SGF, TF, YF

Ingredients

½ cucumber
5 fl oz (175ml) plain organic soya yoghurt
   (Provamel)
2 tsp olive oil

1 tsp gf mint sauce
¼ tsp gf garlic granules
salt to taste

Method

- Peel cucumber, scoop out the seeds and dice.
- Mix together the yoghurt, olive oil, mint sauce and garlic granules and gently stir in the cucumber. Add salt if necessary.
- Chill before serving.

Marilyn Le Breton © Copyright 2001

Creamy herb and garlic dip

CF, FF, TF, YF

Ingredients

8 oz (225g) gluten free soya cream cheese
4 tbsp gluten and dairy free mayonnaise
½ tsp gf dried mixed herbs

4 spring onions (finely chopped)
½ tsp gf garlic granules
seasoning to taste

Method

- Blend together the cream cheese and mayonnaise until smooth and well combined.
- Add the herbs, spring onions, garlic granules and seasoning and stir in well.
- Chill before serving.

Marilyn Le Breton © Copyright 2001

Alternative guacamole dip

CF, EF, FF, SGF, TF, YF

Ingredients

6 oz (175g) frozen peas (defrosted but not cooked)

2 cloves garlic

1 tbsp gluten and dairy free plain soya yoghurt (Provamel Organic Yofu)

1 tsp gf cumin

½ tsp ground black pepper

½ tsp gf dried mint

salt to taste

Method

- Place all ingredients in a liquidiser and blend to a smooth paste.

This can also be used as a salad dressing or sandwich spread.

Anne Pemberton, Leeds © Copyright

Pesto

CF, EF, FF, SF, SGF, TF, YF

Ingredients

2 oz (60g) fresh basil leaves (roughly chopped)

2 garlic cloves (crushed)

2 tbsp pine nuts

4 fl oz (100ml) olive oil

Method

- Place all the ingredients in a blender at high speed until the mixture is very creamy.
- Chill and keep in an airtight jar in the fridge.

Marilyn Le Breton © Copyright 2001

Greek Fava Dip

CF, EF, SF, SGF, TF, YF

Ingredients

8 oz (225g) split yellow peas
1 onion (finely chopped)
3 tbsp organic sunflower oil
1 clove garlic (finely chopped)

1 tbsp lemon juice
1–2 tsp gf dried dill
¾ pint (450ml) water
sea salt to taste

Method

- In a large saucepan cover the split peas, onion, 1 tbsp of the oil, dill and the garlic with the water.
- Bring the water to the boil and then reduce the heat, cover the pan and simmer for 40 minutes.
- Whilst the mixture is still hot, strain off any excess liquid and then puree the remaining mixture in a blender.
- When the mixture has cooled, mix together the remaining 2 tbsp of oil and the lemon juice and mix into the dip well.

Marilyn Le Breton © Copyright 2001

Taramasalata

CF, EF, SF, SGF, TF, YF

Ingredients

8 oz (225g) smoked cod roe
1 garlic clove (crushed)
2 oz (50–60g) fresh gluten and dairy free breadcrumbs

1 onion (finely chopped)
1 lemon (juice only)
¼ pint (150ml) olive oil
6 tbsp water

Method

- Place the cod roe in the blender and puree.
- Add the lemon juice, breadcrumbs, onion and garlic and pulse for a few seconds in the blender.
- Gradually add the oil, blending well after each addition.
- Add the cold water and blend again.
- Chill before serving.

Marilyn Le Breton © Copyright 2001

Mayonnaise

CF, SF, SGF, TF, YF

Ingredients

I egg yolk at room temperature
½ tsp gf mustard powder *or* ¼ tsp gf
    mustard
½ tsp salt
¼ tsp fresh ground black pepper

I tbsp gf white wine vinegar *or*
    lemon juice
¼ pint (150ml) organic
    sunflower oil

Method

- Mix together the egg yolk, mustard powder, seasoning and I tsp of the vinegar/lemon juice.
- Add the oil, little by little, continuously whisking until the mixture becomes thick and smooth.
- Slowly add the remaining vinegar/lemon juice and mix well.

This will keep for 3 days in the fridge in an airtight container.

Marilyn Le Breton © Copyright 2001

Quick fish pâté

CF, EF, FF, SGF, TF, YF

Ingredients

I tin of oily fish (mackerel, pilchards,
    sardines, salmon or tuna)
gluten and dairy free cream cheese

Method

- Remove any bones and skin from the fish and flake down the flesh.
- Mix with cream cheese until the desired consistency has been achieved.
- Chill before using.

Jacqui Jackson © Copyright 2001

Chicken liver pâté

CF, EF, SF, SGF, TF, YF

Ingredients

1 onion (finely chopped)
2 oz (50g) dairy free margarine
1 lb (450g) chicken livers (chopped)
1 garlic clove (finely chopped)

½ tsp mixed gf dried herbs
1 tsp lemon juice
Salt and fresh ground black
   pepper to taste

Method

- Melt the margarine in a pan and gently sauté the onions.
- Add the chicken livers, herbs and garlic and cook on a moderate heat for 10 minutes, stirring occasionally.
- Remove the pan from heat and stir in the lemon.
- Allow the mixture to cool and place in a blender. Blend until it is a smooth consistency.
- Stir in the required seasoning.
- Chill for a minimum of 2 hours before use.

If your child rejects the pâté, don't throw it away. Add a couple of teaspoons (or more) of brandy and you will have a really tasty adult pâté.

Marilyn Le Breton © Copyright 2001

Belgian chicken liver pâté

CF, EF, FF, SF, SGF, TF, YF

Ingredients

1¼ lb (500g) chicken livers
9 oz (250g) dairy free margarine
1 small onion (finely grated)
1 bay leaf

1 sprig of fresh thyme
1 tsp freshly ground mustard
    seeds
½ tsp cloves
seasoning to taste

Method

- Trim the chicken livers to remove any green bits and wash under cold running water.
- Place the livers in a medium sized saucepan and cover with water. Add the bay leaf, thyme and a good pinch of freshly ground sea salt.
- Bring to the boil, cover the pan and simmer for 20 minutes.
- Drain off the water, discard the bay leaf and thyme and leave the livers to cool.
- Beat the spices into the margarine and then stir in the onion.
- In a food processor, blend down the livers until they are a smooth paste.
- Gradually fold the margarine mix into the liver mix (not the other way around).
- Season to taste and chill before serving.

This pâté freezes well.

Maddalena Feliciello, Leeds © Copyright

Sauces, Stocks and Gravies

White sauce

EF, FF, SF, SGF, TF, YF

Ingredients

2 tbsp cornflour
½ pint (300ml) gluten and dairy free milk
    alternative
1 tbsp dairy free margarine

Method

- In a cup or small bowl, mix the cornflour with 4 tbsp of the milk into a smooth paste.
- Place the remaining milk in a saucepan and bring to the boil.
- Add the cornflour paste, stirring or whisking vigorously, to prevent lumps.
- Bring the sauce back to boiling, stirring continuously, until it thickens.
- Reduce heat and cook for a further 2–3 minutes.
- Stir in the margarine; when melted, serve.

Variation

- *You can make a quick pasta sauce using this white sauce. Add some sautéed finely chopped onions and thinly sliced mushrooms. A sprinkle of gf garlic granules adds some extra flavour too.*

Marilyn Le Breton © Copyright 2001

White sauce

CF, EF, FF, SF, SGF, TF, YF

Ingredients

1 oz (30g) DS All Purpose Flour Mix
1 oz (30g) dairy free margarine
½ pint (300ml) gluten and dairy free milk
   alternative
seasoning to taste

Method

- In a small bowl, blend together the flour and sufficient milk to produce a smooth paste.
- Place the margarine and remaining milk in a pan and bring to the boil.
- Gradually, stir in the flour paste and heat through.
- Season and reduce the heat and simmer for 2 minutes.

Dietary Specialities © Copyright Nutrition Point 2001

White sauce

CF, EF, FF, SF, SGF, TF, YF

Ingredients

1 oz (25g) potato starch flour or white rice
   flour
1 oz (25g) dairy free margarine
5–6 fl oz (150–175ml) gluten and dairy free
   milk alternative (warmed)

seasoning (for savoury sauce)
or
gf vanilla extract (for sweet
   sauce)

Method

- In a saucepan, melt the margarine and stir in the flour to form a roux. Allow this mixture to cool.
- Return to heat and gradually add the warmed milk, stirring all the time.
- Simmer for approximately 2–3 minutes.
- If the sauce is too thick, add a little more milk until desired consistency is achieved.
- Add either the seasoning or vanilla extract, stir in and serve.

Barbara's Kitchen © Copyright 2000

Parsley sauce

EF, FF, SF, SGF, TF, YF

Ingredients

2 tbsp cornflour
½ pint (300ml) gluten and dairy free milk
    alternative
1 tbsp dairy free margarine
2 tbsp fresh parsley (finely chopped)

Method

- In a cup or small bowl, mix the cornflour with 4 tbsp of the milk into a smooth paste.
- Place the remaining milk in a saucepan and bring to the boil.
- Sprinkle in the parsley and mix well.
- Add the cornflour paste, stirring or whisking vigorously, to prevent lumps.
- Bring the sauce back to boiling, stirring continuously, until it thickens.
- Reduce heat and cook for a further 2–3 minutes.
- Stir in the margarine. When it has melted, serve.

Marilyn Le Breton © Copyright 2001

Onion sauce

EF, FF, SF, SGF, TF, YF

Ingredients

2 tbsp cornflour
½ pint (300ml) gluten and dairy free milk
    alternative
1 tbsp dairy free margarine
1 onion (finely chopped)
1 tsp dairy free margarine

Method

- Melt the margarine in a pan and sauté the onions over a very low heat for 10–15 minutes, until they are translucent and soft. Do not let the onions brown.
- Drain off excess oil and reserve onions.
- In a cup or small bowl, mix the cornflour with 4 tbsp of the milk alternative into a smooth paste.
- Place the remaining milk in a saucepan and bring to the boil.
- Add the onions and stir in well.
- Add the cornflour paste, stirring or whisking vigorously, to prevent lumps.
- Bring the sauce back to boiling, stirring continuously, until it thickens.
- Reduce heat, and cook for a further 2–3 minutes.
- Stir in the margarine. When it has melted, serve.
- If a very smooth sauce is required, place sauce in a food processor and blend down.

Marilyn Le Breton © Copyright 2001

Quick tomato sauce

CF, EF, FF, SF, YF

Ingredients

14 oz (400g) can chopped tomatoes
1 tsp gf dried mixed herbs
1 tbsp tomato puree
1 tsp caster sugar

¼ pint (150ml) homemade
  vegetable stock
1 large clove garlic (finely
  chopped)

Method

- Place all ingredients in a large pan and bring the liquid to the boil.
- Reduce heat and simmer for 15–20 minutes until the liquid has reduced and the sauce has thickened.
- Place sauce in a food processor and blend down until smooth.

Sauce keeps for 5–7 days in an airtight container in the fridge.
Makes a great dip or burger relish as well as a sauce.

Marilyn Le Breton © Copyright 2001

Tomato sauce

CF, EF, FF, SF, YF

Ingredients

15 oz (425g) can chopped tomatoes
2 tbsp tomato puree
2 tbsp olive oil
1 small onion (chopped)
1 garlic clove (crushed)

2 tbsp chopped parsley
1 tsp gf dried oregano
2 bay leaves
1 tsp sugar

Method

- Heat the oil in a pan over a medium heat and fry the onion until it is translucent.
- Add the garlic and fry for a further minute.
- Stir in the chopped tomatoes, parsley, oregano, bay leaves, tomato puree and sugar. Bring the sauce to the boil.
- Reduce heat and simmer uncovered for 15–20 minutes until the sauce has been reduced to half. Taste and adjust seasoning if necessary.
- Discard bay leaves prior to serving.

Jacqui Jackson © Copyright 2001

Quick curry sauce

CF, EF, FF, SGF, TF, YF

Ingredients

2 tbsp organic sunflower oil
1 onion (chopped)
1 clove garlic (finely chopped)
2 tsp gf dried coriander
1 tsp gf dried fenugreek seeds
1 tsp gf ground cumin
2 tsp gf dried turmeric powder

2½ oz (70g) lentils (red or yellow)
1 pint (600ml) homemade vegetable stock
seasoning
¼ pint (150ml) plain, organic soya yoghurt

Method

- Heat the oil in a pan, add the onion and garlic and sauté for 5 minutes, or until they have softened.
- Add the spices and cook for a further 2 minutes, stirring occasionally.
- Add the lentils and stock and bring the liquid to the boil.
- Reduce the heat, cover the pan and simmer for 30 minutes or until the lentils are very soft.
- Take off heat and season. Stir in yoghurt just before serving.

Marilyn Le Breton © Copyright 2001

Chicken stock

CF, EF, FF, SF, SGF, TF, YF

Ingredients

I small fresh organic chicken

Method

- Trim the breasts from the chicken and freeze for later use.
- Chop up the rest of the chicken and place in a large saucepan.
- Cover the chicken pieces with water 2" above the chicken.
- Bring the water to simmer.
- Continue to simmer for 2–3 hours. Do not let the water boil.
- Skim off the froth from the surface.
- Strain off the liquid and leave overnight in the fridge.
- Scrape off the fat from the top.

Makes 2–3 pints of stock.

Chicken stock

CF, EF, FF, SF, SGF, TF, YF.

Ingredients

whole chicken carcass (with some meat
    still attached)
1 large onion (sliced)
2 carrots (sliced)
2 celery sticks (chopped)
1 bay leaf or gf bouquet garni
3 pints (1.7 litres) water

Method

- Break up the chicken carcass into a large saucepan and add the water, vegetables and herbs. Stir together well.
- Bring the stock to the boil and then reduce the heat. Partially cover and simmer for 2 hours.
- Remove from heat and skim off the fat that has risen to the surface.
- Strain the stock through a fine sieve and allow the liquid to cool.
- When it is cold, scoop off the fat.

Makes approximately 1½ pints (900ml) and freezes well.
For ease of use, pour into an ice-cube tray and place in freezer bag when frozen.
Will defrost quickly when needed and only a little is wanted.

Marilyn Le Breton © Copyright 2001

Beef stock

CF, EF, FF, SF, SGF, TF, YF

Ingredients

I lb (450g) beef (roughly diced)
I onion or 2 leeks (chopped)
I carrot (chopped)

2 celery sticks (chopped)
I gf bouquet garni
3 pints (1.7 litres) water

Method

- Heat a little sunflower oil in a large saucepan and brown the meat.
- Add the water, vegetables and herbs and stir in well.
- Bring to the boil, reduce heat and partially cover the pan.
- Simmer for 2 hours.
- Remove from heat and skim off the fat and scum.
- Strain through a fine sieve and allow liquid to cool.
- When cold, scoop off the fat.

Makes I ½ (900ml) pints and freezes well.

Marilyn Le Breton © Copyright 2001

Vegetable stock

CF, EF, FF, SF, SGF, TF, YF

Ingredients

I large onion (chopped)
2 carrots (sliced)
I leek (sliced)
3 celery sticks (roughly chopped)

I turnip (chopped)
I parsnip (chopped)
I gf bouquet garni
3 pints (1.7 litres) water

Method

- Put all the ingredients into a large saucepan and stir together.
- Bring to the boil. Partially cover and simmer for I hour.
- Remove from heat and remove all the scum from the top.

Makes approximately 2½ pints (2.4 litres).
Freezes well.

Marilyn Le Breton © Copyright 2001

Brown onion stock

CF, EF, FF, SF, SGF, TF, YF

Ingredients

2 tbsp sunflower oil
2 large onions (chopped)
3 cloves garlic (roughly chopped)
2 sticks celery (chopped)
2 carrots (finely chopped)
2 tsp gf dried mixed herbs
seasoning
2 pints (1.1 litres) water

Method

- Heat oil in a large pan and fry onions over a medium heat for approximately 10 minutes, stirring all the time, until they have caramelised (turned dark brown). Do not let the onions burn.
- Add the garlic, celery, carrots and seasoning. Cook over a high heat for 5 minutes, until the vegetables have begun to brown.
- Add the water and bring liquid to the boil.
- Reduce the heat and allow the stock to simmer gently for 30 minutes.
- Strain the vegetables and reserve the stock.
- Either use as is or to reduce the amount and intensify the flavour, return stock to a clean pan and boil rapidly until the amount required remains.

Keeps for 3 days in the fridge.
Freezes well.

Marilyn Le Breton © Copyright 2001

Onion gravy

CF, EF, FF, SF, SGF, TF, YF

Ingredients

3 large onions (chopped)
3 tbsp sunflower oil
2 cups water *or* I cup water and I cup
    gluten and dairy milk alternative
3 tbsp gf flour
seasoning to taste

Method

- Sauté the onions in the oil until they become a rich brown colour.
- Drain off the excess oil and blend in a food processor with I cup of water and the flour until a smooth paste.
- Return mix to pan and add seasoning and remaining cup of water (or cup of milk).
- Bring to the boil and simmer for 3 minutes.

Debby Anglesey © Copyright 2000

Pastry

Pastry

CF, EF*, FF, SF, SGF, TF, YF

Ingredients

1 cup white rice flour
½ cup tapioca starch flour
¼ cup potato starch flour
¼ tsp salt
2 tsp xanthan gum

4 oz (125g) dairy free margarine
1 large egg (beaten) *or* ¼ cup of
   extra iced water
1 tsp cider vinegar or water
3 tbsp ice cold water

Method

If using a food processor (the easiest way)

- Place all ingredients into the machine and using the 'pulse' setting, combine.

By hand

- Mix together the flours, salt and xanthan gum.
- Rub in the margarine, but not too much. The mixture should resemble baked beans rather than breadcrumbs.
- In a separate bowl, whisk together the egg (if using), vinegar/water and iced water.
- Slowly stir the egg mix into the flour mix, until a ball is formed.
- Knead the pastry with a little gf flour for 2–3 minutes.
- Cover the pastry and place in the fridge for 1 hour to rest.
- If the pastry is a little hard when removed from the fridge, knead again a little.
- It can be frozen at this stage.
- Roll out on a floured surface, as required.
- The pastry be cooked at GM7, 425F, 220C, for 10–12 minutes if blind baking.

Barbara's Kitchen © Copyright 2000

Editor's note: This is a really good, easy, tasty pastry. For those of you who have tried and been reduced to tears by making pastry, I definitely recommend this recipe. It is as easy to handle as traditional shortcrust pastry, can be rolled thinly without having to be placed between parchment paper and doesn't crumble or break. Just remember to handle sparingly and to keep as cold as possible.

Pastry for sweet dishes

CF, FF, SF, TF, YF

Ingredients

8 oz (225g) gf flour mix
1 tsp xanthan gum
½ tsp salt
2 tsp icing sugar

1 egg yolk (beaten and chilled)
4 oz (125g) dairy free margarine (chilled)
1–2 tsp iced water

Method

- Mix and sift together the flour, xanthan gum, salt and icing sugar.
- Add the margarine as one lump. Using 2 knifes in a scissor action, cut the fat into the flour.
- Lightly rub the remaining lumps with finger tips until the mixture resembles breadcrumbs. Do not over rub.
- Make a well in the centre and add the egg. Bring the mixture together and add a little of the iced water as necessary.
- Wrap in clingfilm and chill before use.
- Chill again after rolling out.
- Cook at GM5, 375F, 190C.
- If baking blind brush the bottom of the flan with egg white to provide a protective film.

Variations

- *Various flavourings can be used such as gf vanilla extract.*
- *1 oz (25g) of the flour mix can be substituted with 1 oz (25g) of ground almonds.*

Maddalena Feliciello, Leeds © Copyright

Potato pastry

CF, FF, SF, SGF, TF, YF

Ingredients

4 oz (125g) cold mashed potato
2 oz (50g) gf flour (Doves Farm)
2 oz (50g) gram flour
2 oz (50g) potato flour

1 tsp xanthan gum
3 oz (90g) dairy free margarine
seasoning
1 medium egg (beaten)
cold water to bind if needed

Method

- Mix together the flours and xanthan gum.
- Rub in the margarine.
- Stir in the egg.
- Mix in the mashed potato with a wooden spoon.
- Mould with hands to form pastry adding a little water if necessary.
- Cook at GM6, 400F, 200C for 20–25 minutes.

Angela Deakin © Copyright

Shortcrust pastry

CF, FF, SF, SGF, TF, YF

Ingredients

1 sachet DS All Purpose Flour Mix
4 oz (125g) dairy margarine
1 small egg (beaten)
2 tbsp water

Method

- Empty the flour sachet into a bowl and fork in the margarine until the mix resembles breadcrumbs.
- Stir in the egg and the water to give a soft but not sticky dough.
- On a gf floured surface, knead the dough for 1–2 minutes.
- Roll out and use as desired.

Dietary Specialities © Nutrition Point 2001

Candy

Our sincerest thanks go to Diane Hartman for her huge contribution to this section.

Candy Making Tips

- Rinse the pan with ice cold water immediately before adding ingredients; this will prevent them from sticking to the pan during cooking.

- When the candy mixture begins to boil, remove the spoon. Thoroughly wash and dry spoon before returning it to the pan. Otherwise, residual sugar crystals on the unwashed spoon will cause the entire batch of candy to become grainy.

- Do not attach the candy thermometer to the pan until after the mixture has begun to boil.

- Allow the candy thermometer to stand in a glass of warm water before introducing it to the hot liquid; this will prevent the thermometer from cracking when it is immersed in the boiling mixture. Drastic changes in temperatures can result in glass products breaking.

- To check the accuracy of your candy thermometer, bring a saucepan of water to the boil. Water should begin to boil at 212F. If it begins to boil at a different temperature (e.g., 210F), adjust the thermometer accordingly. Weather conditions, especially heat and humidity, can adversely affect candy making. Accuracy is vital, therefore it is worthwhile following this procedure every time you make candy.

- A wooden spoon or a dowel rod placed across the pan will help to prevent the mixture from boiling over. The spoon handle or rod will break the bubbles as they rise to the top of the pan.

- Use a pan that has adequate space to allow for the expansion of the contents. Some of the ingredients will increase in volume as they boil or become heated.

- Do not stir the mixture once it begins to boil. Stirring will result in a grainy and poor textured candy.

- A double boiler should be used for melting chocolate; this helps to prevent the chocolate from scorching or burning.

- When using melted chocolate for dipping and coating candy, add one tablespoon of cf margarine to every cup of chocolate used. This will help it stick evenly to the candy and provide a glossier finish.

- Parchment paper provides an excellent non-stick surface for candy and can withstand moderate heat. Wax paper should not be used for items that are potentially at a high temperature.

- Designate a pair of sterile, stainless steel scissors for cutting 'taffy' and caramel into bite sized pieces.

Hard butterscotch candy

CF, EF, FF, SF, TF, YF

Ingredients

2 cups gluten and dairy light brown sugar
½ cup dairy free margarine
¼ cup water
1 tbsp apple cider vinegar

Method

- In a medium saucepan, combine all of the ingredients and bring mixture to the boil.
- Attach the candy thermometer after the mixture begins to boil.
- Cook without stirring until the temperature reaches 'crack' stage.
- Carefully pour the hot mixture into a well-greased shallow cake tin or cookie tray.
- Score the top of the mixture into the required sizes when it is partially hardened.
- Crack into pieces along scoring, when cool.
- Or pour into well-greased candy moulds and allow mixture to cool for several hours, prior to removing.

Caramel candy

CF, EF, FF, TF, YF

Ingredients

3 cups granulated sugar
¼ cup water
I cup gluten and dairy free brown sugar
I cup soya milk or liquid Dari-free

¾ cup gluten and dairy free milk substitute mixed with ⅓ cup melted dairy margarine
I tsp gf vanilla extract

Method

- In a large saucepan combine all of the ingredients, except the vanilla extract.
- Dissolve the sugar, by cooking over a low heat and stirring constantly.
- Increase the temperature to medium and bring the mixture to 235F (softball stage).
- Remove from heat and stir in the vanilla extract.
- Pour mixture into a chilled and greased 7"x11" baking tray.
- Allow candy to cool and cut into small pieces.

This mixture is also good for coating apples, immediately after adding the vanilla extract.

Diane Hartman © Copyright 1999

Honey and lemon candy sticks

CF, EF, SF, TF, YF

Ingredients

2 cups sugar
½ cup honey

½ cup water
⅛ cup lemon juice
I tsp gf lemon extract

Method

- Combine all the ingredients and bring to the boil, stirring occasionally.
- Remove spoon and attach candy thermometer to pan.
- Cook until mixture reaches crack stage.
- Allow the mixture to cool for 20–30 minutes in pan and then transfer onto a well-greased slab or platter.
- Pull the mixture until it is glossy and then form into sticks.

Diane Hartman © Copyright 1999

Maple cream centres

CF, EF, FF, SF, TF, YF

Ingredients

2 lbs (900g) maple sugar

¼ tsp cream of tartar

I cup water

Method

- Combine ingredients together in a medium saucepan.
- Stir constantly and bring to the boil.
- Attach the candy thermometer and allow the mixture to the boil gently, until it reaches the softball stage. Do not stir.
- Remove from heat and allow the mixture to cool for approximately 30 minutes.
- Using a mixer, beat until creamy.
- Transfer the mixture to a well-greased shallow baking tray, cover and chill for approximately I hour.
- Cut the candy into squares and turn the pan out onto a large cookie tray.
- Dip the chilled squares into melted gf/cf chocolate if desired.

Diane Hartman © Copyright 2000

Peppermint sticks

CF, EF, FF, SF, TF, YF

Ingredients

2 cups caster sugar

½ cup honey

¼ tsp cream of tartar

½ cup water

I tsp gf peppermint flavouring

Method

- Combine all the ingredients in a saucepan and bring to the boil stirring occasionally.
- Remove the spoon and attach the candy thermometer to the pan.
- Do not stir the mixture. Allow it to reach the crack stage.
- Remove from heat and allow to cool for 20–30 minutes.
- Transfer the candy onto a well-greased slab or platter and pull it until it becomes glossy.
- Roll the candy into sticks.

Diane Hartman © Copyright 1999

Mock tootsie rolls

CF, EF, FF, SF, TF, YF

Ingredients

1 cup clover honey
1 cup gluten and dairy free cocoa powder
    (Ah! Laska Baker's Cocoa)
1½ cups Dari Free substitute milk powder
1 cup icing sugar

Method

- Heat honey in the microwave on high power for 20–30 seconds (do not allow to boil).
- In a large bowl, combine together the honey and all the other ingredients until smooth and creamy (this does take some time). Using lightly greased hands is preferable as it keeps the mixture warm and easier to work.
- If the mixture appears dry and crumbly, do not be tempted to add any further liquid.
- The mixture is ready when it appears dull and is still slightly tacky.
- Transfer the mixture to parchment paper and form into small rolls.
- Wrap each roll in greaseproof paper and twist the ends (so they are wrapped like boiled sweets).
- Store in an airtight container in the fridge.

Miscellaneous Food Items

Rice milk

CF, EF, FF, SF, SGF, TF, YF

Ingredients

2–3 cups cooked rice (white or brown or a
    mixture)
1 cup very hot water

Method

- Place the cooked rice into a blender.
- Add the water and blend.
- Add more hot water if necessary to achieve the desired consistency.
- Strain the mixture through a fine sieve or muslin cloth.
- Store in an airtight container in the fridge for a maximum of 4 days.
- Shake before use.

Barbara's Kitchen © Copyright 2000

Coconut milk

CF, EF, SF, SGF, TF, YF

Ingredients

12 oz (350g) dessicated un-sulphated
    coconut
1½ pints (900ml) boiling water

Method

- Stir the coconut into the boiling water.
- Allow to seep in for 30–60 minutes.
- Strain off and keep the water. Press the coconut with the back of a spoon, to extract as much of the liquid as possible.
- Store in the fridge in an airtight container. Keeps for 3–4 days.

Marilyn Le Breton © Copyright 2001

Potato milk

CF, EF, FF, SGF, SGF, TF, YF

Ingredients

1 medium potato (peeled and cooked: check there are no blemishes or green spots)

1 tbsp oil

1 cup of hot water

Method

- Roughly chop the potato and place in a food blender with the oil and water.
- Blend down and slowly add more water if necessary to achieve the desired consistency.
- Strain through a fine sieve or muslin cloth.
- Store in an airtight container and keep in the fridge: will keep for a maximum of 4 days.
- Shake before use.

Barbara's Kitchen © Copyright 2000

Herb dumplings

CF, EF, FF, SF, SGF, TF, YF

Ingredients

1½ oz (50g) tapioca starch flour
1½ oz (50g) white rice flour
1½ oz (50g) dairy free margarine
2 tsp gf baking powder

1 tsp xanthan gum
½ tsp gf mixed herbs
pinch of salt
water to soften dough

Method

- Gently mix together the flours, baking powder, xanthan gum and salt.
- Chop the margarine into the flour until a crumble texture has been achieved.
- Add the mixed herbs and enough water to make the flour into a dough.
- Divide the dough into 3 and shape into dumplings.
- Place the dumplings on top of the stew or casserole when only 15 minutes cooking time remains.

Barbara's Kitchen © Copyright 2000

Yorkshire pudding

CF, FF, SF, SGF, TF YF

Ingredients

3 dessert spoons gf flour mix
2 large eggs (room temperature)
¼ tsp gf baking powder
pinch of salt

½ pint (300ml) gluten and dairy
free milk alternative
oil

Method

- Pre-heat oven to GM7, 425F, 220C.
- Mix all the ingredients together to form a smooth, runny batter.
- Leave the batter to stand for at least 10 minutes.
- Place a small amount of oil into the bottom of 4 Yorkshire pudding tins and heat these in the oven until the oil is smoking.
- Stir the batter again and divide between the 4 tins.
- Bake for approximately 15 minutes. Do not open oven door during this time.

Barbara's Kitchen © Copyright 2000

Yorkshire pudding II

CF, FF, SF, SGF, TF, YF

Ingredients

2 oz (60g) white rice flour
2 oz (60g) tapioca starch flour
2 tsp xanthan gum

2 medium eggs
gluten and dairy free milk
alternative: enough to make
a batter mix

Method

- Pre-heat oven GM7, 425F, 220C.
- Mix all the ingredients together to form a smooth, runny batter.
- Leave the batter to stand for at least 10 minutes.
- Place a small amount of oil into the bottom of 4 Yorkshire pudding tins and heat these in the oven until the oil is smoking.
- Stir the batter again and divide between the 4 tins.
- Bake for approximately 15 minutes. Do not open oven door during this time.

Barbara's Kitchen © Copyright 2000

Mini Yorkshire puddings

CF, FF, SF, SGF, TF, YF

Ingredients

¼ pint (150ml) water
2 oz (60g) dairy free margarine
2½ oz (75g) DS All Purpose Flour Mix
2 medium eggs (beaten)

Method

- Pre-heat oven to GM6, 400F, 200C.
- In a saucepan, gently heat together the water and margarine, until the margarine has melted and the water is boiling.
- Remove from heat and add the flour. Stir in well, until a soft ball of dough is formed in the pan.
- Cool the dough slightly and then beat in the eggs. The mixture should be smooth and firm enough to stand in soft peaks.
- Divide the mixture between 12 well-greased muffin tins. Use the back of a wooden spoon to spread the mixture evenly across the tins, dipping it slightly in the centre of the tin.
- Bake the puddings for 20–25 minutes until well risen and golden.
- Serve immediately.

Suitable for freezing. Freeze individually, in polybags. Re-heat for 5–8 minutes in a hot oven.

Dietary Specialities © Copyright 2001 Nutrition Point

Wild rice stuffing

CF, EF, FF, SF, SGF, TF, YF

Ingredients

4 ⅔ cups homemade chicken stock (see Stocks section for recipes)
½ cup gluten and dairy free milk alternative or water
⅔ cup uncooked wild rice
½ tsp salt
¼ tsp pepper
½ tsp gf dried thyme
½ tsp gf dried sage

1 ½ cups shredded or julienne carrots
¼ cup finely chopped celery
½ cup chopped onion
1 cup sliced fresh mushrooms (optional)
1 ½ cups uncooked, instant white rice
2 tbsp oil or dairy free margarine

Method

- In a large saucepan combine together the stock, water/milk alternative and herbs and bring to the boil.
- Add the wild rice, cover the pan and simmer for 10 minutes.
- Add the celery, carrots, onions and mushrooms (if using). Simmer for another 20 minutes or until the vegetables are tender.
- Stir in the white rice and margarine (or oil). Replace the lid and simmer for a further 5–7 minutes.

Allow the stuffing to get completely cold before using. If the mixture is still warm there is a danger of food poisoning.

Diane Hartman © Copyright 1997

Sage and onion stuffing

CF, SF, SGF, TF, YF*

Ingredients

2 large onions (finely chopped)

2 oz (50g) dairy free margarine

4 tbsp fresh sage (chopped) *or* 3 tsp gf dried sage

4 oz (125g) gluten and dairy free breadcrumbs

½ lemon (zest only, finely grated)

1 organic egg (beaten)

Method

- Gently fry onion in the margarine until soft.

- Add sage, breadcrumbs, lemon zest and egg and mix them in together well.

- Allow the stuffing to get completely cold, before using.

Marilyn Le Breton © Copyright 2001

Turkey stuffing

CF, EF, FF, SF, SGF, TF, YF

Ingredients

5–6 cups gluten and dairy free bread, torn into 2" pieces

2 tbsp oil

3 cups celery (chopped)

2 cups onion (chopped)

1 tsp salt

1 tsp gf dried coriander

1 tsp gf dried thyme

1 tsp gf dried sage

ground black pepper to taste

1½ cups of homemade gluten and dairy free chicken stock (see Stocks section for recipes)

Method

- Heat the oil in a large frying pan over a medium heat and sauté the celery and onions until the onions have softened.

- Add the salt, coriander, thyme, sage and pepper and stir in.

- Pour in the stock and simmer over a low heat for 15–20 minutes.

- Add the bread pieces and stir in well so that they become soaked in the liquid.

- Either bake in the oven for 40–50 minutes at GM6, 400F, 200C or, if using to stuff poultry, allow to cool completely before use to prevent food poisoning.

Miss Roben's © Copyright 2001

Peanut butter

CF, EF, FF, SF, SGF*, TF, YF

Ingredients

3 cups roasted and shelled organic peanuts
2–3 tbsp organic sunflower oil
1 tsp salt

1–2 tsp unrefined caster sugar (optional)

Method

- In a food processor, blend down the nuts, salt, 2 tbsp of sunflower oil and 1 tsp of sugar (if using).
- Add the rest of the oil, until you achieve the desired spreadable consistency.
- Add the rest of the sugar to achieve the desired taste.

Store in the fridge in an airtight container.

Variations

- *Other nuts can be substituted weight for weight for the peanuts; cashews are particularly good.*

Chestnut puree

CF, EF, FF, SF, SGF, TF, YF

Ingredients

2 cups chestnuts (shelled and skin removed)

water
salt to taste

Method

- Place the chestnuts in a saucepan and add just enough water to cover them.
- Simmer over a low heat for approximately 1 hour or until the chestnuts have softened. Check them during cooking to ensure the mixture does not get too dry.
- Place in a food processor and blend down to a smooth puree.
- Add salt to taste.

Keep in the fridge in an airtight container.

Custard

FF, SF, TF, YF

Ingredients

½ pint (300ml) gluten and dairy free milk alternative
1 tbsp cornflour
1 tsp gf vanilla extract
1 egg beaten
½–1 tbsp unrefined caster sugar

Method

- Mix together in a heatproof bowl, the egg, cornflour and vanilla with a little of the milk, to form a smooth creamy paste.
- Heat the remainder of the milk, until it almost reaches boiling point.
- Pour the milk into the paste and stir constantly.
- Return the custard to the saucepan and re-heat, until the custard thickens.
- Serve immediately.

Eve Jackson © Copyright 2001

Chocolate custard

EF, FF, SF, TF, YF

Ingredients

2 tbsp gluten and dairy free cocoa powder
3 tsp cornflour
2–3 tbsp unrefined caster sugar
1 pint (600ml) gluten and dairy free milk alternative

Method

- Sift together the cocoa powder, cornflour and sugar.
- Blend into a smooth paste with a little milk.
- In a saucepan, heat the remaining milk, until it is almost boiling.
- Pour the milk onto the cocoa mixture and stir continuously.
- Transfer the mix back to the saucepan and bring to the boil, stirring constantly.
- Cook for 2 minutes.

Marilyn Le Breton © Copyright 2001

Pure sweet mincemeat

CF, EF, SF, TF, YF

Ingredients

1 lb (450g) cooking apples (peeled and cored)
1 lb (450g) gf un-sulphated raisins
1 lb (450g) gf un-sulphated currants
4 oz (215g) ground almonds
1 lb (450g) gluten and dairy free soft brown sugar
1 lemon (grated rind and juice)
½ orange (grated rind and juice)
1 tsp gf mixed spice

Method

- Finely chop the apples.
- Mix in all the other ingredients and stir together well.
- Gently simmer until the fruit softens and all liquid is absorbed.
- Leave to stand for at least 2 hours before using.
- Keep in the fridge, in a sterilised sealed jar until ready to be used.

Barbara's Kitchen © Copyright 2001

Non-Food Items

Again, our thanks go to Diane Hartman, for her help with this section.

Bubbles

CF, EF, FF, SF, SGF, TF, YF

Ingredients

¼ cup gluten and dairy free liquid soap
2 tsp glycerin
2 cups cold water

Method

- Place all of the ingredients in a plastic bottle with a screw lid and shake gently to combine.

Diane Hartman © Copyright 1998

Play dough

CF, EF, FF, SF, SGF, TF, YF

Ingredients

2 cups gf flour mix
2 cups cold water
I cup salt

4 tsp cream of tartar
2 tbsp oil

Method

- In a large microwaveable bowl, combine all ingredients together and mix well.
- Microwave on highest power setting for 4–5 minutes, stirring every minute.
- Cook until the mixture reaches a consistency that is too thick to stir.
- Allow dough to cool and then knead until smooth.
- Store in an airtight container.

Diane Hartman © Copyright 1999

Play dough

EF, FF, SF, SGF, TF, YF

Ingredients

½ cup white rice flour
½ cup maize meal flour
½ cup salt

2 tsp cream of tartar
I cup cold water
I tsp sunflower oil

Method

- Combine all ingredients in an heavy based sauce pan.
- Cook over a low heat and stir very occasionally.
- When combined together to form a lump/ball, remove from heat and allow to cool.
- When cool enough to touch, work the dough through with your hands a few times.
- Store in an airtight container. There is no need to store this in the fridge.
- If left for a while the play dough will have a 'crusty' appearance. This is just the salt crystallising on the surface. Work the dough through your hands a few times before using.

Marilyn Le Breton © Copyright 2001

Play dough

CF, EF, FF, SF, TF, YF

Ingredients

2 cups white rice flour
I cup salt

4 tsp cream of tartar
2 tbsp oil
2 cups water

Method

- Mix all of the ingredients together in a large pan and stir over a medium heat.
- Continue to stir until the mixture thickens and pulls away from the edge of the pan.
- Allow the dough to cool.
- Knead the dough briefly.
- Store in an airtight container.

Barbara's Kitchen © Copyright 2000

Starch modelling clay

CF, EF, FF, SF, SGF, TF, YF

Ingredients

1 cup potato starch
2 cups bicarbonate of soda
1⅓ cups cold water
food colouring as desired

Method

- In a medium sized saucepan, mix together the potato starch, bicarbonate of soda and water.
- Stirring constantly, cook the mixture over a medium heat for 4 minutes (or until it resembles mashed potato).
- When cooled it is ready to use.

If dough should become sticky when modelling, dust hands with potato starch and continue to work it. If the dough should become too stiff to work, add a few drops of water and work this through with your hands, before continuing. If using cookie cutters or other shape cutters, dip the cutters into potato flour prior to cutting.

To harden the shaped dough, allow to air dry for several days. When completely dry, the dough shapes can be preserved by painting. Store any unused dough in an airtight jar or a zip-lock bag.

Useful ideas

Diane says this clay works well for making beads and hanging ornaments. For ornaments use a small sized cookie cutter and a metal kebab stick to piece a hole where desired. For round beads, dry the dough on the kebab stick and carefully slide off, once hardened.

This recipe can also be used to make pretend food, fridge magnets, etc.

Diane Hartman © Copyright 1998

Clay

CF, EF, FF, SF, SGF, TF, YF

Ingredients

1 cup of fine grade sand (available at
hardware stores, DIY and garden
centres)
½ cup potato starch
½ cup boiling water

Method

- Mix the sand and potato starch together well.
- Carefully add the boiling water and blend in well.
- Cook the mixture over a medium heat, stirring constantly, until it has thickened.
- If the mixture becomes too thick then add a few more drops of water, a little at a time.
- Allow mixture to cool and model as required.
- The shaped clay can be left to air dry for several days.
- This clay will produce a finished product that looks like rock.

Diane Hartman © Copyright 1998

Salt dough

CF, EG, FF, SF, SGF, TF, YF

Ingredients

1½ cups gf flour mix
1½ cups salt
1 cup cold water
2 tbsp oil
colouring as required

Method

- Mix together the flour and salt.
- Add the water to the flour mix and blend together well.
- Pour the oil over the mixture and with hands knead into the dough.
- Remove dough from bowl and place on a lightly floured surface. Knead dough until it is firm.
- Place dough in a large zip-lock bag and cool in the fridge for 1 hour before using.
- Divide dough as desired and knead colouring into the dough.
- Shape dough as required.
- Dough can be hardened, by allowing to air dry for several days.
- When dry the dough can be decorated, and a coat of clear varnish will preserve it.

See *Starch modelling clay recipe for useful ideas.*

Diane Hartman © Copyright 1998

Appendices

Travelling with a Food Allergic Child

Travelling with a child who has multiple food allergies will involve a great deal of advance planning and patience. Many individuals with multiple food allergies will be unable to rely on restaurant fare to meet their dietary needs. Cross contamination risks pose a significant threat to those with severe allergies. In some instances, the only solution is food prepared at home.

Remember to check your child's medical bag before departing. It is a good idea to take a prescription for each medication, stored in a different place to the medication itself. In event that the bag containing the medication goes missing or is damaged, this will provide you with a back up source, enabling you to re-fill the prescriptions. It may be difficult to reach your child's doctor or the surgery may be closed.

The method of travel, destination and length of trip are all factors to consider when planning a trip. The following information will provide you with some ideas and tips on safe travel.

Air Travel

Air travel with a food allergic child can be a challenge. Contact the airline several weeks before the trip to enquire about allergic foods on the menu. Nuts are frequently served on aircrafts. However, some airlines will arrange for a nut free flight when given adequate notice. The first flight of the day will typically pose the least risk. Airlines will generally clean the plane before the first flight and therefore many of the allergic residues will be removed. If possible, board the plane before the other passengers and wipe down any of the surfaces your child may come into contact with. Keep all emergency medication with you throughout the flight.

If you are unable to pack large quantities of food due to baggage limitations, consider shipping a carton of safe foods to your destination. Most hotels will accept your delivery, if you contact them in advance and explain your situation. Dry ice will keep perishable items safe for a limited time.

Car Travel

Space permitting, consider taking multiple coolers in various sizes to store food items. Reserve the largest cooler for those items requiring freezing temperatures, so that adequate space for ice is available. It is important to provide enough ice to maintain a safe temperature and prevent spoilage. Half-gallon containers (4 pints), partially filled and frozen with water or safe juice, will work well as an ice source. These large blocks of ice do not melt quickly and will also provide safe cold drinks when thawed. It is a good idea to fill the space around the ice containers with loose ice cubes, so that all the surfaces of the food are surrounded by a cooling source.

It is always better to pack more food than is needed, than to run out of an item that is unavailable at your destination. Safe canned foods will offer an emergency source, but don't forget to pack a can opener.

Review maps or contact a travel service (AA/RAC in the UK, AAA in the USA) to locate rest areas and other possible places to eat. It is also advisable to request a listing of hospitals on your route. If an unexpected reaction to food should occur, this will save time locating a suitable medical facility. Mobile phones are also a valuable facility for summoning emergency help.

Camping stores and large department stores sell portable propane camping stoves, which can be useful for meal preparation away from home. There are disadvantages to these stoves, however. They require a few minutes to set up and will also need time to fully cool before packing into the car again. However, they do provide a portable method of preparing hot meals.

Hotels and Motels

Hotels frequently offer rooms with a microwave or refrigerator for a nominal fee. In many cases, it is worth the extra expense for the convenience, and is especially useful if your child is unable to eat restaurant meals. Small appliances are also useful to pack, if space allows.

It is also a good idea to locate stores that sell speciality food items. If you have access to the internet, you may be able to run a search using an online directory. This will allow you to locate stores and contact them to see if they stock specific products. If in the event your supplies should run out, or if your trip is unexpectedly extended, you will have a source from which to replenish your child's food.

Restaurants

If your child will be eating restaurant food during your trip, contact potential restaurants before arriving on holiday. Carefully explain your situation and forward a list of your child's allergies and intolerances (including all hidden ingredients) before reaching your destination. Phoning the chef who will be on duty when you expect to visit the restaurant will allow you to judge if the restaurant will be able to provide your child with safe food. Upon arriving at the restaurant, provide a card listing all your child's allergies and ask to speak to the chef. It is important to emphasise the severity of your child's allergies, so that the utmost care is taken to prevent cross contamination.

Diane Hartman © Copyright 2001

Travelling and Holidaying with an AiA Child

First of all, this can be done! It may take some time and forward planning, but it is possible.

There are two golden rules for travelling with an AiA child:

1. Never, ever underestimate the amount of food and drink your child will consume.

2. Don't ever take a risk with feeding your child. One slip-up with food may damage your child and ruin the holiday for the entire family. Paranoia is the watchword here.

Days out and travelling

Make sure you pack more food and drink than will be needed for your day out. It is far better to waste food than to sit in a car or on public transport with a hungry or thirsty child. Travel delays, breakdowns, traffic jams and accidents may mean you being away from home and a safe source of food for far longer than you intended.

It is a good idea to invest in two cooler boxes (a small one for days out and a larger one for longer stays away from home and holidays) and some ice packs. Make sure that the food and drink are kept within easy reach, not in the boot of the vehicle where you cannot get to them if caught in a traffic jam.

Holidaying in the UK

Self-catering holidays are the easiest to manage (although they might not fit the term 'holiday' for the primary care giver!): all that is needed is a little advanced planning. Most specialist mail order companies are happy to deliver to your holiday address, so you need only take a little food with you.

Contact your local supermarket to find out which is their nearest store to your holiday destination. Most supermarket chains now do home deliveries, so order the food and drink you require before leaving and arrange for it to be delivered to your holiday address. If this is not possible, phone the store and check the availability of the items you need (not every store will stock the same goods). Explain the situation with regard to your child's food intolerances and ask that if they cannot deliver, would they put the food to one side for you to collect.

Take any cooking and baking equipment you may need with you. Although self-catering apartments might have such equipment, by taking your own you will prevent any cross contamination of food items. Such equipment might include: toaster, saucepans, frying pan, chopping board, bread machine (if your child prefers home baked bread), deep fat fryer, and cooking utensils (such as wooden spoons).

Remember that it is your holiday too, and resign yourself to the possibility that your child will not have the healthiest and most nutritionally balanced diet for the duration of the holiday. If it is easiest option and everyone is happy with it, then let it be burger and chips, chicken nuggets and chips, sausage and chips and cold meat and chips every night for dinner. Our AiA children are infamous for their faddy foods and self-limiting diets, and a change in routine and surroundings may be unsettling. An overstressed cook and overstressed child at the dinner table do not make for a good holiday.

Marilyn Le Breton © Copyright 2001

School Lunch Suggestions for the AiA Child

One of the most frequent questions asked of the AiA parent help-line is, 'what on earth can I feed my child at school?' Hopefully, this section will allieviate the panic that surrounds this issue.

One thing that I do not advise is to expect the school's catering department to provide your child with lunches. However willing the department is to do this, it is prone to too many disasters. Remember how panicked you felt implementing the diet? Remember how many 'mistakes' you made in the early days? Remember how you have constantly refined the diet as new information has come to light or as you have discovered or tested for additional food intolerances? You have your child's well-being at the heart of all you do. But, however willing someone else is to try to help, it is not fair or reasonable to expect the same level of dedication, understanding and up-to-date knowledge from another. In a school's kitchen there are far too many potential problems: issues of cross contamination in storing, preparing, cooking and serving the food. Just one spoon moving from the non-gf/cf food to your child's own food will have dramatic consequences for them. And a catering manager who swears nothing untoward happened to your child's lunch (because he or she is unaware) will have you hunting for a new food intolerance.

Some schools are happy to re-heat a meal in a microwave. If you don't ask, you won't find out. So packed lunches it is! All the following are suggestions only. Suitability will depend on the range of foods your child is able to tolerate and their willingness to eat them. The items marked with a * indicate that you can find a suitable recipe in this book:

- Sandwiches and rolls filled with suitable safe fillings (cold meats, soya cream cheese★, nut butters★)
- Cold cooked meats
- Chicken nuggets or chicken dippers★, complete with individual serving of sauce or dip★
- Cold baked chicken
- Cold cooked sausages
- Hot dogs
- Cold pasta salads★
- Sausage rolls★
- Soups★ in food flask
- Cold rice salads★
- Scampi
- Pancakes★ (e.g., plain, buckwheat, spicy chickpea), chapatis★ or pitta bread★ rolled up with various fillings (meat, salad, soya cream cheese★, spicy chickpea mix★) for mock tortillas
- Risottos (cold)★
- Meatballs (cold)★
- Falafels (cold)★
- Rissoles (cold)★
- Scotch eggs★
- Pakoras★
- Quiche★
- Luke's potato salad★
- Suitable crisps★, poppadoms, or prawn crackers
- Rice crackers
- Gorilla Munch or other suitable cereal (served dry as a snack)
- Nuts (plain or salted only)
- Spicy nut and seed mix★

- Gluten and dairy free crackers
- Plain or salted popcorn
- Suitable soya yoghurts*
- Suitable soya or rice based puddings
- Vegetarian jelly
- Suitable fruit in jelly
- Suitable fruit in juice or syrup
- Suitable cakes* or brownies*
- Suitable biscuits*
- Suitable donuts*

Marilyn Le Breton © Copyright 2001

Allergen Free School Lunches

Food preparation for a child with food allergies and intolerances is a challenge in itself. But when you have to prepare safe and appealing meals for your child's lunchbox, it can become a real dilemma. For many children, it may be the first time that they realise that they are 'different'. Some children will simply refuse to eat foods if they look different from the items that their classmates are consuming. But there are some simple things that may make this transition easier.

Prior to your child's first day at school, spend some time discussing why he or she must eat foods that appear different from classmates' lunches. Ask your child to give you some ideas about the types of foods that he or she would like in his or her lunchbox and begin experimenting in advance. Make lunch fun and listen to your child's views on the items to pack.

Advance preparation will help reduce some of the last minute lunchbox frustrations. Allow your child to accompany you in selecting lunch gear. Consider allowing him or her to choose a special lunchbox/bag, food containers, drink bottle and cutlery to help alleviate the disappointment at not being able to eat a school lunch.

Find ways to make lunch exciting and to add variety, if possible. Since most children will be eating hot cafeteria lunches, think about investing in a thermal container that will keep foods hot so your own child can enjoy a hot lunch too. Soups, casseroles and stews can be modified to conform to most allergen free diets. They can even be made in advance and frozen. This will enable you to provide a quick, hot lunch with little effort. Suitable meatloaf, breaded meat, stuffed tortillas and noodles are also items to consider for your child's lunch fare. These items are simple to prepare and can also be easily converted to meet most allergen free requirements. Side dishes can be simple or complex. A safe fruit dessert, muffins, steamed vegetables and cookies may be a welcome accompaniment. Be creative and add interest by adding a variety of foods.

Think about what kinds of safe treats you can provide for the school to store: this will allow your child to have a safe treat for class parties and special events. Package the items and label them, so that they will not be confused or lost. It is best to provide extra treats so replacements are readily available if one is dropped or contaminated in some way. Also plan to provide a replacement lunch in case your child should forget his or her own. A can of safe soup or other non-perishable item is easy to store, but a lunch can be kept in the school's freezer if that is the only safe alternative.

Diane Hartman © Copyright 2000

Details of Commercial Contributors

Barbara the Bread Consultancy

Website: www.barbaraskitchen.co.uk
Email: enquiries@barbaraskitchen.co.uk
Tel/Fax: 01443 237997

Barbara the Bread provides specialist intolerance and allergy services for individuals, groups and the catering industry:

- Giving specialist food intolerance cookery demonstrations
- Hosting tailor made training programmes for coeliac disease sufferers
- Running food intolerance cookery classes for the catering industry and individuals.

Wholesome House Ltd.

Head Office:
Unit 1
Ely Valley Business Park
Pontyclun
South Wales
CF72 9DZ
Tel: +44 (0) 1443 22 55 10
Fax: +44 (0) 1443 22 29 59

Store:
46 Bedford Street
Leamington Spa
Warwickshire
CV32 5DT
Tel: +44 (0) 1926 888288
Fax: +44 (0) 1926 429 660

Specialist suppliers of a huge range of products for allergies and intolerances including:

- A full range of flours for the specialist market
- Barbara the Bread starter packs
- American measuring cups and spoons
- Xanthan gum and gluten free baking powder
- Delivery to holiday destinations on request.

Nutrition Point Ltd

13 Taurus Park, Westbrook, Warrington, WA5 7ZT, UK.
Tel: (+44) 07041 544044
Fax: (+44) 07041 544055
Email: info@nutritionpoint.co.uk
Website: www.dietaryspecialties.co.uk
Suppliers of the following gluten and dairy free packet mixes:

- Blueberry muffin mix (also EF and YF)
- Brownie mix (also EF, SF and YF)
- Chocolate cake mix (also EF and YF)
- Victoria sponge mix (also EF and YF)
- Brown bread mix (also CF, EF and SF)
- White bread mix (also CF, EF and SF)
- Flour mix (also EF, SF and YF)

Innovative Solutions (UK) Ltd

Cenerago House, The Heston Centre, International Avenue, Hounslow, Middlesex, TW5 9NJ, UK.
Tel: (+44) 0845 6013151
Fax: (+44) 0208 756 6332
Email: info@innovative-solutions.org.uk
Website: www.innovative-solutions.org.uk
Suppliers of:

- Gluten free flour blend (contains brown rice flour, white rice flour, tapioca starch flour and potato starch flour)
- Brown rice flour
- White rice flour
- Tapioca starch flour
- Potato starch flour
- Gluten and alcohol free vanilla, lemon and almond extracts

- A variety of organic, dried, un-sulphated fruits
- A selection of other gluten free products

Able to arrange international deliveries.

Lock's Sausages Ltd

West Lane, Edwinstowe, Mansfield, Nottinghamshire, UK.
Tel: (+44) 01623 822200
Fax: (+44) 01623 822200
Suppliers of:

All of the following are nitrate free, preservative free, additive free gluten and dairy free

- Sausages in a variety of sizes and flavours
- Bacon
- Ham
- Burgers in a variety of sizes and flavours

Only able to supply in the UK.

Orgran

49-51 Aster Avenue, Carrum Downs, Victoria, 3201, Australia
Email: romafood@ozemail.com.au
Website: www.ozemail.com.au/~romafood
This company manufactures a variety of gluten free food, the majority of it is also dairy and D-Ga free, including:

- 26 varieties of pasta
- 9 varieties of crispbread and crackers
- 'No Egg' (egg replacer)
- Pizza and pastry mix
- Apple and cinnamon pancake mix
- Buckwheat pancake mix
- Fruit bars

- Canned spaghetti in tomato sauce
- Gluten free bread mix
- Gluten and dairy free plain flour
- Gluten and dairy free self–raising flour
- Gourmet pesto bread mix
- All purpose crumbs

Available at supermarkets, health food stores and specialist suppliers.

Index